Praise for *I*

'It will fascinat
back with shrewd insight to a famous Ashes Test match,
it is simultaneously an account of the social issues of the
time, which are illuminated in numerous, often subtle, ways
throughout.' Mike Brearley

'David Kynaston is amazing: instead of sleeping between
each magnum opus, he turns out a splendid *jeu d'esprit*.
He and Ricketts have masterfully re-created the long-ago
rivalry of the conformist Englishman and the inventive
Aussie, and guess who wins?' Matthew Engel

'This wonderful book recreates a famous Ashes Test played
more than sixty years ago, making it as vivid and enjoyable
to the reader as if they were watching it enacted live on
television. The research is extraordinarily rich, the prose
utterly exquisite. And the narrative of the cricket itself is
both deeply informative and hugely enjoyable… Destined to
become a classic of sporting literature.' Ramachandra Guha

'A scrupulous and subtle evocation of one of cricket's
forgotten classics: the Ashes of 1961.' Gideon Haigh

'Rekindled fantastic memories of a historic afternoon at
Old Trafford…the detail offered by the authors revealed
plenty of stories forgotten or maybe unknown to me.
A comprehensive and interesting read.' Graham McKenzie

'An epic contest superbly retold. In their expert hands,
the match also becomes a trigger for a fascinating slice of

social history, epitomised by the contrasting outlooks of the two captains, Peter May and Richie Benaud in his blue suede shoes. It is a spellbinding read and an essential text for those of us who wonder why the Aussies beat us so often.' Vic Marks

'A highly enjoyable account with helpful historical context of one of the great Ashes Test matches. The authors paint the picture exactly as this superannuated 12-year-old remembers it as he sat on the grass behind the boundary rope, absorbed in the pendulum swings of the cricketing drama being played out in front of him.' Colin Shindler

DAVID KYNASTON was born in Aldershot in 1951 and has been a professional historian since the 1970s. Best known for his multi-volume social history of post-war Britain (*Tales of a New Jerusalem*), he has also written or co-written four books on cricket history – most recently (with Stephen Fay) *Arlott, Swanton and the Soul of English Cricket*, voted Cricket Book of the Year by both the *Telegraph* and the Cricket Writers' Club.

HARRY RICKETTS was born in London in 1950 and, as a boy at Wellington College, broke the school record for wickets in a season. Since 1981 he has lived and worked in New Zealand, where he is well known as a poet and critic. In addition to biographies of Kipling and the War Poets, he has written *How to Catch a Cricket Match*, a guide to getting the most out of watching a day's Test cricket.

They both remember keenly the events of Old Trafford 1961; and they have wanted to write this book together for many years.

RICHIE BENAUD'S

Blue Suede Shoes

THE STORY OF AN ASHES CLASSIC

DAVID KYNASTON & HARRY RICKETTS

BLOOMSBURY PUBLISHING
LONDON · OXFORD · NEW YORK · NEW DELHI · SYDNEY

BLOOMSBURY PUBLISHING
Bloomsbury Publishing Plc
50 Bedford Square, London, WC1B 3DP, UK
Bloomsbury Publishing Ireland Limited,
29 Earlsfort Terrace, Dublin 2, D02 AY28, Ireland

BLOOMSBURY, BLOOMSBURY PUBLISHING and the Diana logo are
trademarks of Bloomsbury Publishing Plc

First published in Great Britain 2024
This edition published 2025

A catalogue record for this book is available from the British Library

ISBN: HB: 978-1-5266-7029-8; PB: 978-1-5266-7030-4; EBOOK: 978-1-5266-7028-1;
EPDF: 978-1-5266-7027-4

2 4 6 8 10 9 7 5 3 1

Typeset by Newgen KnowledgeWorks Pvt. Ltd., Chennai, India
Printed and bound in Great Britain by Clays Ltd, Elcograf S.p.A.

To find out more about our authors and books visit www.bloomsbury.com
and sign up for our newsletters
For product safety related questions contact productsafety@bloomsbury.com

There is no such thing as a crisis in cricket; there is only the next ball.

– W. G. Grace

For as long as I can remember, cricket has been said to be in a crisis or at a crossroads.

– Peter May

His seriousness of purpose, his fearlessness, his intelligence and lack of self-doubt: if you were trying to clone a captain, Benaud's would be the DNA you would want.

– Marcus Berkmann

Hindsight never loses, does it?

– Ben Stokes, on being asked after the 2023 Ashes if he had any regrets

To Lucy and to the memory of Belinda

Contents

PART ONE

I

Captains of the Ship

In cricket, as in life, Peter May and Richie Benaud came from completely different hemispheres. One was a quintessential Englishman of his era, imbued with the old certainties (of class, of empire, of conduct) and seldom if ever questioning them; the other was a quintessential Australian, imbued with an unsentimental pragmatism and capacity to take risks that throughout his life made him open to change. In short, two great cricketers, embodying two very different cultures, sporting and otherwise.

'The archetypal clean-cut Englishman' was how indeed one notable Australian cricket writer, David Frith, would characterise May after his death. 'Tall, square-shouldered, erect, slightly stiff of movement, self-effacing and taciturn, shy of smile but steely in reaction to adversity.' Perhaps the only mystery about P. B. H. May was where his cricketing talent had come from. He was born in Reading on the last day of the 1920s; his father ran the family firm of wholesale ironmongers and builders' merchants; his parents were Methodists; the young Peter grew up in a very orderly household, with handsomely bound volumes of Kipling adorning the sitting room; and, sent to board at Charterhouse in Surrey, he was a schoolboy prodigy with the bat, before further great feats almost inexorably followed in the 1950s for Cambridge University, for Surrey, and, of course, for England.

A trio of reminiscences suggests something of the person. 'Genuine modesty' would be the admiring words of the writer Simon Raven, his contemporary at Charterhouse. So much so that 'the quiet and sometimes embarrassed manner in which Peter behaved in the midst of his triumphs reminded one of the poet Horace when he disclaimed personal merit for having written his poetry and gave credit for all to his Muse'. Charles Williams, an Oxford Blue and subsequent historian of the passing of the amateur, recalled 'a modest and agreeable companion' who was 'polite, well-mannered but strangely inarticulate'. And Micky Stewart, a Surrey team-mate, remembered someone who, as captain, struggled somewhat to connect with the professionals because he 'didn't have the experience of mixing with a cross-section of society'. One way and another, the Peter May of the 1950s was someone very much of his time: a privately educated southerner, playing cricket as an amateur, enjoying a comfortable enough berth at Lloyd's in the City of London, and knowing little of other worlds. It is easy enough to condemn him for his lack of imagination, let alone imaginative sympathy; but in those deficiencies he was no different from many thousands of upper-middle-class Englishmen of arguably any era, let alone his.

If there was a mystery about Richie Benaud, it was that of his attractively exotic surname, explained by the fact of French Huguenot ancestors. He was born on 6 October 1930 (less than a year after May) in a small town near

Sydney; his paternal grandfather was a watchmaker and jeweller, his father a schoolteacher employed by the New South Wales Department of Education in a series of country towns; he spent his early years in the bush, before (when he was seven) his cricket-minded family moved to a Sydney suburb; his secondary education, after passing an entrance exam, was at Parramatta High, a state school; his first-class cricketing career began on New Year's Eve 1948 (May's nineteenth birthday); and from 1950, at a time when even Australian international players relied on outside jobs for most of their income, he worked in a clerical capacity for a Sydney paper, the *Sun*.

It was there, in 1956 after returning from a tour of England, that this all-rounder in every sense asked to be moved to the editorial department. 'Sure, said the editor, who offered him a sports column and, if he liked, a ghost writer to do the actual work,' relates his *Wisden* obituary some sixty years later. 'No, said Benaud: he wanted to learn the trade the hard way. The competition between Sydney's evening papers in the 1950s made old-time Chicago look soft, and Benaud asked to be assigned to the police round, the toughest, most competitive area of all. It was not unhelpful being a celebrity, but he did the hard yards ...' This was not, to put it mildly, a working environment quite the same as the hermetic, club-like Lloyd's in the old, unreconstructed City – long before Big Bang and the accompanying Americanisation of the Square Mile's culture would bring an end, in the 1980s and beyond, to centuries of relatively undemanding gentlemanly capitalism in which what mattered more than anything was to be a good, reliable chap who had been to the right sort of school. Both men were, in their fashion, always immaculately turned out: the sober May in the sports-jacket-and-tie English manner, while the dapper Benaud had early adopted the sartorial tastes of his first New South Wales captain, Arthur Morris, including the latter's penchant for suede shoes.

Fortunately, to add further flesh to the contrast between the two men, we have from the *Observer* in early 1959, when they were both in their late twenties and by now the two captains in the middle of an Ashes series in Australia, an engagingly written joint profile (anonymous, but probably by a cricket-loving English journalist, Michael Davie) of 'the world's best all-rounder' and 'the world's best batsman':

Benaud, a smoothly tanned, bright-blue-eyed cove with a complicated Australian profile, is so relaxed that you sometimes feel you want to stir him with a stick to make sure he is still going. He walks with the slow-motion gait of a bushman who is working in a temperature of 120 degrees and is expecting to run out of water. He is gentle, genial and approachable outside, and very single-minded inside. He is thoughtful, mature, a spruce dresser and as clean as the Pacific surf. He has false teeth because his own were smashed by a cricket ball.

May is a text-book contrast. He has a fine-drawn, rather unemphatic face. He is as taut as a wire; he is never still. On the field he is always pulling at his collar, clasping and unclasping his hands or nibbling the side of his thumb. Even if he is not playing, he keeps up an anxious stream of half-involuntary exhortation from the pavilion – 'Well done, Colin!' 'Oh! Back up, Ted!' 'Let her go, Brian!' He hums at breakfast.

Benaud, though of a quiet disposition, is spiritually one of the boys – 'We're all good mates.' May, though he is not exactly shy, has a kind of English frozen-upness about him: to join a hearty cricketers' group at a bar is for him the social equivalent of climbing the Matterhorn. Benaud handles journalists easily; May evidently feels that talking to writers is as unpredictably risky as throwing an egg into an electric fan.

And in the latter's spare time? 'May writes numerous letters, mostly duty ones, and likes reading Trollope and listening to Sinatra and Ella Fitzgerald.' Well, it was never likely to be Elvis; but it is tempting to think of him, through a tough tour, reading *The Warden* and finding solace as well as perhaps inspiration in that good man's unwavering dislike of life's self-promoters and publicity seekers.

*

May was still an undergraduate when in July 1951 he made his Test debut against South Africa at Headingley. His century – a seemingly nerveless innings of 138, as it happens completed on the day one of us was born – was no more than his growing body of admirers had expected. 'His equanimity from first to last, his subordination of self for side, and his sound technique stamped him as a player well above the ordinary,' recorded *Wisden*.

Benaud's debut, six months later in a dead rubber against the West Indies, was less auspicious: modest scores (3 and 19) with the bat, and his leg-breaks given barely four overs right at the end of the match. A dropped catch behind the wicket denied him the scalp of Everton Weekes, instead having to settle for the much lesser prize of Alf Valentine, a number 11's number 11, to finish proceedings. If May at this point was clearly ahead of Benaud, a brief period of near-parity then followed: for the Englishman, in his last year at Cambridge, a so-so series against the Indians in 1952; for the Australian, no great shakes against the visiting 1952–53 South Africans. With an Ashes series now looming – and England hoping in Coronation summer to regain them at long last after nineteen largely Bradman-dominated years – neither could yet be sure of his Test place.

In the event, 1953 did not prove the easiest of summers for either of them. May, after failing twice for Surrey against the tourists (including a salutary and very thorough going-over by Ray Lindwall), then failed again in the first Test and was dropped for the next three. Benaud did play in three out of the first four, but to little effect, with the nadir being the last day at Lord's when the Australian bowlers failed to achieve the win that everyone had expected to be theirs. Early in the day, noted *The Times*'s still anonymous cricket correspondent (not yet John Woodcock), 'Compton, with three crushing off-drives to the boundary in a single over, seemed to destroy all Benaud's confidence in his own length and leg-spin'; and he went wicketless until almost the very end, when it was too late.

After four draws, the fate of the Ashes rested on The Oval. May was recalled and, batting at his favoured first wicket down, made significant contributions of 39 and 37 to England's historic eight-wicket win, with *The Times*'s man gratified that he had 'showed the true quality that is within him'. No such praise for Benaud, relegated to twelfth man and left to serve the drinks; though a few weeks later, in a lengthy conversation at Scarborough, he was advised by the great inter-war Australian bowler Bill O'Reilly to concentrate less on variety and more on making his stock ball, the leg-break, as accurate as possible – advice, recalled Benaud many years later, which 'really taught me how to bowl from there on'.

A year and a half later in 1954–55, as Len Hutton's team successfully defended the Ashes down under, it was still advantage May. Now vice-captain, despite precious little captaincy experience, he top-scored for England with 351 runs in a largely low-scoring series, playing match-changing innings in two of the Tests and arguably a third. Alan Ross acclaimed at Sydney his century 'of crisp drives, powerful on-side placings and, most important of all, a certainty suggesting that he knew himself the equal, if not the superior, of Australian bowling', while his team-mate Frank Tyson was struck by 'a savagery' in his shots to the midwicket fence 'which seemed out of place in such a cultured individual'; Neville Cardus at Melbourne relished how 'the swift power of his strokes reduced even Australian fieldsmen to open-eyed immobility'; and John Arlott at Adelaide, as England struggled to their target of 94 to clinch the series, was grateful for his 'common sense and good judgement'. Again, few plaudits for Benaud, who over the five matches took ten expensive wickets (though including May's twice) and averaged only 16 with the bat. Would he ever come good at the highest level with his spin bowling and attacking strokeplay? Arlott typically took the long view. 'Benaud continues to promise more than he performs,' he reflected at the end of the series, 'but the promise is so great that it is not difficult to understand why the selectors persevere with him.'

The perseverance continued in 1956 – another series win for England, completing an Ashes hat-trick – but was ill rewarded with four underwhelming matches out of five. The shining exception was the second Test at Lord's. 'Benaud is 25 and looks every inch a cricketer,' mulled Cardus after watching him in the nets two days before the start. 'It will be no matter for wonder if at any moment he confounds those of his critics who have more or less "written him off".' So he now did: taking a miracle catch in the gully to dismiss Colin Cowdrey; confounding a well-set May with his top-spinner; and making a splendidly buccaneering, match-securing 97.

One swallow, though, did not make a summer, and the cardinal fact of the series was that the Australian slow men, Benaud and his captain Ian Johnson, were on helpful pitches comprehensively outbowled, with Benaud's nugatory eight wickets coming at a pricey 41. Or in Ross's damning words, 'they had as much opportunity as Laker and Lock, but, lacking both spin and length, made nothing of it'. No such problems for captain May, in charge since Hutton's retirement the previous year – and a wholly uncontroversial appointment, following England's brief flirtation with having a professional at the helm. Now, not only did he retain the Ashes, but a succession of imperious displays saw him comprehensively the leading batter of the series, with his average of 90 three times that of the most successful Australian. 'For May, there cannot be too great praise,' wrote Ross after it was all over. 'He captained England with growing certainty, never once failed as a batsman, and shed around him that aura of confidence which is a captain's most priceless asset.'

Yet from this point, the May–Benaud balance began to shift. It was a shift reflected, certainly as seen in retrospect, by two contrasting tours of South Africa. The first, the English tour of 1956–57, had May remaining in provincial and other lesser games the nonpareil, racking up hundreds almost at will; but, in the Tests, he scored a single half-century and averaged only 15, while his captaincy came in for criticism as he let slip a 2–0 lead to draw the series. Still, insisted Ross in an overview, 'his Test run of failures was more an accident of nature or an act of God than attributable to any decline in concentration or power'. As for Benaud, touring with Australia exactly a year later in 1957–58, this was the series in which at last he came fully into his own as an all-rounder, with his contribution crucial to his side's convincing 3–0 victory: leading wicket-taker and third in the batting averages, well above Australia's new captain, Ian Craig, or indeed the last survivor of Bradman's 1948 'invincibles', Neil Harvey. 'The outstanding personality ... a tour of unbroken success ... a great favourite with the crowds': *Wisden*'s words, long in the waiting, could hardly have been more fulsome.

Towards the end of 1958, after Craig had fallen ill, the Australian selectors had to decide who would captain the team in the forthcoming Ashes series. Harvey was the obvious choice; but despite a feeling in some quarters that Benaud lacked the temperament and was too aloof for the job, they plumped instead for him to take on May. An implicit rivalry between the Australian and the Englishman was now about to become explicit and take centre stage.

*

Richie Benaud had originally been a batting all-rounder rather than a bowling one; and, throughout his career, such was the power of his aggressive if inconsistent strokeplay that bars would tend to empty when he came to the crease. Certainly he had his moments: not only that resplendent 97 at Lord's in 1956, but three years earlier, in the festival match at Scarborough when he imbibed wisdom from O'Reilly, a stunning 135 in comfortably less than two hours against a T. N. Pearce's XI attack comprising Alec Bedser, Trevor Bailey, Roy Tattersall and Johnny Wardle – a spectators' feast, full of boundary-clearing pull-drives, only ended when May caught him in the deep.

But, of course, it was as a bowler that Benaud truly began to make his mark during the second half of the decade.[*] 'It was smooth, fluent, graceful, compact and overall very pleasing to the eye' is how his biographer Mark Browning describes his action. 'He was side-on in his delivery stride, head still and looking over the left shoulder at his target, back foot parallel to the bowling crease, wrist cocked. His arm made a complete and smooth full circle coming through on high.' Ross in 1955 noted that 'his action is too unvaryingly low for my taste', so almost certainly it was only later that it became higher; and indeed, Browning emphasises how Benaud 'constantly refined and improved' his action 'until he was satisfied it could not be bettered'.

He was seldom a huge spinner of his leg-breaks or googlies. Rather, he relied upon a mixture of accuracy, variation and ingenuity to get on top of the batter, with that

[*]For a notably close analysis of Benaud's development as a bowler, see: Amol Rajan, *Twirlymen: The Unlikely History of Cricket's Greatest Spin Bowlers* (2011), pp. 249–56.

ingenuity, that ability to outwit his opponent, much helped by an elephantine memory about each batter's strengths and weaknesses. He was always learning, always open-minded: Bruce Dooland, a fellow Australian wrist-spinner, playing for Nottinghamshire, taught him the 'flipper' when the tourists were at Trent Bridge in 1956; while later that year, when the Australians were in the nets at Madras, he tried bowling off five paces, as opposed to his usual nine or ten, and the results were transformative (including taking twenty-three wickets in the current three-match series against India). Above all, in his search for just that bit more dip, just that bit more bounce, he *practised* – to the extent that, before he even played his first match on the breakthrough 1957–58 tour of South Africa, he had bowled some 1,500 balls, including hours at a time in an otherwise empty net. Cricket for Benaud was a way of life; on the field, his adhesive hands were always hungry for the ball; and at the end of a day's play, he had (to use a mark of praise beloved by football managers) left behind nothing on the pitch.

For all his inner steel, however much masked by an outward diffidence, the Englishman was a somewhat different sort of cricketer. 'As a fielder May was steady but not spectacular, and he never bowled,' *The Times*'s obituarist (Woodcock?) would recall:

His genius was confined to his batting. At the wicket he was tall and upright, with the blade of the bat noticeably shut in his stance. There was nothing in his rather stiff-legged walk to the middle, or in his manner when he got there, which announced his standing among the cricketers of the world. The quality emerged only when he began to play.

And what quality that was – at times almost peerless. 'An outstanding performer in the classical amateur tradition,' remembered the *Daily Telegraph*'s also anonymous obituarist, but probably E. W. Swanton. 'Six foot in height, broad in the shoulders and long in the leg, May always played with a perfectly straight bat,' he went on. 'His trademark as a batsman was his superb style and strength when driving off the front foot through mid-on; but he had all the strokes.'

Most contemporary assessments were just as admiring. 'He hits with great power off the back foot and, driving as well as he does anything remotely over-pitched, he never allows the innings to grow becalmed,' noted Ross ahead of the 1954–55 series. 'He is deceptively slim, a beautiful on-side player, and he has the virtues of elegance and attack one hopes of from a No. 3.' That promise was wholly fulfilled, most crucially at Sydney in the second Test, when May's second-innings 104 in a low-scoring match got England back in the series after the self-inflicted Brisbane humiliation. 'May scored continually in the area between square leg and mid-on,' recorded Ross as he watched him take on Lindwall and Bill Johnston. 'His bat swings naturally across his body, and anything not well pitched-up outside the off stump he was able to force into that space. When Archer came on, he hooked him hard for four. Bowlers tend to pitch short to May, for he lays into the over-pitched ball with uninhibited savagery.'

Just occasionally there was a murmur of criticism, with Swanton in 1957 even daring to suggest that May had fallen foul of the regrettable, morally indefensible tendency of right-handed batters (not Swanton's word) to have 'left hands wrapped so far round the handle as almost to risk a broken wrist, right hands down by the shoulder of the blade, and bodies slewed round towards the bowler, so square-on that the cover drive is virtually impossible'.

But through the 1950s such complaints were rare indeed, with the praise reaching a climax in 1957 at Edgbaston, where May's monumental 285 not out, admittedly helped by gross umpiring indulgence over pad play, thwarted the West Indian spinners. That, though, was an understandably defensive innings, and more often than not he was in attacking mode when at the crease. By 1958, ahead of the Ashes tour, he was arguably at his absolute peak as a batter: not only comfortably England's top scorer in the series against New Zealand, but for Surrey – in a dismally wet summer in which bowlers were largely on top – a batting average of 55, with Bernard Constable following next on 32.

No innings that year was more masterful than his 174 at Old Trafford, out of Surrey's total of 314. 'He turned Higgs and Statham repeatedly with an ease matched only by its elegance,' reported the *Manchester Guardian*'s Denys Rowbotham. 'He lay back and bludgeoned Statham's few short balls with a suave imperiousness which disguised the degree to which sometimes they lifted.' Near the end, batting with the last man, he opened 'his broad shoulders with a vengeance, drove Higgs mightily over mid-off for six, and then high to long-on for four. He next late cut Higgs and then swept him and finally lofted Statham over deep mid-off, this time scarcely credibly off the back foot.' Altogether, concluded Rowbotham, it had been 'a great privilege to see a great batsman play a great innings'.

That season, May's second as Surrey captain, saw the county's record-breaking seventh successive Championship title win. His approach was undeniably less bold than that of his predecessor, Stuart Surridge; but such was hardly surprising given that May, since taking over the England captaincy from Hutton in 1955, had very deliberately – and so far very successfully – modelled his methods, essentially cautious and risk-averse, on that predecessor. Even so, it had been an ominous moment when the series in South Africa in 1956–57 revealed the downside of this largely attritional style of captaincy.

Going into the third Test, at Durban, England were two up with three to play and thus had the clear opportunity to clinch matters – even more so by the final day, as South Africa needed 190 to win in 250 minutes, with a strong likelihood of the slow left-armer Johnny Wardle, who had already taken twenty wickets in the series (including five in the first innings here), bowling them out. Instead, May opted to shut up the game and, setting defensive fields, play for a draw. He rotated his quicker bowlers at one end (they, of course, took much longer to get through their overs) and used Wardle and the more economical Jim Laker at the other. Moreover, May apparently discouraged Wardle from employing (as potentially too unpredictable?) the back-of-the-hand deliveries with which he had been regularly bamboozling the South Africans. After this let-off, the home team recovered to win the fourth and fifth Tests, and square the rubber.

Playing in the England side in that series was the Essex amateur, and future chairman of the England selectors, Doug Insole. 'His tactical approach was straightforward,' he remembered about May's captaincy. 'He was not adventurous, but it might be said that he had no need to be. The attacks at his command, for Surrey and England, were very strong, and he depended on his established bowlers to do their job. He would set out with a plan and he was not easily deflected from it.' But, of course, the ultimate test for any captain is how to respond when, for whatever reason, his subordinates are failing to execute the plan and, seemingly inexorably, the match is slipping away.

*

Most of the 1950s had been England's decade – from March 1951 through to August 1958, fourteen series played, of which ten were won and none lost – but then came the rudest of shocks, as Benaud's men pulverised the tourists 4–0 in the 1958–59 Ashes. Inevitably, there were some extenuating factors: the absence of Wardle (originally picked, but his selection rescinded after some inflammatory newspaper articles appeared under his name); a crop of injuries; the presence in some of the Tests of Australian bowlers with suspect actions; and indifferent umpiring generally. Furthermore, the tabloid press pack hounded May on personal as well as cricketing grounds, which probably played a part in his form in the Tests being less commanding than usual, although he still managed an overall average of 40, second only to Cowdrey on the English side.

Ultimately, however, it was England's whole approach – playing consistently dreary, defensive, joyless cricket – that was the root cause of the thumping defeat. In the first Test, during one ninety-minute session of 21 eight-ball overs in what admittedly was a slow-scoring match, May, Cowdrey and Tom Graveney (England's premier shot-makers) managed less than a dozen runs between them; while at the other end, the all-rounder Trevor Bailey, often usefully obdurate in the middle order but now promoted to three, was in the middle of grinding his way to 68 in more than seven excruciating hours at the crease. On the first day of the fourth Test, with England by then 2–0 down, May rather desperately put Australia in; and yet that day, in a must-win game, England only bowled a meagre 56 eight-ball overs.

Among the many unimpressed observers was the sharp-eyed Australian cricketer-turned-journalist-cum-broadcaster, Jack Fingleton. 'I often thought on this tour that Hutton's legacy of defensive play and England's great faith in "Stayput" Bailey cost May pretty dearly,' he reflected afterwards. 'When the Australians defeated the defensive policy of the circular field and bowling down the leg-side, May didn't have much else to turn to, so much, in recent years, have these tactics been resorted to in English cricket against Australia. I have never liked them because they are so barren …'

For Benaud, the series was a triumph: not just the 4–0 margin, not just his 31 wickets at less than 19 apiece, but a vindication from day one of his distinctive approach to the vexed art of captaincy. One immediate innovation was to institute a team dinner the evening before the Test, at which all were encouraged to contribute suggestions about the strengths and weaknesses of the opposition. Furthermore, in marked contrast to May's safety-first tactics, Benaud almost constantly looked to attack; he crowded the batters with close catchers; he made astute bowling changes; he rarely allowed the game to stultify; above all, he exuded confidence in himself and in his players, a sense of shared enjoyment. When a wicket fell, rather than a quick, undemonstrative English half-smile or nod, Benaud might give a celebratory jump; there would certainly be open applause, backs slapped.

'Some of the Australian old and bolds did not think very much of these antics,' noted Fingleton. 'They savoured, too, of the soccer field where the players fall upon the neck of the goal-shooter. But, whether one admired Benaud's enthusiasm or not, he was able to infect every member of his side with his eagerness, his zest, his desire to beat England.' Like his opposite number, he played the game hard; but unlike May, the golden amateur who captained like the dour pro, he was a pragmatic maverick who had a keen, instinctive *feel* for the pulse of a match and was prepared to take calculated chances. That capacity to risk made all the difference; and by the end of the series he must have known that he could be Australia's captain as long as he wanted to be – just reward for such a long and difficult apprenticeship.

Over the next two years, things only got better for Benaud. In 1959–60 he took an Australian team to Pakistan and India, winning both series and in eight matches taking 47 wickets at barely 20 apiece, establishing himself as the pre-eminent spinner in the world as well as a captain of infinite resource and sagacity; he spent the summer of 1960 in England, partly engaged in cricket journalism (establishing a long-term relationship with, perhaps rather incongruously, the *News of the World*), and partly in writing his book *Richie Benaud's Way of Cricket*, a very readable treatise full of anecdotes, personal theorising and down-to-earth practical advice; while in 1960–61 there came the remarkable home series against the West Indies, played throughout in such a positive atmosphere that it was instantly recognised as a huge boon for the game at large. The tone was set from the very start. Benaud met Frank Worrell at the airport on his arrival, and the two had the following exchange: 'I hope it's a great year,' said Benaud; to which Worrell replied, 'Well, we'll have a lot of fun anyway.'* And fun they had, along with exhibitions of exhilarating batting, thunderous fast bowling and session after session of high tension, with Australia eventually winning the series 2–1.

The tension was at its very highest as the first Test at Brisbane came to its nail-biting end. Australia on the final day had to make 233 in a little over five hours, but Wes Hall soon had them 57 for five; and at tea, the score was 110 for six with only Alan Davidson and Benaud left of the recognised batters. During the interval, the chairman of selectors, Sir Donald Bradman, told Benaud how much he was enjoying the game, before asking, 'What are you going for, Richie – a win or a draw?' Benaud replied that he was going for a win. Which he and Davidson then did their spirited best to pull off, reaching 226 – just two hits from victory – before Davidson was run out. At the beginning of the final over, to be bowled by Hall, six runs were required from the eight balls with three wickets in hand. Whereupon Benaud was caught behind; Wally Grout was dropped off a sitter; and, with the scores level, Grout and Ian Meckiff were spectacularly run out. It was the first tie in Test match history. The two teams then partied together for hours in

---

*Frank Worrell is sometimes thought of as the first non-white West Indian captain. This feels true, although it is not quite factually accurate since the veteran George Headley captained the West Indies for a single Test against England in Barbados in 1948.

the pavilion (rum and beer) until the curator finally threw them out.

These were not such a happy two years for May. In 1959, at home, a newish-looking England side trounced the talented but incohesive Indian team 5–0. May, initially in good form, missed the fourth and fifth Tests due to an operation for an ischiorectal ulcer. He seemed to have recovered sufficiently to resume the captaincy for the winter tour of the West Indies, but was patently well below par and had to return to England for further treatment after playing only the first three Tests. By then, England had gone one up (having won the second Test, despite a pitch invasion), and they held on to that lead when Cowdrey took over for the last two Tests. The series as a whole was disappointingly attritional, with Gerry Alexander (Worrell's Cambridge-educated predecessor as captain) proving no more tactically adventurous than May or Cowdrey; while May himself scored only 83 runs in his five innings, so ill at ease that it was not until the final one that, in Ross's words, 'at last one heard the ball hit without the feeling one had cotton-wool in both ears'. He then sat out the entirety of the 1960 season – England under Cowdrey's captaincy convincingly winning 3–0 against South Africa – with a view to recruiting his strength ahead of the visit of the Australians in 1961. Altogether, then, far from ideal preparation for the opening men's Ashes series of the new decade; but of May's determination to be at the helm as England at the first time of asking wrested back those Ashes, few who knew him would have doubted.

*

One of us was nine years old that spring of 1961 as bats were oiled and pads were whitened, the other was ten. For the nine-year-old, whose parents in the past few months had divorced and then almost instantly married new partners, cricket offered some kind of security, a safe, self-contained world to enter into, as he pored for hours over his father's *Wisden*s. For the ten-year-old, living in a village near Worcester, the obsession began that Easter holidays, as his father bought netting and poles in order to set up a net on the lawn, where the two would play for an hour or so every day between tea and supper, with Shot the family dog, an assiduous retriever of the ball, stationed at cover point. We were both the sons of cricket-minded military men; we both spent nearly nine months of each year at an all-boys boarding school (one in Shropshire, the other in Kent); and we were both sure that England would prevail in this, the first conscious Ashes series of our cricket-loving lives.

2

Out of Time

'Fixtures for 1961': placed, as ever, right at the back (pp. 1,007–15), following straight on from John Arlott's book reviews, those most tantalising pages of the latest *Wisden Cricketers' Almanack*. The Australians opening their nearly five-month tour at Worcester in late April; the visitors playing each county at least once, plus MCC, the ancient universities, Club Cricket Conference, A. E. R. Gilligan's XI, T. N. Pearce's XI, Minor Counties, Scotland, Ireland – and 'Gentlemen of England'; the five Tests (no play on Sundays) stretching out between 8 June and 22 August; no one-day competitions; the seventeen counties instead each playing 32 (or in some cases 28) three-day championship matches (Saturday, Monday, Tuesday; Wednesday, Thursday, Friday); those venues to include Gillingham, Neath, Hull, Gravesend, Ilford, Yeovil, Newport, Stroud, Worksop, Hinckley, Middlesbrough, Ashby-de-la-Zouch, Cowes, Ebbw Vale, Loughborough, Rushden, Clacton, Glastonbury, Pontypridd, Weston-super-Mare, Wellingborough, Llanelli, Dover, Worthing and Coalville; matches at Lord's to include Eton v Harrow, Oxford v Cambridge, Gentlemen v Players, Beaumont v Oratory, Clifton v Tonbridge, Rugby v Marlborough, Cheltenham v Haileybury, Combined Services v Public Schools, Royal Navy v The Army, Royal Navy v RAF, and H. S. Altham's Public Schools XI v English Schools Cricket Association; and, to round off the season, festival cricket at Scarborough, Hastings and Blackpool. Altogether, it was the familiar, reassuring annual calendar for what could still just about legitimately claim to be the national game. A calendar that, like English cricket itself, seemed immutable.

So, too, in some obvious ways, seemed the England of the early 1960s. An almost universally admired royal family; the world's most stable parliamentary democracy; the widespread exercise of a largely benevolent paternalism; limited social mobility, limited access to higher education; people knowing their place; a puritanical guilt about money; and, despite ominous talk of relative economic decline, a near-unshakeable, Podsnapian assumption, whether conscious or unconscious, that foreigners were essentially inferior creatures and definitely to be pitied rather than envied. Yet, in truth, this was a country on the cusp of major and permanent change.

Here it is hard to avoid a list. *Beyond the Fringe*, opening in London in May 1961, brilliantly and irreverently spearheading a palpable decline in deference; married women increasingly going out to work; the steady growth of non-white immigration (since the *Windrush* in 1948 but picking up in numbers from the mid-1950s) starting to turn a monocultural society into a multicultural one; increasingly 'privatised' lifestyles, epitomised on the one hand by the rise of television and the motor car, on the other by the decline of the pub and the cinema; further traditional staples of urban leisure patterns (football, rugby league, greyhound racing, the *News of the World*, seaside boarding houses) all in decline; lager, filter-tipped cigarettes, American-style tenpin bowling all on the rise; foreign holidays no longer unthinkable. England was becoming, in short, a more fluid, more mobile, more open society: not yet post-industrial, not yet socially liberal (homosexuals still criminalised), not yet youth-oriented (National Service only just abolished, the Beatles in 1961 still a year away from their first single) – but the broad direction of travel was unmistakable. Inevitably, the challenge facing the elders at Lord's and elsewhere was whether they were willing for cricket to go with that potentially unsettling flow.

*

'Rightly or wrongly,' declared an *Observer* profile in 1959, 'most of the men connected with cricket today would regard G. O. "Gubby" Allen as the dictator of English cricket.' The writer was Clive Taylor (who in 1975 would famously characterise the bespectacled David Steele going out to bat against Jeff Thomson and Dennis Lillee as 'the bank clerk who went to war'); and later in his piece he explained from where 'the benevolent despot and indefatigable administrator' derived his ubiquitous influence: 'He is chairman of numerous committees ("far too many to list") but his power arises from four – the MCC cricket committee, the selection committee which chooses English teams at home, the selection committee for teams overseas, and the MCC tours sub-committee.'

Two years later, entering his seventh season as chairman of the selectors, Allen was as powerful as ever – the very embodiment, for all his Australian antecedents, of the cricket establishment. Eton, Cambridge and the City had formed the indispensable background for someone remembered in his *Wisden* obituary as 'a true amateur'; on the notorious 'Bodyline' tour of 1932–33, he had stood out as the one English fast bowler refusing to have any truck with Douglas Jardine's ruthlessly unsporting tactic; four years later, captaining England in Australia, he had gone 2–0 up in the series before a mixture of the weather and Bradman saw Australia winning 3–2; and by the 1950s he had effectively replaced Sir Pelham ('Plum') Warner as cricket's great panjandrum.* 'He was,' recorded *Wisden*, 'clear-minded and unflinching in putting over his arguments, which he would defend with the tenacity and confidence of one who was thoroughly well briefed.' 'I suppose I enjoy it,' Allen himself told Taylor about his chairmanship of the various selection committees, 'but it can be terribly hard sometimes.'

There was no mistaking the identity of His Master's Voice. E. W. ('Jim') Swanton was hardly, as a stockbroker's son, born on the wrong side of the tracks, but his background – Cranleigh School, no university – was appreciably less gilded than Allen's. Indeed, Neville Cardus in 1951 had, not implausibly, attributed the unfortunate impression that Swanton too often gave of 'self-importance and unnecessary resonance of speech and a certain pompousness' to the fact

---

*It should be noted, however, that Bill Bowes always claimed Allen's virtuous demurral to be disingenuous, even dissembling, and that in fact, unlike the professionals Larwood, Voce and himself, Allen simply could not bowl the short-pitched ball so precisely and effectively.

that 'he probably never got over not having been to Oxford and Eton'. By the early 1960s he was at the very height of his influence: not only the cricket correspondent for the *Daily Telegraph* – almost certainly the paper most widely read by cricket-minded people – but also a regular commentator and summariser on both radio and television. If his great rival John Arlott was the poetic voice of cricket, then Swanton's – firm, archiepiscopal, permitting no ambiguity or doubt about his judgements – was the authorised version.

Crucially, he and Allen were almost wholly as one in their worldview: MCC as the unquestioned repository of authority; the importance of the carefree amateur contribution, able to leaven that of the dour professionals; the indispensable retention of cricket's traditional two-class system; and perhaps above all, an unwavering desire that cricket be played with a mixture of attack, of style, and of sportsmanship. As early as 1954, Swanton was complaining bitterly about how 'county cricket, speaking generally, has got into a pawky, dreary, defensive groove'; and over the ensuing years, those complaints, often applicable also in his eyes to the England team, only gathered force and frequency.

Swanton in later life would write Allen's biography, in the course of which he related how, playing for Eton 2nd XI against Eton Ramblers in 1919, his subject had been comprehensively run out following an ambitious call by his partner, Ronny Aird. Once Aird himself was out, an exchange of views had then ensued in the pavilion:

Aird: You must admit that that was bad luck.
Allen: I don't know about bad luck.
Aird: Oh, you must run to a chap in brown suede shoes.

Three and a bit decades later, Aird was ensconced as MCC's secretary, in effect chief executive. He took up his position in 1952, after many years as assistant secretary, and over the ensuing decade served under a distinctive run of presidents:

1952 The Duke of Beaufort
1953 The Earl of Rosebery
1954 Viscount Cobham
1955 Field Marshal Earl Alexander of Tunis
1956 Viscount Monckton of Brenchley
1957 The Duke of Norfolk
1958 Marshal of the RAF Viscount Portal of Hungerford
1959 H. S. Altham
1960 Sir Hubert Ashton
1961 Col. Sir William Worsley, Bart

The only commoner was Harry Altham, revered cricket master at Winchester and notable cricket historian. Sadly, and *pace* Tony Lewis's far from negligible *Double Century: The Story of MCC and Cricket* (1987), we still lack a comprehensive history of the MCC; but there is no reason to doubt this 2012 characterisation by Charles Williams (distinguished biographer of de Gaulle as well as Bradman). Williams portrayed the MCC as a private members' club which in the post-war period – when it was still all-male, with the overwhelming majority of its membership privately educated – as not only intensely conservative (often with an upper 'C'), but also arrogant. Few over the years felt this more keenly than the anti-establishment Arlott. 'Why now?' he would say to Tony Lewis at Lord's in 1980, on the occasion of his last Test in the commentary box, after he had refused the MCC Committee's invitation to join them for lunch. 'They never asked me before ...'

The two-class system was still firmly entrenched in county cricket. Most of the seventeen counties only had a bare smattering of amateurs playing for them; yet in some two-thirds of the counties it was an amateur who, in 1961, captained the team. Eight of those amateurs – Peter May at Surrey, Colin Cowdrey at Kent, Donald Carr at Derbyshire, Ted Dexter at Sussex, Raman Subba Row at Northamptonshire, Mike Smith at Warwickshire, Bob Barber at Lancashire, Colin Ingleby-Mackenzie at Hampshire – had already had at least one summer in charge, while four others were newly chosen for the job: Ian Bedford returned to the fray eleven years after he had last played for Middlesex; at Essex, the veteran all-rounder Trevor Bailey succeeded his fellow amateur Doug Insole; Glamorgan's choice was Ossie Wheatley, a Cambridge Blue; and Gloucestershire controversially replaced Tom Graveney with an Old Etonian, C. T. M. (Tom) Pugh, who (in the words of Michael Marshall, a Conservative MP who in 1987 wrote the enjoyable oral history *Gentlemen & Players*) 'would make a greater name for himself as a rackets player than as a first-class cricketer'.

Practice varied from county to county, but at least in some the reality remained of a social apartheid not so different from the pre-1914 era: separate dressing-rooms for amateurs and professionals; separate places to eat; and separate hotels when playing away. No social contrast starker than at Worthing, where the respective changing-rooms were on opposite sides of the ground, resulting in visiting pros having to wait patiently on the boundary edge until their captain emerged on the other side to take the field. That particular choice detail derives from Stephen Chalke's authoritative history (*Summer's Crown*) of the county championship; and in it, he rightly emphasises the sheer hypocrisy increasingly involved in maintaining the two-class system, as counties found all sorts of ingenious, indirect ways of financially compensating their so-called 'amateurs'. Indeed, not only counties: ahead of the 1958–59 tour, Jim Laker, a hard-headed Yorkshireman to his bones, gave Gubby Allen an uncomfortable quarter of an hour by announcing that he was considering becoming an amateur and, when asked why, explaining that he could earn more on the tour through generous expenses than by drawing professional pay. Of course, 'shamateurism' had a long history – going back to the days of W. G. Grace, the most richly rewarded amateur of all – but seldom had it been quite so shameless, and never so out of joint with the spirit of the age.

That increasingly egalitarian spirit found little if any sympathetic echo in the 1961 *Wisden*. The chapter entitled 'The Universities in 1960' had the following allocation of pages:

Oxford: 12
Cambridge: 13
Other universities: 0

Or take the almanack's coverage of schools cricket in 1960. Nothing – *nothing* – on state schools; but no fewer than sixty-two pages on the public schools, i.e. those private, fee-paying schools educating only some 7 per cent of the nation's children. The sixty-two pages included full coverage of the thirteen days at Lord's of matches between public schools or involving representative XIs of the public schools. Many years later, Williams (privately educated, Oxford Blue, one appearance for Gentlemen against Players) recalled the powerful legacy of the education received by the amateur batters who by the mid-to-late 1950s were becoming 'the stars of English cricket':

> It was not just that they, like me, had been brought up to play on wickets which the state schools could hardly ever achieve. We had been brought up to believe that we were there to run the show. In fact, with the honourable exception of David Sheppard, it was many years before we were to be persuaded that the world as conceived by our tutors had changed and that we should change with it.

May, Cowdrey, Dexter: those three above all. The three great amateur, stroke-playing batters whose inherited sense of entitlement this book's authors at the time never for a moment thought to question.

Looking back, there is no great mystery about why English cricket remained a game largely dominated by a privileged, self-perpetuating elite: inherited wealth, educational apartheid, networks of connections, institutions and clubs (above all MCC) that were virtually closed shops. In many ways, English cricket was a microcosm of what Anthony Sampson spent most of 1961 charting for his coruscating *Anatomy of Britain*, published the following year and which was essentially an attack on how, as he put it, 'the club-amateur outlook' was 'totally out of keeping' in an age suffering from 'an oppressive lack of innovation and zeal'. In short: 'The old fabric of the British governing class, while keeping its social and political hold, has failed to accommodate or analyse the vast forces of science, education or social change which (whether they like it or not) are changing the face of the country.'

Crucially, in cricket's case, there was also the whole ethical-cum-moral dimension, further cementing the traditional elite's near-stranglehold; or, as the cricket historian Duncan Stone has recently argued in *Different Class* (2022), the fetishisation of cricket as more than just a game, but instead a character-building way of life accompanied by largely unwritten codes of behaviour. This fetishisation, which goes back to the late nineteenth century and is intimately bound up with Christianity, public schools and empire, has had in practice a powerfully exclusionary effect. The right sort of chaps could be implicitly relied upon to uphold and enforce those codes. But the others? Not necessarily. Or to cite the four short words that were the key to advancement in the old City of London (where the stockbroker Gubby Allen was so at home): if the face fits …

The literature of cricket – the richest of any game – played its part. *The Cricketer's Companion*, an instant classic of an anthology edited by Alan Ross in 1960, is suggestive: in its non-fiction sections, as much emphasis on the amateurs as on the professionals, even though at almost any one time the former were far less numerous; while prominent in the fiction section are 'Tom Brown's Last Match' (Rugby School v MCC), 'The Hill' (Eton v Harrow), and two matches of essentially country-house cricket. Unaccountably omitted in Ross's poetry section is Henry Newbolt's 'Vitaï Lampada' (1898) – urging the last man in, in a tight finish, to 'Play up!

play up! and play the game' – but he does include Gavin Ewart's much more recent vision of 'The Cricketers' Arms', with its memorable last verse:

An Umpire, keen of eye and ardent,
Dispensing Justice, stands regardant.
Fieldsmen support a blazoned scroll:
FAIR PLAY DOTH ELEVATE
                    THE SOUL.

More generally in the anthology, Gerald Brodribb noted that to date there had been only two cricket novels (Dudley Carew's *The Son of Grief* and Bruce Hamilton's *Pro*) with a professional as their leading character. But though a short story rather than a novel, he might have mentioned John Arlott's wonderfully poignant-cum-humorous 'Ain't Half a Bloomin' Game', in which Norshire's snobbish amateur captain (and 'Flash Harry' of a batsman), K. E. Tallis, is increasingly impatient with the county's George Kennett, an ageing pro struggling for runs near the season's end and in danger of being dropped and no longer retained. In the event, Kennett has an unexpected last hurrah, the two men are reconciled, and Kennett is able to retire with honour satisfied and the prospect of a groundsman's job at a local works ground. In fact, it is a story that – for all its implicit criticism of the two-class system – falls a long way short of calling for abolition; and Arlott himself, notwithstanding his persistent undertow of dislike for cricket's establishment, was in all his instincts liberal rather than out-and-out egalitarian.

English cricket's set-up by the early 1960s undeniably had negative consequences. To name just some: a deep attachment to the two-class system, with an MCC inquiry (chaired by the Duke of Norfolk) into potential abolition having ruled in 1958 that 'the distinctive status of the amateur cricketer is not obsolete, is of great value to the game and should be preserved'; a favouring of amateurs when it came to selection (particularly in the July–August holiday season), accompanied by an instinctive lack of sympathy with the pro's often poorly paid lot; and a reluctance to face up to the implications of social change – a reluctance epitomised on the one hand by the continuing rejection of taking a world lead by having a one-day knock-out competition between the counties, on the other by at best patchy attempts either to encourage women's cricket or to reach out to ethnic minorities.

Was the amateur dominance of the game also responsible for some sort of ultimate softness? It is hard to gauge or quantify an ethos, but the fact was that by this time there was still relatively little competitive cricket played by clubs in London and the South-east, in essence a snobbish reaction against the league cricket widely played in the Midlands and the North, most famously in the Lancashire League. The fact also was that the seven post-war Ashes series prior to 1961 had produced markedly different outcomes depending on what sort of England captain was in charge. Five series with an amateur captain (Wally Hammond, Norman Yardley, Freddie Brown and May twice) had produced a solitary series win (May in 1956); whereas two series with a professional captain had produced two series wins (Hutton in 1953 and 1954–55). Of course, there were variable circumstances at play in all seven series – of course there were – but the contrast is still a striking one.

Is there a case for the defence? We find ourselves conflicted. That world of taken-for-granted privilege, of cricket as its own uniquely meaning-laden game, with its own unique spirit and own unique soul, was the world in which, as privately educated cricket-loving children, we grew up. Inevitably, for all the necessary – and very considerable – criticism, we retain a degree of emotional attachment to it. Moreover, it is always easier to condemn than to understand. We are all products of a particular background and environment. For all their limitations, these amateurs were not bad people, nor were those who defended their continuing dominance. And to assume with lofty, unimpeachable hindsight that they were is all too liable to result in a sterile, one-dimensional reading of the game's history.

We come back to Swanton, that apparently unwavering embodiment of the cricket establishment, and a man who seldom if ever used his unique pulpit on the *Daily Telegraph* to seek to improve conditions for the professional cricketer. But, in reality, he was a more complex person than the cartoon version, the man of whom it was said he was so snobbish that he would not even travel with his chauffeur. Back in 1957, reflecting in his customary tour book on the recent South Africa v England series, he described his 'frequent feelings of utter bewilderment at the Nationalist [i.e. the ruling white party] treatment of the dark population, whether African, Indian, or Coloured', before going on: 'Apart from moral considerations, how anyone can suppose that a persistent policy of suppression and the denial of basic rights to the labour force of a country can end in anything short of a most dangerous crisis in the long run baffles understanding.' These may seem unremarkable sentiments – but in the English cricket world of the time (and for many years later), they were very seldom to be heard.

Or take an illuminating episode in May 1960, when Swanton proposed Brian Johnston to fill one of the five vacancies on the MCC Committee, with his fellow commentator up against five candidates nominated by the Committee itself. Swanton, relate the AGM's minutes, 'felt it was wrong that the Committee should be self-perpetuating by putting up their own candidates'; he 'considered that Mr B. A. Johnston would introduce a fresh independent mind into the Committee'; and he 'expressed the view that a wind of change was desirable on the Committee'. Swanton's arguments failed to sway the members present, accustomed as they were to follow guidance-cum-instructions from above, as well as instinctively nervous about bringing someone from the newfangled and not quite respectable world of broadcasting into the inner sanctum of their club. Accordingly, 159 votes for Maurice Allom (a Cambridge Blue who between the wars had played as an amateur for Surrey and England); 158 for Brian Sellers (legendary amateur captain of Yorkshire in the 1930s, now Yorkshire chairman); 147 for Doug Insole (amateur captain of Essex and former England player); 141 for R. A. Boddington (Lancashire's amateur wicketkeeper for some years either side of the Great War, to be remembered in his *Wisden* obituary as 'a man of great charm'); 120 for David Clark (former amateur captain of Kent); and only 90 for the irreverent Old Etonian, Johnston. Swanton's reaction to this reversal? Mercifully unrecorded; but as a true lover of the game, and as one of its great evangelists, albeit because of his pomposity and snobbishness too often counter-productively off-putting, he had fought the good fight.

*

'Today the 1961 Australians landed at Tilbury,' recorded John Arlott on Friday 21 April 1961. 'They have been eagerly – and anxiously – awaited, for upon them may depend not only the periodic high season which their visit traditionally creates in English cricket, but the entire public image of the game in England. Surely they – particularly those who had made the trip before – must have sensed an unaccustomed urgency – a mixture of hope and anxiety – in those of us who came to greet them.' Why this anxiety? Essentially because, irrespective of the two-class system and all that, two threatening shadows now lay over English cricket.

The lesser, and affecting cricket generally, was that most troublesome of intermittent yet somehow perennial problems: throwing. An article by Leslie Smith in the just-published *Wisden* itemised the recent history: the storm in 1958–59 about whether 'Chuckers' (notably Ian Meckiff) had enabled Australia to regain the Ashes – or, to quote the title of Jack Fingleton's book about that controversial series, *Four Chukkas to Australia*; then, during the Lord's Test of June 1960, the South African fast bowler Geoff Griffin being called almost a dozen times; and that autumn, England and Australia agreeing that in the 1961 season there would be a moratorium during the tourists' matches ahead of the first Test, a moratorium designed to allow umpires privately to report on any Australian bowler with a suspect action, but without the publicity which would result from calling him.

'A sensible compromise' was the verdict of Smith's editor, Norman Preston, on 'the truce'; but Smith himself, who was linked with the Association of Cricket Umpires, reckoned it a shabby agreement 'which, to my mind, reflected no credit on the authorities of the two senior cricketing countries'. In the event, largely for valid cricketing rather than diplomatic reasons, the Australian touring party did not include any bowler at all seriously suspected of throwing; but given that England's leading left-arm spinner, Tony Lock, was still suspected of chucking the occasional one, despite having conscientiously remodelled his action, and that there were others on the county circuit with suspect actions, the issue still had the potential to return.

The other shadow was altogether bigger, blacker and more difficult to shift: in short, the declining popularity of the game. In 1947, most golden of post-war seasons, total attendance (exclusive of members) at county matches had reached 2.3 million; by 1960, after thirteen years of almost continuous decline, the total was barely a million. The most common sociological reason given was changing leisure patterns – above all, the coming of widespread car ownership allowing much greater choice – but few observers disagreed that, ultimately, the main culprit was the declining attractiveness of the cricket itself. 'The prevailing attitude of 1957 can be summed up in one word – security,' declared the Marxist critic C. L. R. James in a widely read *Cricketer* article. And he went on:

> Bowlers and batsmen are dominated by it. The long forward-defensive push, the negative bowling, are the techniques of specialised performers (professional or

amateur) in a security-minded age. As a corollary, we find much fast bowling and brilliant and daring close fielding and wicketkeeping – they are the only spheres where the spirit of adventure can express itself. The cricketers of today play the cricket of a specialised stratum, that of functionaries in the Welfare State. When many millions of people all over the world demand security and a state that must guarantee it, that's one thing. But when bowlers or batsmen, responsible for an activity essentially artistic and therefore individual, are dominated by the same principles, then the result is what we have.

And it is clear that those who support the Welfare State idea in politics and social life do not want it on the cricket field. They will not come to look at it.

Four years later – a couple of months before the start of the 1961 season and even as the latest inquiry continued into how to make cricket a more attractive product – county captains gathered at Lord's. Taking the chair was the inevitable Gubby Allen; and the minutes record how, after setting the ball rolling by referring to 'the need for increasing the tempo of the game', he received a gratifying degree of backing from almost all those present. P. B. H. May and the buccaneering A. C. D. Ingleby-Mackenzie 'felt that a conscious effort should be made by all concerned to give the appearance of enjoyment'; M. J. K. Smith said that 'even with seam bowlers, it was possible to keep up an over-rate of 20 per hour'; Yorkshire's professional captain, Vic Wilson, urged that 'all should agree to sporting declarations in which both sides had a chance of winning'; O. S. Wheatley 'emphasised the need to encourage batsmen low in the order to hit the ball'; and E. R. Dexter 'found general support in suggesting that from the very beginning of a three-day match, as many quick singles as possible should be taken'. Only one captain, right at the end, dared to strike a dissenting note: 'He felt that we must face the fact that there were inherent weaknesses in the game and, on occasions, the game must inevitably be dull – in fact, it sometimes paid to play dull cricket.' Heresy, indeed; and the dissenter was that supreme hard-boiled pragmatist, T. E. Bailey.

Still, the majority will was clear, with the public statement coming out of the captains' summit affirming boldly, if not entirely accurately, 'their unanimous determination to provide entertaining cricket' and 'to do their utmost to increase the tempo of the game'. *Wisden*'s editor, for one, was sceptical. 'It is useless them going to Lord's in the winter and agreeing that it is essential for every county to adopt a dynamic attitude to the game from first ball to last whether batting, bowling or fielding,' complained Preston in that year's edition, 'and then deliberately ignoring the agreement on the field.' But his greatest ire was reserved for the other ranks: 'There are too many county professionals who reckon they have done a satisfactory job if they scrape 1,200 runs in a season for an average of about 30.00. They pay no heed to the way they make their runs and it is time they were clearly told that unless they are prepared to think of making the occasional hundred in two and a half to three hours, their services will no longer be required.'

Nor by this time, and in fact for the best part of the previous decade, was the English team remotely immune from similar charges, under first Hutton's cautious, overly defensive leadership and then more recently May's and Cowdrey's. England's funereal over rate in the 1950s was a particularly sore point with the Aussies. Yet now there was a very visible – almost embarrassingly visible – challenge to that approach. 'CRICKET ALIVE AGAIN: ONUS NOW ON ENGLAND AND AUSTRALIA' was the title of the article immediately following Preston's unhappy ruminations. In it, Fingleton wrote in the immediate aftermath of the 'incredible' Australia–West Indies tie in Brisbane about the crucial lesson to be drawn:

> Cricket matches are always at their best when they are hard-fought. I have no stomach for anything else, but there comes a time when the desire to win defeats itself in a dull negation of the game and its virtues. We, England and Australia, must in the near future have more confidence in each other, more trust. Often, as might have happened in Brisbane, there is as much virtue in losing as in winning if the game has been played honourably, with courage, with character and with challenge.

Challenge indeed ... The rest of the series had, of course, also been a triumph, universally hailed as one of the finest in modern times and culminating in a world-record attendance at Melbourne. 'The need for English county sides and Test teams to follow the lead set by the Australians and West Indians is strongly felt by both the Press and the public of this country,' reflected Arlott on the day of the Tilbury landing. 'Failure to make use of an opportunity which might not readily recur may well prove disastrous.'

Even before he got off the boat, Benaud was giving a press conference where he made it clear that if the forthcoming series failed to live up to hopes, it would not be the fault of the visitors. 'We will not be diverted from playing attractive cricket, even if the opposition do not do likewise. We have made a policy and will stick to it …' And: 'We want to win very badly, but if we lose, we want to lose playing attractively.' For his favourably impressed observers, it was almost as if the Australian captain had arrived in order to fulfil his destiny as the saviour of English cricket. 'Now here he is,' wrote Swanton in the next day's *Telegraph*, 'having done so much to rehabilitate cricket's good repute in his own country and expected to play the leading part in boosting it here. The accent everywhere is on the game rather than the result.' Was it too good to be true? 'Many platitudes are uttered before the start of a new series and many things said tongue in cheek,' the well-seasoned Swanton readily conceded. 'Yet,' he went on, 'Benaud's ambition to play enterprising cricket need not be doubted.'

Six of the seventeen-strong touring party had toured England before. Benaud himself; his vice-captain Neil Harvey, at this time second only to Don Bradman as Australia's heaviest-ever run-scorer; batters Peter Burge and Colin McDonald; and all-rounders Alan Davidson and Ken ('Slasher') Mackay – the former's left-arm fast bowling likely to be the Australian attack's most potent weapon, the latter's idiosyncratic left-hand batting style described by Arlott on the previous tour as 'fascinatingly repulsive'.

Of the other eleven, Bobby Simpson was an opening batsman with a useful line in leg-spin bowling and slip-catching; Brian Booth and Bill Lawry (a teacher and a plumber respectively) were uncapped batters with good Sheffield Shield records; the experienced Wally Grout held wicket-keeping world records, with Barry Jarman as his understudy; Lindsay Kline and Ian Quick were slow bowlers in whom only relatively moderate hopes were invested; and so, too, with the fast-medium bowlers Ron Gaunt (a surprise choice as a renowned 'dragger'), Frank Misson and Graham (Garth) McKenzie, at nineteen the 'baby' of the party.* That still left, from those eleven newcomers, the man widely anticipated as the star of the whole show: the gloriously attack-minded Norman O'Neill, who had made a huge impact in the 1958–59 series in Australia. 'The batsman English cricket followers have been waiting to see as he promises to be Australia's leading batsman for the next decade,' declared Gordon Ross in the tour's official souvenir brochure; while Swanton simply declared, following the tourists' arrival, that 'few heights are beyond him'.

'What of the English team?' wondered Arlott at this expectant spring moment. In his eyes, 'near-certainties' for the first Test were, in likely batting order, the six batters Geoff Pullar, Raman Subba Row, Ted Dexter, Peter May ('if fit'), Colin Cowdrey and Ken Barrington, together with the opening bowlers Fred Trueman and Brian Statham, while the off-spinner David Allen was 'almost in that category'.

---

*Before the 1962 'front-foot rule' was brought in, bowlers (for a delivery to be legal) only had to have their rear foot behind the line of the bowling crease adjacent to the stumps. A 'dragger' was a bowler who, while technically complying with the law, raked the toe of their rear foot through the line of the bowling crease in the delivery stride, often with their front foot considerably in advance of the front line (the popping crease) as the ball was propelled down the pitch. During the 1958–59 tour, the very tall Australian fast bowler Gordon Rorke had so pronounced a 'drag' that various English batters accused him of treading on their toes.

Who, if needed, would be the third seamer? Arlott's best bet was Middlesex's Alan Moss, though with Hampshire's David ('Butch') White and Worcestershire's John (Jack) Flavell among those in the frame. As for the keeper, it probably came down to a choice between Jim Parks, the superior batter, or John Murray, better behind the stumps, albeit 'many county players would declare Keith Andrew by far the best wicketkeeper in the country'. And captain? The general assumption, unquestioned by Arlott, was that it would be May if available, or Cowdrey if not.

But around this time, the South African player John Waite published a book, *Perchance to Bowl*, whose final chapter looked ahead to the imminent Ashes series and argued that Trevor Bailey (dropped after the 1958–59 debacle) ought to be recalled to the England ranks as captain. 'I believe him to be the ideal man for this tremendous task,' he told his English readership. 'Yes, pit Trevor Bailey's cricketing wits against the cricketing wits of Richie Benaud this year, if you hope to win.' An intriguing thought, but seldom canvassed by the home pundits, let alone seriously contemplated by the selectors. Overall, Arlott for his part saw two things as indispensable if England were to regain the Ashes against an Australian side probably stronger in batting than bowling: first, that the old firm of Trueman and Statham, both now in their thirties, 'sustain their former pace through all five Tests'; and second, that May be available, and in good enough form 'to give the English batting sufficient weight to guarantee against defeat'. 'It is important,' added Arlott reassuringly, 'that he plays Benaud so well.'

A last word at this stage went to Neville Cardus, almost sixty years since he had seen in the flesh his first Test – at

Old Trafford in 1902, as England, seemingly poised to win, had lost to Australia by a heartbreaking 3 runs. As ever, he invoked the human dimension:

> A game, like any other activity in life, is pretty much what we make of it, the players and the public. Imagination from players and crowd alike is needed to bring about greatness. Fresh pages in cricket's history are waiting to be written upon. Let our pens be golden. Let us all be made to realise, every ball, every over, that cricket is not an exact science, that it is the sum total of the skill, the impulse and the mortal error of everybody taking part in it. Playthings of fortune! On whom this summer will she smile; on whom will she frown? Peter May, Richie Benaud, Neil Harvey, Colin Cowdrey, 'Lord Edward' [i.e. Dexter] and the rest, including, most likely, some new aspirant? The stage is ready, inviting, beautifully set.

3

Halfway to Paradise

The Australian tour – notable throughout for the collegiate, egalitarian spirit among the players consciously engendered by Benaud – began its first-class programme on Saturday 29 April, as usual in the shadow of Worcester Cathedral. Except there was precious little sun, and instead three damp, bitterly cold days, with rain on the Tuesday preventing what might well have been a tight finish. Remarkably enough, YouTube has about a quarter of an hour of intensely evocative silent film, including many shots of huddled spectators. Two of the match's spectators were us: entirely coincidental, and seven years before we first met. One, aged ten, was reassured by his father that Tom Graveney – Worcestershire's new acquisition, not allowed this season to play championship matches, and thus effectively debarred from England consideration – was not really playing and missing, but instead deliberately playing above the ball in order to gauge the pace of the wicket; the other, aged nine, had been very kindly taken by his Shropshire grandmother, but that did not prevent his vexation when she accidentally sat on his newly acquired *Wisden* and permanently creased a corner of the cover.*

A rather more important drama centred on the Australian captain. Bowling a wrong 'un to Graveney late on the first day, Benaud felt something go in his right shoulder. Fairly soon he was in intense pain; and that night, back at the team's Droitwich hotel, he found himself barely able to raise his bowling arm. He managed six overs on the final morning, even bowling Martin Horton; but that evening, as the rest of the party went on to Chesterfield, he was heading to London and, following a diagnosis of an inflamed tendon, intensive treatment. After weeks of wearing a sling and shaving left-handed in order to alleviate the soreness, accompanied by sustained media attention that prompted the Australian cricket writer Ray Robinson to call Benaud's shoulder 'the most discussed since Venus de Milo's', it was seven matches before he bowled seriously again, against Gloucestershire at Bristol – where, though he took two wickets, there was, noted Bill Bowes (Yorkshire and England bowler-turned-journalist), all too little 'fizz' in his thirty-three overs. 'My shoulder is getting better every day,' he publicly insisted not

---

*Graveney, a professional, had been captain of Gloucestershire and their star batter. In 1960, the county dropped from second to eighth place in the county championship, and the Gloucestershire committee replaced Graveney as captain with the amateur C. T. M. Pugh, a vastly inferior player. Graveney in disgust moved to neighbouring Worcestershire; but, according to the quasi-feudal regulations of the time about players moving against their county's wishes, had to serve a year's residential qualification. This allowed him, for instance, to play for his new county against the visiting Australians – but barred him from appearing in any county championship matches. There had been no comparable penalty when the Gloucestershire off-spinner 'Bomber' Wells moved to Nottinghamshire the previous season by mutual consent.

long afterwards, but most observers reckoned he was likely to remain essentially crocked for a while yet.

Problems, too, during these early weeks for his probable opposite number. May began his comeback (no cricket in England since 1959) with 68 at Fenner's against his old university; there followed a near-century against Worcestershire, and other good scores, including an authoritative 58 for Surrey against the tourists, before later that day (15 May) he pulled a muscle in the groin and was out for the rest of the month. Or as Swanton gloomily put it, 'a period of rest, just at the stage when May needs all the time on the field he can get'.

Over the three and a half weeks after the tourists' opener – as Spurs became the first twentieth-century team to complete the double, as *Beyond the Fringe* made its first great impact, as the weather gradually picked up – the new season started to take shape. 'Why has he played for England only once?' wondered the former Australian fast bowler Ray Lindwall as Derbyshire's Les Jackson bowled a typically immaculate spell (10-7-9-1) in the only sixty-five minutes of play at Chesterfield; Roy Marshall's match-winning 153 at The Oval ('a glorious display of majestic batting', *Wisden*) suggested that Hampshire might be a considerable force in the championship; next day, also at The Oval, Bill Lawry took 165 off a presumably weary Surrey attack, a feat he celebrated by downing half a gallon of milk in the dressing-room; England's greatest off-spinner, Jim Laker, was struck at the end of that match by how, without Benaud, 'the spin-bowling department' of the tourists appeared 'ominously bare'; playing at Peterborough, Gloucestershire's new amateur captain, Tom Pugh, ducked into a full toss from the young Northamptonshire fast bowler David Larter, had his jaw broken in two places and was given out lbw; 'if he keeps his head and his health he is surely a young player to whom the future beckons,' reckoned *The Times*'s John Woodcock, after Cambridge's nineteen-year-old freshman Mike Brearley had in two innings taken 162 runs off the tourists, admittedly on a Fenner's special on which four Australian batters had already scored centuries on the first day; and on the last Friday of the month, the 26th, there was an almost universal shaking of heads, as all but one of the latest round of matches ended in tame, unenterprising draws. Still, consolation that evening for over 14 million viewers as, on one of the only two TV channels, Tony Hancock, no longer living in East Cheam, sat in his Earl's Court flat and wrestled unavailingly with Bertrand Russell's *Human Knowledge: Its Scope and Limits* – so unavailingly that he soon got up and ran across the room pretending to bowl Benaud-style while giving his own commentary ('Here's Richie Benaud now, bowling from the pavilion end ...') with an Australian accent.

Next day, pitted against an MCC team of batting probables and (largely underperforming) bowling possibles, the Australians began their first match at Lord's – where, a month earlier, their keeper Wally Grout had had his first underwhelmed glimpse on arrival for a practice session in the Nursery end nets. 'I immediately saw how the gate takings could be greatly increased,' he would recall. 'Tear down the Long Room and build a decent stand.' In the middle, two centuries on the Saturday: one for the already increasingly inevitable Lawry ('more a run-getter than a craftsman, and at the moment he is working a productive borehole,' noted

Woodcock) and the other for O'Neill, fulfilling Swanton's pre-match acclamation that 'here at last is a player fit to rank with the great'.

O'Neill himself, in the course of delighting a crowd of some 22,000, was less than impressed by the defensive field placings ('at times he had five men on the fence') of MCC's captain, Colin Cowdrey. Monday, though, was Cowdrey's turn to make a fine century, prompting Woodcock not only to observe that 'soon he was in such command that people shook their heads at the authority of his strokes', but to speculate that 'perhaps he wanted to show that O'Neill is not the only lion in the jungle'. And Benaud? On the face of it, the match was a triumph – a crowd-pleasingly bold declaration, the tourists winning by 63 runs with just over half an hour to spare, five wickets for himself on the last afternoon – but he was still in constant pain when he bowled and still unable to bowl his googly. Even so, he had, in Woodcock's words, 'exposed again the old English anxiety against leg spin'.

By the start of June, most cricketing thoughts were firmly on the Ashes series, due to start at Edgbaston on Thursday the 8th. The Saturday before, May was back in action for Surrey, making 30 at Northampton, while at Hove the main event was always going to be Dexter versus Benaud. 'The feeling of tension was inescapable,' recorded Arlott. 'Dexter lost all his usual regal air of command and eventually, after some uncertain defence, was drawn forward into the dipping flight of a leg-break which whipped through his over-stretched defensive stroke for Grout to execute the stumping for which he was obviously poised in advance. Benaud's delight emphasised his recognition of this wicket as a psychological victory ...' In the event, though, that was not the main drama, as O'Neill in the field tore a tendon below the knee and was immediately rated as highly doubtful for Edgbaston.

One uncertainty, though, was resolved that evening: albeit his groin had stood up well enough during his innings, May remained unconvinced that, especially after his long absence from Test cricket, he was fully ready for the rigours of a five-day contest, and accordingly he rang Gubby Allen asking not to be considered. England's captain for the first Test would therefore be Cowdrey, May's automatic and seemingly willing deputy over the last two years.

The following day, Sunday the 4th, the selectors – Allen in the chair, joined by Glamorgan's Wilf Wooller, Essex's Doug Insole and the old Yorkshire and England opener Herbert Sutcliffe – gathered at Allen's flat in Queen's Gate and chose their party of twelve: Cowdrey, Pullar, Subba Row, Dexter and Barrington as the five obvious batters; Mike Smith in place of May; Murray to keep, after Parks had failed twice with the bat for MCC at Lord's; Trueman and Statham as the two automatic fast men; David Allen and Ray Illingworth as the two possible spinners; and Essex all-rounder Barry Knight to provide additional pace if required.

'Not an exciting English side,' thought Arlott, and 'like any Australia may pick, it is not so strong in bowling as some of its recent predecessors'. Woodcock for his part reckoned Dexter lucky ('hardly merits a place on current form'); pointed out about Knight's inclusion that Essex had 'another, better-known all-rounder, by the name of Bailey'; and noted the omission of Yorkshire's Brian Close, twelve years after the all-rounder had first played for

England and who 'still has more ability than most'. What might ultimately make the difference? Woodcock had little doubt about the crucial factor from an English point of view: 'In Cowdrey and Dexter there is greatness. The others have prolific county records. Yet what is needed against Australia, as much as all the inherent skill a man can have, is the character to become the master of his nerves and the nerve to make the most of his ability.'

The English skipper's mental state appears to have been distinctly unsettled in these days leading up to the Test. Cowdrey himself in later years described the discovery over that weekend that he was going to be taking charge, with little time for adequate preparation, as a 'shattering fact'; while more than half a century afterwards, John Murray related to his biographer Christopher Sandford the story of how, probably on the Wednesday, Cowdrey had given him a lift up from London in his silver Mark VII Jaguar:

It was an odd sort of drive up. Every ten miles or so he'd pull off the main road and turn down some country lane where he'd stop at somebody's bloody great manor house, say 'Won't be a minute', and I'd sit there in the driveway while Colin went in to see whoever it was. Then he used to pull out these sheets of paper from the glove compartment and show them to me when we stopped at red lights. Basically they were diagrams of the Edgbaston playing area and Cowdrey would say things like, 'If Trueman bowls to Lawry from the pavilion end, do we want to start off with a leg gully, or a man closer to backward square leg?' Well, what the hell do I know? ... This went on all afternoon, until we finally pulled up at the team hotel in Droitwich.

I got out and started hauling my kit from the back seat of the Jag. There might still be time for a swift net before dinner, I thought. Just then Gubby Allen came trotting down the front steps wearing a beautiful pinstripe suit with a carnation in the buttonhole and offered us both a glass of sherry ...

For the England team, Dexter was passed fit (having been troubled by a knee for much of the season), which meant no place for the young Surrey batter John Edrich, called up just in case, while Knight was left out (Dexter now as the third seamer). For the Australians, a tough workout on Wednesday saw O'Neill pronouncing himself fit, and Benaud – whose relationship by this time with the tour manager Syd Webb, a sixty-year-old from the unreconstructed disciplinarian school of Australian cricket administrators, was becoming increasingly difficult – declared he himself would also play, despite his continuing shoulder problems. 'It's still pretty sore, but I've got to reconcile myself to the fact that it will continue to be sore and there's nothing I can do about it,' he told a journalist. 'I've played in difficulties before,' he added. 'Either I played in pain, or didn't play at all. I intend to play on.'

What did the pundits think? Jack Fingleton had already predicted that 'the series looks like being a colossal one for scoring', so presumably he expected a draw; another Australian, Percy Beames, much-respected cricket correspondent of the Melbourne daily the *Age*, explicitly predicted a draw and emphasised the thin resources on a good pitch of the respective attacks, albeit wondering whether Benaud, hitherto 'not over-exerting himself', might 'quite easily be keeping something special back by way of surprise'; Jim Laker in the *Daily Sketch*, calling the Australian attack 'the WEAKEST ever to visit these shores', anticipated 'a high-scoring match with the extra penetration of Trueman, Statham and Co SEEING ENGLAND THROUGH'; Arlott declined to commit himself to a specific match prediction; Swanton enjoined his readers that there was 'absolutely no need to be despondent', given the largely untested Australian attack; Woodcock concluded his preview by declaring that the Test, like all the others in the series, would ultimately be judged 'not so much by its outcome as by the methods that are used'; and Len Hutton, talking to the *Evening News*'s Julian Holland, uttered four words based on a cricketing lifetime of bittersweet experience: 'Don't underestimate the Australians.'

*

Thursday was a day of weddings: of Shirley Bassey in Cardiff, of Petula Clark in Paris – and, at York Minster, of Katharine Worsley, as the daughter of MCC's President-elect (Sir William Worsley) married the Duke of Kent, a wedding whose extensive coverage on BBC TV was a significant blow to cricket lovers, royalist or otherwise. 'The greenest Test wicket I have ever seen,' observed Hutton at Edgbaston itself about one of the classic good tosses to lose, not helped by a forecast of showers. Cowdrey won it and decided to bat. 'A more adventurous captain,' thought Hutton, 'might well have put Australia in to bat', adding that Trueman and Statham on that wicket 'would have been to me an overwhelming temptation'; but most observers were unlikely to have quarrelled with the cautious reflection of another distinguished captain, Frank Worrell, that Cowdrey 'would have been open to much criticism' had he done so and 'his gamble had failed'.

Indeed, on the basis of the first hour of play, interrupted by a rain shower, even Hutton was compelled to concede ('what a deceptive game cricket can be!') that there were few signs of any great movement off the pitch. In practice, though, it was the first shower, followed by other showers in the course of the day, that made all the difference, as the uncovered wicket became increasingly problematic and the ball started to lift. Subba Row hung in tenaciously, but Pullar and Dexter were both out before lunch; Cowdrey gave a masterly defensive display ('watches everything on to his bat,' said Hutton, 'as though he were playing with a paddle and a football') before unluckily playing on to Frank Misson; and by half an hour after tea, with Subba Row and Barrington at the crease, England had recovered to the extent of 121 for three. At which point, with Alan Davidson not proving the expected threat, the relatively gentle medium pace of Ken Mackay took three wickets in four balls: Barrington, in attacking mode, caught at gully; Smith, crowded by Benaud, caught at silly point off an inside edge; and Subba Row, caught at slip for a worthy 59.

Should Cowdrey have now declared in order to take immediate advantage of a manifestly bowler-friendly wicket? Some apparently thought so, but among others not Swanton or Bowes or the high-class cricket reporter Ron Roberts or the former England leg-break bowler Ian Peebles ('would have been a very chancy affair'). However, what about later in the session when Murray's was the next wicket to fall? Swanton after close of play would ponder the tantalising possibilities:

This was the point, with 153 for seven on the board, at which various theorists would have had Cowdrey either declare or order full steam ahead. There were 50 minutes to go, the ball was still 'seaming', and no doubt Statham and Trueman would have enjoyed a bowl.

To declare would have been a magnificent gesture in its way, and it is possible we might now be hailing Cowdrey as a genius if he had done so. On the other hand the weather forecast is uncertain, and the runs made by the England tail, both this evening and presumably tomorrow, will be valuable if the Australians have to bat in similar conditions.

What I personally hoped Cowdrey would do was to send in Trueman after Murray left, with orders to chance his arm. England might, perhaps, then have collected as many as there are on the board now and still given themselves half a dozen overs at the enemy.

In fact, what transpired was altogether tamer: Illingworth and Allen adding only 3 runs in twenty minutes before the Yorkshireman was out; and then his fellow Tyke barely playing a shot in anger until almost the very end, as England closed at a disappointing 180 for eight. 'How Trueman must have fretted,' mulled Arlott, 'at having to bat where he might have bowled so menacingly.'

Little menace, alas, on the Friday. The wicket restored by an overnight's covering followed by morning sun, the England innings quickly wrapped up, Trueman and co. toiling as Australia racked up 359 for five by the close – it was a day that, among other things, kept faith with Benaud's promise that the tourists would try their hardest to score at a rate of at least a run a minute. After the plumber from

Victoria had laid the foundations ('each time I see Lawry,' remarked Hutton, 'the more convinced I become that he is going to be one of the biggest thorns in England's side for many years'), the glory belonged to Harvey and O'Neill, whose third-wicket stand of 146 in less than two hours marked what Beames acclaimed as 'one of the fiercest attacks seen on English Test bowling for many years'. 'Cut followed push, peerless cover drive rippling glance, punched on-drive flowing off-drive, imperious force impish chop,' wrote the *Guardian*'s admiring Denys Rowbotham. 'Feet moved ever more quickly to the ball's pitch. Bodies lay back more audaciously to cut and force.' For a no less appreciative Swanton, it was a case of 'the old hero and the new': Harvey displaying 'that crispness and economy of effort that one associated with the masters', O'Neill at his 'superbly powerful and confident' best less than a week after his injury at Hove. The finest raptures, though, belonged to Arlott:

Suddenly, after years, the mantle of care and anxiety had dropped away from Test cricket and the game was gallant – even heroic – once more. Small wonder that representative cricket in recent years has been glorified numbers, by the records that have been broken – measures of quantity instead of quality. This cricket made the scoreboard a secondary interest. Here were two batsmen who would have been a credit to any 'Golden Age' ... Not even the absent sun could so completely have warmed both the ground and the players; the scoreboard passed out of mind, and we lived for an afternoon in an age when men played cricket with all their gifts because they enjoyed it – and did not give a damn for the selection committee – nor even the critics.

Those last, though, were not so completely dazzled as to lose their critical faculties, as they laid into the bowlers for failing to attack off stump and also into the fielders (Dexter in the covers the shining exception) for a listless display of 'fumbling and slow-footedness', reviving in Swanton painful memories of 'the blackest of all dark days at Leeds in '48', when, set 400 to make in a day on a turning wicket, Bradman and Australia romped home by seven wickets. Nor was Cowdrey's captaincy exempt, with Wilfred Rhodes – who at Edgbaston fifty-nine years earlier had taken 7–17 against Australia and now, in his blind old age, sat between Sydney Barnes and Frank Woolley and relied on their descriptive powers – telling Fingleton that there should have been a man deep at point for Harvey. Was Cowdrey perhaps under explicit orders from Gubby Allen not to resort to defensive tactics? Given the mauling that England were taking, he could easily have set a six-three or seven-two field and instructed his men to bowl outside the off stump; while the fact was that in the two hours between lunch and tea, as the runs flowed, England bowled forty overs. Arlott, for one, would not have had it otherwise; while another telling detail (equally hard to imagine in the 2020s) was Beames's pleasure in Harvey and O'Neill 'driving, cutting and hooking in a way that brought roars of admiration from the 18,000 crowd'.

'A dank, dismal and drizzly day' was, in Alan Ross's words, the backdrop for Saturday's weather-interrupted play, watched by a 'large, gloomy crowd wrapped in scarves and coats, and at intervals hoisting multi-coloured umbrellas'.

What action there was had at its centre the idiosyncratic Mackay, compiling a half-century and prompting Hutton to remark that 'he does not seem to bat well enough to get himself out'.

The ever-reliable Statham apart, none of the England bowlers impressed, with not just Swanton predictably critical of Trueman ('soon seemed depressed by the prospect of bowling to such efficient players on so good a surface'), but also the instinctively less anti-Trueman Woodcock ('looked as though he was growing old before his time'). Allen and Illingworth continued to make little impact; after five overs the day before, Dexter with his suspect knee was not trusted with any more; and Barrington with his leg-breaks was not trusted with any. An hour before the close, Benaud – not out 36 and going well – declared at 516 for nine, Australia's highest Test total in England since their 701 at The Oval in 1934, five series and three reigns earlier. A selfless declaration, but Pullar and Subba Row had been batting for only a couple of overs before bad light and more rain brought play to an end.

Next morning, as Cowdrey and the Australian twelfth man, Brian Booth, read the lessons at a 'Sportsmen's Service' in a Birmingham church, the Sunday cricket writers read the tea leaves. In the *Sunday Times*, Peebles surveyed England's 'pretty grim' position and concluded that 'the English climate looks like our only, if not very secret, weapon'; in the *Sunday Telegraph* (only four months old), Michael Melford held out the hope that 'a draw and some redemption of a melancholy performance so far is not impossible'; and in the *Observer*, Ross's view, that 'one would be brave to predict' England escaping defeat, was balanced by Worrell's: 'The

Australians, by their adventurous strokeplay, are now in a commanding position, but on this wicket there is no reason why the England batting side should not respond equally strongly.' What all agreed upon was the significance of the Edgbaston moment. Needing to win the series in order to regain the Ashes – a series in which, by general consent, the batting was still likely to dominate the bowling – England could ill afford to go one down.

Monday was another wet sort of day, with the score standing at 106 for one when rain drove the players conclusively in some twenty minutes after lunch. Pullar had survived until shortly before the interval, while Subba Row (68 not out) was cementing his reputation as, in Woodcock's words, 'one of the hardest of all to uproot once he settles in'. He also, either side of lunch, performed a valuable team service in protecting Dexter from Benaud – given that, as Hutton put it, the new batter 'sent our hearts to our boots' whenever he did have to face him. 'He continually played back and was repeatedly beaten. He must learn that the only way to play a bowler like Benaud is to go forward to him as do Cowdrey and May.'

The Sussex man also had a slice of good fortune shortly before the rain, as he slashed a short one from Davidson straight to second slip, where Mackay seemingly lost the ball against the crowd and ducked out of its way. This was Dexter's sixth Test innings against Australia, and so far his top score was 11. Unsurprisingly, it was at this point, recorded Woodcock, 'impossible to find an Australian with any noticeable respect for Dexter's cricketing ability. Both on tour in Australia and against them here this season he has struck them as having feet of clay.' Five not out overnight, and England still 215 behind, this proud young man must have badly wanted to prove them wrong.

Tuesday – a sunny day, a well-behaved pitch – paid for all. After Subba Row had completed his century and been out for 112, Dexter stayed firm and batted almost all day for his 180, as England comfortably enough in the end earned their draw. 'To watch Dexter, as he played today, is like drinking champagne,' declared an uncharacteristically lyrical Hutton. 'His artistry completely eclipsed the artisan Subba Row.' Woodcock described more fully the making of what was an English batter's second-highest score against Australia since Hutton's monumental 364 back in 1938:

> Strangely enough, he never stung them with quite the fullest powers of his driving. He was hitting the ball too much into the ground for that, and the pitch was a shade too slow. There was, however, an aggression and an authority about his play that revealed to the Australians a batsman of singular strength and style. His detachment, amounting almost to disdain, must have maddened his opponents. He was concentrating on laying a bogey, upon overcoming an inferiority complex against leg-spin bowling, and in doing so he gave no chance until his score was 179.
>
> Had Dexter got out at any time before three o'clock, Englishmen might have been gnawing at their nails for much longer than they were. Instead, he found a balance between attack and defence and conveyed an air of permanency which surprised even those who knew his talents …

The batting disappointment of the day was Cowdrey, playing on (for the second time in the match, this time to Mackay) for a dispiritingly timid 14. 'Miserable with anxiety,' observed Arlott, he had played every ball 'as if it were a bomb likely to explode at the slightest hint of violence'. Not that his opposite number was happy either, on a day when his team had failed to clinch victory and he himself had struggled horribly with his shoulder, able to bowl only two overs in the whole of the afternoon (perforce leaving leg-break duties to Simpson) and barely able to get his arm over. Soon after the close of play, at a press conference, Benaud even gave a demonstration of how the pain was such that he was quite incapable of turning his wrist over and bowling a wrong 'un; 'I am convinced his shoulder trouble is now very serious,' duly noted Beames; and inevitably, the question of whether he would be able to play in the Lord's Test in nine days' time was already coming into focus.

That Tuesday evening had one revealing episode, unreported at the time. Barrington during the afternoon had, in the course of just over three hours, played a staunch, uncomplaining second fiddle to Dexter, scoring barely a quarter of the runs in their fourth-wicket partnership of 161. 'Diligent' and 'invaluable' were Arlott's just adjectives of praise, yet it transpired that not everyone agreed, as Barrington himself would recall some years later:

I had travelled back to London with Dexter, and my wife and I were having dinner at his flat when 'Gubby' Allen, chairman of the England selectors, rang him up. Judging from what I heard of the conversation (and I could not possibly *help* hearing) Mr Allen had quite rightly telephoned to congratulate Ted on his knock, but he then seemed to want to know what I had been doing batting all that time for 48! Ted put the facts before him.

I thought I had played with common sense. My aim at first was to stay there at all costs. After all, Ted was going for his shots, and though he was playing magnificently he was inevitably giving the bowlers a chance. If he had got out anything could have happened. I concentrated on defence so much that when the game was safe I found I just could not time any attacking strokes. Of course, by that time it did not matter.

Was anyone else, in the context of the match and indeed the series, really complaining? Admittedly, albeit from an Australian point of view, the journalist A. G. ('Johnny') Moyes did observe of Barrington's innings that 'there were times when he collected runs as though he had to produce a ration book in order to be served'; but the undeniable crux was – as Moyes himself added, however grudgingly – that 'he stayed, and no doubt that was what England wanted and needed'.

Lord's now awaited. 'CRY RINGS OUT FOR A BAILEY OR LOCK' had been the headline for the weekend assessment by a former Middlesex and England fast bowler, the often humorous amateur J. J. Warr; and during the next county round, playing at Hove, Tony Lock complemented his attacking 67 not out with eight wickets in Surrey's match-winning performance. Once the contest was over on Friday afternoon, he headed straight to Lord's, where that evening at the Nursery end – with a handkerchief to aim at, Murray behind the stumps, and Swanton among those watching – Gubby Allen put him through his bowling paces. That test passed, Lock next day went with confidence into Surrey's home match against Yorkshire and took four for 25 – just as, up on Burton-on-Trent, the other old warhorse possibly ripe for recall, Trevor Bailey, was taking five for 27 for Essex against Derbyshire.

Fingleton on Sunday morning, with four days to go, offered a general *tour d'horizon*. Following two high totals at Edgbaston, he anticipated another draw; there was little case, over two years since their last Test, for bringing back either Bailey ('one can't see him containing O'Neill, Harvey and company') or the remodelled Lock ('he might get Test wickets but he will take, I am sure, a hammering'); Edgbaston had shown there was no point England again playing two off-spinners in order to exploit bowlers' rough outside left-handers' off stump ('everybody, umpires as well as captains, now scrupulously watch the pitch and warn off invaders'); Australia should take a chance and pick Graham McKenzie ('an up-and-comer'); and 'as at Birmingham, this might be a good toss to lose, because of early life in the pitch and because the pitch is covered overnight'. Also in the papers was the news that Samuel Beckett was planning to attend the Lord's Test, prompting Philip Larkin to react in inimical fashion to Monica Jones: 'Waiting for Benaud ogh ogh'.

Later that Sunday the England selectors released the names of their chosen party of thirteen. May was back, but not as captain, with Cowdrey continuing in that role. As far as one can tell, Gubby Allen had wanted May restored to the captaincy at once; but he had resisted, on the grounds that, although he had scored a big century at Taunton on the eve of the Edgbaston Test, another injury (a damaged calf muscle) had caused him to miss the previous and the current round of county matches. 'It is reasonable that, wrestling with both form and fitness, he should be relieved at least of the captaincy,' concurred Arlott. 'His presence must certainly strengthen the side's confidence and, even on his county form, he will give power as well as dignity to the batting.'

Arlott, though regretting the omission of Allen rather than Illingworth, was also positive about the choice of Gloucestershire's David Smith, who in effect replaced Knight as back-up seamer. What about the oldies? No place for Bailey, but Lock did now get the nod, causing a somewhat unenthusiastic Woodcock to describe him as 'no longer the terror he was in the fifties, when from his elbow came those vicious and irresistible spells'. Some, of course, might secretly have pined for a fleeting glimpse or two of that elbow – but, if so, in vain. 'It was agreed that the chairman should speak to Lock on the eve of the match,' recorded the minutes of the selectors' meeting, 'and obtain from him an assurance that he would not bowl his "away swinger" [so-called] or "chinaman" as both were regarded as "suspect" and, in the circumstances, no possible causes for concern can be given.' Or as Tony Lewis wryly put it years later in his bicentenary history of MCC, 'it must have been like going into battle and finding that you have left half of your ammunition behind'.

Over the next few days, contrasting fortunes for the two Edgbaston captains: Cowdrey warming up nicely with centuries on successive days for Kent against the tourists; but Benaud, despite intensive medical attention, having to concede on Wednesday that he would be unable to play – a bitter personal blow to be denied captaining Australia in a

Test at Lord's, with his unhappiness no doubt compounded by an increasingly public dispute with manager Webb about which of the two men was responsible for speaking to the press (something at which Benaud, with his journalistic background, was a complete natural). While as for his longer-term playing prospects, 'The End for Benaud?' would be the headline for a *Daily Mail* piece by Alex Bannister, who reckoned, such was the nature of his shoulder injury, that he was 'unlikely to be an effective Test bowler for the rest of this tour'. In the here and now, meanwhile, Harvey instead was set to captain; McKenzie was brought in; and Davidson, though both injured (back) and asthmatic by the end of the Kent match, was persuaded by Benaud that he owed it to Harvey to play.

Also on the eve of the match, Bowes inspected the wicket with the groundsman and his assistant. 'They assured me it was a good pitch and said one, "If they don't average 300 runs per innings in the Test match they won't be trying".' The barometer was steadily rising, and next morning Keith Miller in the *Daily Express* took an even more confident line – 'this second round in the Ashes battle looks like being the biggest batting party since the war' – while at the other end of the political spectrum the *Guardian*'s headline was 'Batsmen Promised Rich Harvest in Second Test'. Rowbotham emphasised the Australian attack's vulnerability in the absence of a front-line spinner, on a wicket 'which may have a little pace in it early this morning but thereafter seems unlikely to help seam bowling'.

Woodcock agreed. After dismissing a Benaud-less Australia as having 'as plain and straightforward an attack as ever took the field in those green and baggy caps' (a view echoed by Beames's confession that 'our attack is not capable of putting us in a winning position unless it gets worthwhile help from the pitch'), he went on: 'If ever there was a time to be a batsman against Australia this must be it, and a failure in temperament is what England may have most to fear.' As for England's final XI, to be announced shortly before the toss, Swanton anticipated no great rewards for the faster bowlers and accordingly called for 'a balanced attack' – which in practice meant playing both spinners (Illingworth and Lock) and relying on Dexter to provide the requisite back-up to Trueman and Statham, with Smith and his seamers left on the sidelines. 'Who will win?' asked Swanton. 'If the wicket remains reasonably good I believe the most probable result is a draw. If there is to be a result England are the likelier winners.'

Shortly before the toss, England did duly name that balanced attack, with no place for Smith. What then ensued was neatly summed up in the tour diary of Australia's continuing twelfth man, Brian Booth: 'England won toss and batted all out for 206. Alan [Davidson] took five for 42. Pitch proved a bit lively and balls jumped off a good length – from "the ridge".' Over the years the so-called 'ridge' at the Nursery end had come and gone, but this particular iteration seems to have been its apotheosis. 'However mildly the Lord's wicket may have behaved this season, the English batsmen found it a cruel place today,' observed Arlott. 'The Lord's "ridge" may be, as some claim, no more than a figment of the imagination but without doubt one ball in every two overs or so of pace bowling from the pavilion end lifted quickly and steeply enough to cheat the middle of some very accomplished bats.'

Under cloud cover, and on a fast wicket that posed problems of uneven bounce at the other end also, among those accomplished bats to succumb were Subba Row (leg before to a grubber from Mackay), May (getting a touch to a beauty from Davidson), Barrington (playing needlessly at a lifter) and Cowdrey (hitting three successive boundaries off McKenzie, but then an extra-quick short one flicking his glove). Further down the order, Murray's innings ended when he played what Swanton disparagingly called 'the fashionable sweep' at a straight ball from Mackay and missed; while it was only a robust last-wicket stand of 39 by Trueman and Statham that got England to a just about semi-respectable total.

Swanton overall was inclined to blame the challenging pitch, with many balls lifting to rib-high, rather than the batting – though he did have stern words for Dexter's gum-chewing at the crease ('a recent habit this, that somehow does not accord with his public image'). For Australia, Davidson had bowled magnificently, pulling out all the stops for his temporary captain, or in Beames's words 'fiercely aggressive, swinging the ball in the heavy atmosphere and making it rise awkwardly to different heights'; while the absence of a specialist spinner was rendered irrelevant by the wicket. The visitors had an hour's batting left, Statham and Trueman each claimed a rapid scalp, but Lawry and Harvey survived to the end. All in all, reflected Woodcock ruefully, 'it was a state of affairs which at the start of today no one could have envisaged'.

Friday – a near full house; blazing sunshine; shirt sleeves and summer frocks – was Lawry's day, as he played one of the great Lord's innings, eventually out at a quarter to six after making 130 out of 238 for seven. Hutton early on, recognising once again a soul mate, remarked with satisfaction to his amanuensis that 'when a leading New South Wales all-rounder [Keith Miller?] heard the news of the Australian party to come to England, he made a bet that Lawry would not make 300 runs in the whole tour'; during that passage of play, with the wicket at its most dangerous and Trueman and Statham at their liveliest, he was, in Rowbotham's words, 'cool and phlegmatic under the severest of pressure, and his courage in getting over and behind deliveries short of a length, any one of which for an hour might have lifted sufficiently enough to knock his head off, was every whit as admirable as it sounds'; after he was eventually out, his right arm and right side were a mass of black; the *Sun-Herald*'s Tom Goodman, an Australian cricket writer who also wrote for the *Sydney Morning Herald* and was not a man given to hyperbole, acclaimed a 'memorable' display of 'high technical skill, shrewd judgment and intense concentration'; and the *Daily Mirror*'s Brian Chapman let himself go: 'Lawry, Lawry, Hallelujah! Yes, the tall, thin man of Australia, Bill Lawry, with a beak like Disney's perky doll Pinocchio, trod the glory road at Lord's ...'

Frustratingly for England, after Grout had quickly followed Lawry, the ninth-wicket pair of Mackay and McKenzie then added an undefeated 48 in the last three-quarters of an hour, leaving Australia 80 runs on with two wickets left. The English spinners Lock and Illingworth had bowled a tidy but unthreatening thirty-one overs during the day, and it was all too clear that on this Lord's wicket Cowdrey had badly missed a fourth seamer to keep

Trueman, Statham and Dexter fresher as the hot day wore on. Appropriate enough viewing that evening was Hancock in *The Blood Donor*, imperishable apogee of the supreme serio-comic embodiment of frustration; while Woodcock pondered somewhat gloomily that England would need to bat 'uncommonly well' on the morrow if they were to set Australia a challenging fourth-innings target.

As it turned out, a sweltering day – hottest for over a year – marked one of the nadirs of post-war English cricket, watched by a semi-disbelieving full house of 32,000. First, after McKenzie (on his twentieth birthday) was out fairly quickly, Mackay and Misson added 49 for the last wicket, stretching Australia's lead to 134; and later, the cream of English batting – Dexter, Cowdrey, May – was swept away for only 46 runs between them. Cowdrey's innings of 7, so soon after his two centuries against the tourists, was a peculiarly painful experience, evoked by the ever-humane Arlott:

Every spectator on the ground suffered with him while he played as if, instead of one of the master batsmen of his time, he was as humanly fallible as those who watched him. Although he was clearly not timing well, he next tried, as in the first innings, to hit his way out, but simply could not get the ball away. To add to his discomfort, McKenzie, deriving considerable pace and lift from the pitch, got home on his thigh with a genuinely fast ball. Bogged down without a run for almost twenty minutes, Cowdrey hooked a four and then played a grotesque, one-handed wave at a short ball from Misson and was almost caught at square-leg. It could not go on: and his friends were almost relieved when, checking the drive he aimed at a near half-volley from Misson, he was caught by Mackay at cover …

Instead, after this comprehensive failure of the three great amateurs, 'only Barrington, chunky, earthy, and workmanlike, remained to demonstrate that it was possible to bat normally', as the day closed with the Surrey pro 59 not out and England a precarious 44 on, with just four wickets left. The collective failure was all the more disappointing because, as Arlott emphasised, this was by now 'a pitch from which the ball still moved abruptly at times but which was no longer throwing up quite such extravagant lifters as earlier'. Probably no one felt the course of events more acutely than the home captain. 'Lord's was a picture that any cricket-lover would like to imprint on his brain for nostalgic reveries in his old age,' Cowdrey recalled fifteen years later. 'The sun really did blaze down from a cloudless sky and that great and wonderful crowd really was packed to its eaves.' Yet in the event, and it is hard to read the nine words without wincing, 'that Saturday was the blackest day of my life'.

On Sunday morning the mood of the English cricket writers – the more upmarket ones anyway – was one of regret more than anger or bitterness. 'There is no doubt that the pitch has dictated the pattern of the game,' noted Peebles, before adding mildly enough that 'it has been the same for both sides, and Australia have shown themselves to be the better one in these trying circumstances'. 'England started the match by winning a toss it would have been better to lose and the Fates have not smiled on her since,' observed Warr. 'However, this does not detract from the general air of purpose and determination about Australia's cricket throughout.' So, too, Ross, declaring that for all England's 'shortcomings' it was 'Australia's perseverance and mental resilience that must at the last be applauded'.

Swanton on Monday morning was also inclined to resist the blame game: 'By and large England have batted poorly, even taking the difficult conditions into account. The fact must be stated, but it is no use harping on it.' Instead, the major contrasting broadsides came from Laker and Woodcock. 'I feel that the real cause of it all was the brighter cricket campaign which is hanging over everyone's head this season,' declared the unromantic Yorkshireman in the *Sketch*. 'Cowdrey's batsmen had a twofold object. First, they had to score sufficient runs to give their bowlers a chance, and second they had to score them in a manner which would serve as the best advertisement for the game. As a result, we saw batsmen chasing and snicking balls that would have only been of interest to a tail-end club player …' For Woodcock, clearly in a weekend mood of some despair, Saturday's miserable chain of events had 'brought out the worst features in English cricket, both in terms of character and technique':

What is so thoroughly depressing from an English point of view is the extent to which we have been outfought. When, on paper, there is nothing to choose between two sides, the deciding factors are courage, common sense and character, assuming that the luck breaks even. In this case England, had they been more fortunate in the field, might have earned a lead themselves. But their batting, for the umpteenth time in recent years, has been wretchedly irresolute.

In their last seven meetings with Australia England have been outplayed; in that time they have passed 300 only once in 13 innings. With the exception of the second innings at Edgbaston, collapse has followed collapse until now they are expected.

In short, 'when the heat has been turned on, the English temperament has failed'.

Was there any chance of fourth-day redemption? It seemed highly unlikely when, after twenty minutes, the new ball was taken and, in helpfully cloudy and humid conditions, it duly did for the rest of the English batters. The debutant McKenzie (five for 37) led the Australians off; and England's miserable total of 202 left the visitors with a mere 69 to win and go one up. But there ensued, between 12.45 and 1.30, three-quarters of an hour of the most thrilling play imaginable. Statham and Trueman gave it absolutely everything, the crowd started roaring, and within minutes the score had been transformed from 15 without loss to 19 for four, with McDonald, Lawry, O'Neill (his second failure in the match) and Harvey all back in the hutch.

From 'disappointed resignation', noted Woodcock, the atmosphere had changed to 'electric tension'. Then – off the last ball before lunch, with Australia still in some danger at 33 for four – came the match's single most dramatic moment. Burge mishit a Statham bouncer; Lock ran from backward short leg towards the square-leg umpire and made a desperate dive; but though he got a hand to the ball, the impact of his fall cruelly jolted it out. 'The Tony Lock of a few years ago – before he developed this troublesome knee – would have started a yard quicker, moved much faster and all but swallowed the catch,' reckoned a regretful Arlott. In effect it was England's last chance, as after lunch some bold strokes from Burge – following captain's orders – took the game away; and though Simpson was out, Australia got home with five wickets to spare.

The instantly memorable passage of play before lunch only temporarily stilled mutterings in the Pavilion, where older members perhaps recalled similarities with the closing stages of the Australian win at Lord's in 1930: a small target, a flurry of excitement (Bradman sensationally caught in the gully by Percy Chapman), but then the easing to victory. 'The England side is giving no satisfaction – no guts, no concentration, not playing like a side etc. etc., you hear all round,' the retired Eton schoolmaster George Lyttelton reported to his friend Rupert Hart-Davis. Typically interesting analysis on the day came from Sir Len. 'England have batted badly in three of the four innings to date, but in addition, they have batted without luck,' he asserted, before going on:

> It seems to me that the English batsmen, almost without exception, are suffering from the campaign for brighter cricket. They get too many easy runs in County matches. They come into a five-day Test against the Australians with a three-day mentality ...
>
> The Australians, on the other hand, have a much tougher approach. That is why a side as relatively poor as the present touring party, has so humbled England.

Even so, Hutton remained convinced that, *au fond*, England had 'the better side'. Accordingly: 'If the batsmen pull themselves together and follow the lead Trueman and Statham gave them, England can still win the series. It only needs the England captain to lose the toss at Leeds to convince me that fortune is back on our side.' The dry humour was all Hutton's own; but looking ahead to the third Test, due to start at Headingley in ten days' time, a last word at this stage went to a fellow Yorkshireman, Brian Sellers. 'We know,' he apparently told anyone willing to listen, 'how to prepare a proper wicket up north.'

*

July began with the birth of Diana Spencer, a field day (five wickets and 53 not out) for Brian Close at Hull in Yorkshire's match against Somerset, and Benaud at Old Trafford still able to do little more than turn his arm over against Lancashire. Five days to go until Headingley; and in Leeds itself this Saturday, the Great Hall at the university was crammed to capacity for a lecture by T. S. Eliot, looking back on his literary criticism over the past forty years. 'When asked whether I still hold the same belief I can only say I don't know or I don't care,' he disarmingly told his audience. 'There are some matters in which I seem to have lost interest. There are errors of judgement and, what I deplore even more, errors of tone.'

Next day came the Sunday ritual of England's chosen party: on a 3–1 vote by the selectors (as it subsequently transpired), May to replace Cowdrey as captain for the rest of the series; Allen instead of Illingworth; and, attracting the most attention, a place in the twelve for Close. J. M. Kilburn in the *Yorkshire Post* was broadly supportive, referring hopefully to his 'increased maturity of outlook'; Woodcock was more circumspect ('his ability is a by-word and if he had the temperament to match it, he might have played not six but 60 times for England'); but Swanton was outright unhappy, stating his preference for Middlesex's Fred Titmus and calling Close 'unpredictable'. There were few more damning words in the Swantonian lexicon.

On Tuesday, while Benaud bowled fourteen innocuous overs at Old Trafford ('merely pushed the ball through in a gentle arc and a very slow pace', according to the watching South African journalist and broadcaster Charles Fortune), Statham reported himself an injury doubt because of a strained side. His potential replacement was named as Les Jackson, who in his last four matches for Derbyshire had taken 28 wickets, to add to his 584 in the past four seasons. 'If the wicket at Headingley is at all green – which is improbable – Jackson will exploit it unfailingly; if it breaks up, his ability constantly to hit a worn spot will make him dangerous; if it is simply good for batting, he will be as steady as a rock' – in every sense he was Arlott's sort of cricketer, the ultra-experienced pro as supreme craftsman.

What in fact *would* the wicket be like? Arlott himself paid on Wednesday, like virtually all the players and most of the press, a fascinated inspection. 'Such grass as there is has been cropped extremely closely – far too closely, one would think, for it to hold the soil together for five days,' he noted. 'But if there were grass – however short – all over, it would not seem so threatening; there are whole wide spaces of earth totally bare and already, if the human eye can be trusted, on the verge of becoming dust. It is all very perplexing.' 'Test pitch rather patchy and dusty' was how Booth put it in his tour diary. 'Boys weren't too happy with it.' Indeed they were not. 'This game will be all over in three days,' predicted Harvey; Benaud took one look and, before heading to the races at Pontefract, decided there was enough chance of it proving spin-friendly that, despite his shoulder problem, he had to play this time (or as he confidently announced, 'I'm fit, I'll play'); and the recently retired Ray Lindwall had firmly in mind those fuzzy-end-of-the-lollipop events five years earlier when he pronounced darkly, 'They've done it again.'

In the English camp, where it was now definite that Statham would not be playing, both Close and Barrington reckoned the pitch would take spin, while Cowdrey – perhaps somewhat demob-happy after surrendering the captaincy – simply said that he was off to a nearby beach for batting practice. Which side would benefit? 'Traditionally these are conditions that favour England,' reflected a still emotionally bruised Woodcock. 'When the ball plays tricks visiting batsmen are usually at a disadvantage, but England have missed the boat against Australia at so many recent ports of call that to support them now becomes a matter more of hope than faith.' Swanton would have sympathised, but in his eyes it all came down to the toss: 'The side that goes in first will probably win.'

Even as a crowd of over 20,000 enjoyed a day of brilliant sunshine and eventually dramatic cricket, Yorkshire on 6 July 1961 was not just about events at Headingley. Some ten miles away, in Bradford, the Methodist Conference that was being held in the city received a deputation representing the 8,000 Pakistanis and Indians who in recent years had arrived to work in the local textile industry. The deputation's leader was Syed Tremasi, whose focus of complaint was the city's mill owners and workers. 'Our boys there [i.e. in the mills] are treated as third-class human species,' he stated, almost certainly with much justification. 'The use of offensive language towards us is quite common and has caused fights. We are looked upon as inferior.'

It was probably by the time the day's play was over that a *Yorkshire Post* leader writer had framed a response for next day's paper: 'Coloured people, like Southerners before them, have failed to understand the real nature of Bradfordians, whose highest praise is to say that something is "fair to middling" and whose use of language can be direct and brusque.' With that and suchlike, including a reference near the end to 'the grievances of a minority of coloured people who fear dangers which hardly exist', the paper for the time being deflected the matter. Supremely unconcerned at this stage about such prejudicial treatment was the world of Yorkshire cricket; but as even it eventually came to realise, the issue of racism had deep, deep roots and could not be wished away.

At Headingley itself, the Thursday was very much a day of two halves. After England had left out Close (a decision attributed by Arlott to an abiding suspicion of Yorkshire frailty against leg-spin, in this case Benaud's and Simpson's), and Benaud had won the toss and decided to bat in confident expectation of a badly deteriorating pitch later in the match, Australia made solid, unspectacular progress over the first two sessions, reaching 183 for two at tea, with Harvey and O'Neill both well established. Lock and Allen had done the bulk of the bowling, and it was Lock who had taken the openers' wickets. But everything changed after tea, as May took the second new ball. At which point, Australia proceeded to lose seven wickets in startlingly quick succession, most of them to the local hero, and against the soundtrack of a roaring, jubilant, on-their-feet 20,000 crowd:

- O'Neill neatly caught by Cowdrey in the gully off Trueman.
- Harvey brilliantly caught low down at backward short leg by Lock, again off Trueman.
- Burge falling to Jackson, another accomplished, unflashy catch by Cowdrey in the gully.
- Simpson leg before to Trueman as he played across a straight one.
- Mackay leg before to a Jackson shooter.
- Benaud, reaching out, bowled first ball by Trueman and giving the pitch a meaningful, Paddingtonian stare before departing.
- Grout caught behind, by Murray, as he drove at Trueman.

With Australia 208 for nine, the game had been turned on its head – though Davidson and McKenzie did now bat steadily against Trueman and Jackson, putting on 29 for the last wicket; and May was required to turn to Allen, who in his first over (and England's 110th) bowled McKenzie as he pushed forward to an off-break. Pullar and Subba Row then quietly batted the day out, finishing at 9 without loss.

How to explain Australia's dramatic collapse? 'It was as if the top of this dry, bare wicket had crumbled before the end of the first day,' reckoned Rowbotham. 'It was probably not Trueman's and Jackson's pace off the pitch which undid Australia so much as the disparity between that and their pace through the air. The ball, in short, was losing more pace after pitching than the batters anticipated, and they played too soon and reached too far. Trueman and Jackson in this sense allied pace through the air and accuracy of length in order to prompt vulnerable forward shots.' Woodcock for his part did not pull his punches, calling it 'without doubt one of the worst pitches ever prepared for a big match'. Given which, it was entirely plausible this Thursday evening that Australia's total of 237 was not so dusty after all.

The visitors had batted in brilliant sunshine, whereas Friday was a day of largely unbroken cloud, as a crowd of 23,400 intently but occasionally impatiently watched England build their admirably doughty reply in difficult conditions. 'They all played with rigorous self-discipline and considerable skill,' noted Kilburn of the batters, with significant if not major contributions coming from Pullar (53), Subba Row (35) and May (26). But the undisputed star of the day was Cowdrey, in an infinitely happier frame of mind than during that wretched innings on the Saturday at Lord's. 'Like a rock, his method standing up to everything and anything,' applauded Rowbotham, while Arlott praised how, though 'taking no risks whatever', he nevertheless 'pounced unerringly on the ball that would give him safe runs'. Eventually, half an hour before the close, Cowdrey was caught by Grout off the thinnest of leg glances and, apparently without referring to a hesitant umpire Langridge, walked. 'Such is the excellent habit of the modern cricketer,' reflected an entirely approbatory Swanton. 'The episode, of course, was completely in character. But such a gesture cannot be wholly easy to make when one is seven runs short of a century against Australia.' In an alternative, less adulatory, version, Cowdrey himself hesitated, aware of the umpire's hesitation, and only left when Grout behind the stumps quipped ironically: 'Are you reading the lesson this Sunday, Colin?' Either way, as the old-school Beames recorded with some pride, the Australians applauded him all the way back to the pavilion.

The day finished with England 1 run on and a reassuring six wickets left. Australia by common consent had failed to take advantage of a helpful wicket, with Kilburn referring to 'the general ineffectuality of the bowling'. It was certainly not Benaud's best day: still prevented by his shoulder from bowling his googly, and as captain his field placings criticised by Worrell as 'not sufficiently flexible' on a low-bouncing wicket, with 'fielders on the boundary who were much too square and slips which were much too fine'. Indeed, one Australian journalist, Goodman, even asked, 'Should Benaud have played?' Altogether, on a day on which Eton v Harrow at Lord's had been watched by the Duke of Windsor as well as by several Old Etonian members of the Cabinet including Prime Minister Harold Macmillan, and on which a product of Tonbridge School and Oxford University had resolutely held the fort, it had been from an English perspective a notable hurrah – if not quite last hurrah – for the amateur tradition.

Saturday morning was mainly Australia's: Davidson and Benaud imposing a stranglehold, wickets falling and only an aggressive 30 by Lock, in barely a quarter of an hour and entirely off Benaud, enabling England to obtain a valuable but not necessarily decisive lead of 61. The initiative then stayed largely with Australia, so that by twenty to four they were 98 for two, with Harvey and O'Neill both going well. At which point, with the match potentially slipping away from England, May called on Trueman for his second spell; captain and bowler decided between them that medium-paced off-cutters might be the way to go on this very distinctive pitch; and there ensued another near-incredible collapse:

- Harvey, holing out to cover off a ball from Trueman (still on his long run) that stopped on him.
- Burge, leg before to a sharp off-break from Allen.
- O'Neill, scooping Trueman (by now operating off his short run) to Cowdrey at forward short leg.
- Simpson, bowled by Trueman as he tried to drive.
- Benaud, completing a pair as he reached forward to Trueman and was bowled middle stump by a break-back.
- Mackay, caught behind by Murray as he prodded at Trueman.

With the crowd almost beside itself, Trueman had taken five for 1 in the greatest spell of his life; and Australia at tea were 109 for eight – in a contest which had again been turned on its head, this time in a mere twenty-five minutes. After tea, a wicket each for Jackson and Trueman, leaving Trueman with figures of six for 30, and eleven for 88 in the match. 'Fred bowled well – aye, he did that – ah'll not take that away – but they batted bad,' Arlott heard an old Yorkshireman say, his eyes glistening with delight. England were left with 59 to win; and they achieved this with few alarms, losing just two wickets and thereby levelling the series, with two Tests to play. It had been a day for the history books; and likewise, as would eventually transpire, the moment this Saturday evening when, by a swimming pool at Cliveden, the

Secretary of State for War, John Profumo, was introduced by Stephen Ward to a semi-naked Christine Keeler.

Benaud, by now allowed by his reluctant manager to give post-match press conferences, had been at his most diplomatic when asked about the Headingley pitch ('Our fellows will just have to adapt themselves to English conditions ... We have to play on whatever pitch is prepared for us'); but over the next day or two, 'desert', 'rubble heap', 'disgrace to Yorkshire cricket', 'shameful', 'a cart-track', 'the Sahara' were but some of the condemnatory comments being publicly directed at it. 'Unfortunately,' Swanton told his perhaps (or perhaps not) suitably chastened English readers on Monday, 'the Australians, accustomed as they are to true wickets, were handicapped so greatly by this treacherous one as to modify, or even destroy, any elation in the victory. It leaves a taste of ashes in the mouth ...' Indeed, he added next day in a further piece, 'on Saturday night one could hardly look an Australian fairly in the eye'. Woodcock sounded slightly less disappointed, though he did concede that 'a visiting side in a fine spell of weather is entitled to expect a reliable batting wicket, at any rate for their first innings'.

The *Yorkshire Post* was unrepentant. Kilburn on the Monday attributed the Australian second-innings collapse to 'a disintegration of inadequate technique' and more generally declared that 'the pitch conditioned the play, but it certainly did not either determine or spoil the match'; the same day his sports editor, after a dig at 'pompous critics for whom nothing is good north of the Thames', argued that 'under the circumstances of the weather we have suffered this spring', namely eight weeks of a cold wind from the north-east, 'the groundsman made the best of a bad job'; and Kilburn next day returned to the fray: 'Headingley's pitch clearly fell short of perfection, mainly because the height of the bounce and the pace of the ball could not be calculated, but it did provide the desirable elements of safety, it did provide success for widely differing types of bowling, it did permit the leading batsman to play the most significant innings and it did not favour either one side or the other beyond their relative ability to make use of it.'

Tellingly, both Beames ('Australia was found wanting in batting skill on a pitch that looked more dangerous than it played') and Goodman ('some dismal batting by Australia in both innings') in effect agreed; while a last word went to a *Yorkshire Post* reader, K. B. Barker of Ossett (setting for Stan Barstow's recent novel *A Kind of Loving*). Not only had there been, he insisted in a letter on Wednesday, the right balance between bat and ball, but 'three incident-packed days' had produced each day 'a jolly good day's entertainment for the spectators'. He surely had a point; and he did not need to add that the outcome as well as the drama had merely heightened anticipation for the contestants' next encounter, due at Old Trafford in just over a fortnight.

*

'At 6:30pm the team went to Clarence House entertained by the Queen Mother,' recorded Brian Booth on the same day as Barker's letter. 'The Queen and Duke arrived – then Princess Margaret and Antony Armstrong-Jones – they are all charming people and talked freely with all present – made you feel most welcome.' A rather different sort of welcome two days later, as the tourists, on their way to play Nottinghamshire, stopped off at Coventry:

> We were entertained to lunch by Standard Car Co.
>
> After lunch – tour of inspection of assembly line – cars coming off the line – driven off and tested.
>
> All the workers stopped work and gave us some barracking re the Tests – signs all over the place e.g. 'Mind the Ridge', 'Trueman for President' etc. Chap in mock pads and bat shaped up for us to bowl as we came along – very interesting.

Main event during the gap between the Tests was that most time-honoured of fixtures, Gentlemen v Players. The first day, Wednesday the 19th, coincided with the annual meeting (also at Lord's) of the tellingly named Imperial Cricket Conference, where the question of whether England should continue to play against South Africa (no longer a member of the Commonwealth) was kicked into the long grass; missing from the match was Cowdrey, apparently suffering from a throat infection (or tonsillitis according to at least one other report); while on the field of play Dexter's pair meant that since his monumental match-saving innings at Edgbaston he had scored only 155 runs in twelve completed innings.

Apart from May's fine first-innings 79 against a high-class attack on a green, ridged pitch, the outstanding individual performances both came from the professionals, who won by 172 runs, the biggest margin of victory in the Lord's fixture since the 1940s. On the Wednesday, in Woodcock's words, 'the season's heaviest wicket-taker, [Jack] Flavell, showed there was no fluke about his record', as 'he moved the ball about enough at a lively pace to have everyone in trouble'; while on the Friday, the Worcestershire man backed up his three first-innings wickets with figures of 12-7-15-4 in the Gentlemen's second innings, including the prize scalp of the England captain, 'thoroughly surprised by a deadly delivery which knocked out his middle stump as he played back' (*Wisden*). The other player seizing the main chance was Close, who on that last day followed up a hard-hitting 94 not out with his own eye-catching figures of 11-3-23-5 as he forsook his usual off-breaks and bowled medium pace into the ridge. At this timely moment, Woodcock was especially impressed by his batting: 'It is unfortunate for Close that in his immature days he was labelled as an irresponsible batsman. This no longer applies.'

Saturday the 22nd was 'Slasher' Mackay's day as, pressed into service as an opener for the tourists against Middlesex at Lord's, he scored a surprisingly rapid 168. The watching – and largely admiring – Alan Ross allowed himself to speculate about the likely team selections for Old Trafford, starting with 'Australia's problems':

> Could a place be found for Booth? Who to open? Simpson or McDonald? What more could be hoped for from Benaud? The answers are still not easy to come by.
>
> As far as England were concerned, it seemed likely that Close would join the Headingley eleven, with Statham, if fit, back in place of Jackson. Dexter's total failure outside the Tests may be disconcerting to many, if not to himself, but if there is any principle worth sticking to at all, it is that one must keep faith with genuine class.

Fingleton agreed. 'Dexter's bad trot has brought out the usual growls when a good cricketer falls on evil times,' he noted in next day's *Sunday Times*. 'His 180 at Birmingham should guarantee his place for the series, apart from the rich prospects he has of succeeding at any time. He is a cricketer of character and challenge and these attributes will be needed, I think, by the winning side at Old Trafford.' The England selectors did indeed, in their announcement later that day, include Dexter in their party of thirteen. Statham was now fit to play; in the expectation of a hard, fast wicket, Jackson, the late call-up for Headingley, was omitted for Flavell ('well, it's better late than never,' he said on being told of his selection); the word from Cowdrey was that he would be well enough to play, in which case the general view was that Dexter or Barrington would drop out; and few of the pundits thought that Close, after his stirring deeds at Lord's the previous week, would be left out of the starting XI this time round. For, as Woodcock on Monday morning once again assured his *Times* readers about a cricketer who had only played five further Tests since his debut in 1949, 'he has now reached, as a batsman, the years of discretion'.

That day, and Tuesday morning, a fully recovered Benaud was back to his best, finishing with match figures against Middlesex of nine for 70 and, no less impressively, a total of fifty overs bowled in which he had been able to perform freely his whole repertoire. Indeed, one journalist in the know even described him as, before breakfast on the Tuesday, 'working off the natural stiffness in the hotel corridor outside his bedroom [at the Waldorf] bowling imaginary leg breaks, googlies and his own special "flipper"'. In Manchester itself by this time, much nervous attention naturally focused on the prospective wicket; but the *Manchester Evening News*'s John Kay was confident, in his Tuesday profile of the groundsman Bert Flack, much maligned in 1956 when Jim Laker had taken his record-breaking nineteen wickets, that this time round it would be 'a pitch fit for the kings of cricket to play on':

> Today and tomorrow Bert will put in the finishing touches. Then he will doff his cloth cap, wipe his brow, and pull deep on his much-loved pipe. He will go home to his little house at the main Old Trafford gates – so aptly named 'The Wickets' – and settle down with the contentment of a man who has done a good job well.

The Australians practised on Wednesday morning. With gale-force winds, and the clouds dark overhead, it was a session notable for Davidson hitting the ball so hard that he split his bat and also for, just weeks after Pullar on the same ground had been dropped five times by the tourists in their match against Lancashire, half an hour's extra catching practice. Later in the day they announced their XI: with McDonald (wrist) and Misson (jarred ankle) both unfit, Simpson would open with Lawry, and McKenzie (despite some shin soreness) would keep his place to open the bowling with Davidson; while Booth was set to make his Test debut, taking Simpson's place in the middle order. When England practised in the afternoon, the main focus was on Cowdrey. Earlier in the week, playing for an MCC XI against Cranbrook School in Kent, he had made only 8 in thirty-five minutes; driving up to Manchester he had still felt unwell; and to a watching Bill Bowes, it was 'patently obvious' that he was 'in no condition to play', notwithstanding the player's protestations. '"I feel all right," he said, and wobbled his knees, "but doesn't it take it out of you?"'

It was time for predictions – each of them made in the knowledge that an Australian win would enable them to retain the Ashes even before going to The Oval. From a visitor's perspective, Percy Beames reckoned it 'highly questionable whether either side will be able to win this Test'; the *Daily Mail*'s Crawford White thought England had 'balance and strength enough to beat Australia'; the *Daily Worker*'s Philip Sheridan was, five years on, 'afraid that the Australians have too strong a motive – REVENGE – to fail twice in succession at Old Trafford'; the *Daily Herald*'s Charles Bray expected that 'Manchester will revert to its old habit of drawn Tests'; Jim Laker in the *Daily Sketch* declined to make a forecast, but noted his 'feeling there are the makings of a wonderful game of cricket here'; 'Benaud May Turn Fourth Test Topsy-Turvy' was the headline for the *Daily Mirror*'s Brian Chapman, identifying the at last 'really fit' Australian captain as the factor 'which may well tip an otherwise evenly balanced scale'; the *Guardian*'s Denys Rowbotham, more tentatively, suggested that Benaud 'could conceivably turn the match Australia's way'; Jim Swanton, by now happy enough at the prospect of Close playing ('a chance to prove that at the age of 30 he has outgrown the accusations of irresponsibility that were not unjustified in his precocious youth'), pessimistically thought an England win only the third-likeliest outcome;

and John Woodcock, though expecting the bat generally to be on top, like Chapman and Rowbotham saw Benaud as potentially the pivotal figure: 'If he is allowed to play on England's nerves his recovery could decide the series. At any rate it is a threat to be considered.'

PART TWO

4

Day One: Thursday 27 July

Australia haven't won a Test at Old Trafford since 1902 when Victor Trumper scored a century before lunch on the first day, and Neville Cardus saw poor Fred Tate drop a vital catch, and later be bowled neck-and-crop with just 4 runs needed for a famous victory. Memories are long in the North, and there may well be spectators here who still recall that heart-wrenching day. Certainly there will be many in the crowd who vividly recall first-hand the visitors' humiliation just five years ago.

The toss could be crucial. The morning is windy, the sky somewhat overcast. Local wisdom likes to say that if you can see the Pennines, it's going to rain; if you can't, it's already raining. No rain yet, but there is a distinct hint of damp in the air. For Australian readers, the *Canberra Times* reports reassuringly that 'sharp attention for weeks has been focussed on the work of Manchester Groundsman Bert Flack and his staff'. And, indeed, the pitch, after the less than satisfactory strips at Lord's and Headingley, looks fast and true; though its tinge of green should offer some assistance to the opening bowlers.

The Australian XI is known, but England still have a good deal to weigh up. Among the batters, so much depends on the state of Cowdrey's throat; there is to be a last-minute decision. Assuming that both he and the now heavily favoured Close do play, will it be Dexter or Barrington omitted? Neither has been in irresistible form. Dexter has his aggressive flair and lively, medium-paced bowling to commend him; Barrington has his general adhesiveness, exemplified by the two fifties he made in the Gentlemen v Players match, and perhaps his slip-catching. Among the bowlers, the choice is almost certainly between Flavell or Lock, with Allen's off-spin likely to be preferred against Australia's four left-handers.

In the event, Cowdrey, after a short run around and some brief fielding practice, declares himself unavailable; so Close, Dexter and Barrington are all included, Lock is left out and Flavell gains his first cap. The two sides in probable batting order look like this:

ENGLAND	AUSTRALIA
Geoff Pullar	Bill Lawry
Raman Subba Row	Bobby Simpson
Ted Dexter	Neil Harvey
Peter May *	Norman O'Neill
Brian Close	Peter Burge
Ken Barrington	Brian Booth
John Murray †	Ken Mackay
David Allen	Alan Davidson
Fred Trueman	Richie Benaud *
Brian Statham	Wally Grout †
Jack Flavell	Graham McKenzie

On paper, and in English conditions, England appear to have the stronger bowling combination, though the masterly Davidson, the lively McKenzie, the ultra-steady Mackay, together with a now fully operational Benaud (plus additional leg-spin from Simpson), can never be discounted. Furthermore, Australia bat all the way down, while, with Trueman at nine, England have something of a tail. That Australia are the superior fielding side is beyond question.

So, the toss could indeed prove crucial. Conventionally, captains prefer to bat first, on the premise that runs on the board (hopefully plenty of them) will allow their team to dictate terms. But, during this series, calling correctly and batting have not produced happy results: 195 (England); 206 (England); 237 (Australia). All the same, May, with some anxiety about what swing-and-seam wizardry Davidson might conjure up, will very probably elect to bat, if given the choice. After all, the only time in the 1958–59 series he gambled and put Australia in, it backfired badly: Australia compiled 476, won the match easily and reclaimed the Ashes.

Whether Benaud, for his part, will make the same decision is less clear. He is not a conventional captain, as Jack Fingleton reminded cricket followers last weekend in the *Sunday Times*, suggesting that, should Benaud win the toss, he might well decide to insert England on a pitch which will 'possibly … play lively on the first day'. Fingleton recalled two occasions on which Benaud did just that with great success: at Melbourne during the 1958–59 Ashes tour and, just a few months ago, in the fifth and decisive Test against the West Indies, also at Melbourne. Benaud, he pointed out, 'often flies in the face of convention and elder statesmen'. Which is no doubt true. However, not on this occasion. May flips the coin, Benaud calls correctly and, conventionally, he opts to bat.

MORNING SESSION

Shortly before 11.30, the umpires, John Langridge in a white cap and bareheaded W. E. (Eddie) Phillipson, wend their way to the middle. They are watched by a cloth-capped, heavily overcoated crowd of 12,000, many wearing ties. May leads his team onto the field, followed by Lawry and Simpson. Simpson opened with great success in the series against the West Indies, and Lawry, though only playing his fourth Test, is well on the way to establishing himself as the team's banker. This may be the first occasion the right-hander and left-hander have opened together in a Test, but they have already had several substantial first-wicket partnerships against county sides. As he leaves the dressing-room, Lawry remarks to his skipper with a slight turn of his head: 'We'll see what we can do, Rich ...'

Trueman prepares to bowl from the Stretford end, with the pavilion to his left and the wind from the west behind him.* May has set an attacking field: two slips and two gullies; three short legs (forward, square and backward); cover and mid-on; no long leg, no third man. Lawry takes guard, hunches over his bat. Lanky, ungainly, disciplined, he favours a low grip on the handle. Murray behind the stumps begins his invariable routine with a wide circling of his arms, before the finale much admired by the cricket-loving comedian Arthur Askey: 'Both hands to the peak of his cap, a slight jerk, then gloves together jamming them in

---

*In 2010–11, the square was rotated through 90 degrees and now the pavilion is immediately behind the bowler's arm.

place, an abridged rendering of "Chopsticks" on the tips of his fingers and Murray is ready.'

Trueman to Lawry, announces the excited voice of BBC commentator Brian Johnston. *And what we're looking for, I think, is to see whether this wicket has pace in it. It has been promised to be a good, fast, true wicket. And it's got a certain amount of grass on it. So, it could possibly help the opening bowlers; got a bit of green on it.*

Trueman, the hero of Headingley, sweeps in along his honed, curved run. He usually manages to move the new ball in the air, and his outswinger can be lethal. His nickname 'Fiery Fred' is well-earned; he is always more than happy to test a batter with his bouncer. Now – with Arlott among those watching, perhaps already knowing that one day he would write the definitive description – Trueman gathers himself into his delivery stride, moving slightly wide on the return crease, hoping presumably to create an angle across the left-hander. He turns sideways on, his left shoulder aimed down the wicket. The seam, pointing towards the batter, is held between the first two fingers of his right hand; the metal-capped toe of his right boot rakes the ground behind the bowling crease. His left arm is flung up and across his body, so he is looking over his left shoulder; his back arched and braced, his left boot (pointing towards what would be leg slip to a right-hander) thuds into the pitch; the right arm swings through; the ball hurtles towards the batter; the momentum propels Trueman forward; he lands heavily on his right boot and seems to leave a light mark on the surface. His is one of the most perfect and classical actions in contemporary cricket: a thing of beauty and power.

Anti-climactically, his first ball is well off target. It pitches outside the leg stump. Lawry moves carefully to the off. The ball at no great pace goes through to Murray, standing back. Trueman flexes his shoulders and swings his arms. Lawry next plays a defensive push right under his eyes, and May fields in the finer of the two gullies. The fifth ball is a straight full toss which Lawry works efficiently into the leg side, all along the ground. *There's Flavell chasing it down to the Pavilion boundary. He'll catch it all right* and returns the ball to Murray. Flavell's first touch in Test cricket. Lawry and Simpson run three, Lawry loping, Simpson scampering. Simpson takes guard. The last ball of Trueman's over is a well-pitched-up inswinger just outside the leg stump. Simpson, trying to leg-glance, seems to play a fraction early, and the ball ricochets off the back of his bat. Trueman throws up his arms in frustration. *That's gone down to the third-man boundary. A very lucky one. He just got a bat to it.* Seven off the first over.

Statham, on his home ground, bowls into the wind from the Warwick Road end (where the railway station is). He is aptly nicknamed 'the Greyhound': lean, poised, he seems to flow over the ground as he approaches the wicket. If Trueman is all *Sturm und Drang*, Statham is the epitome of Pinteresque understatement. His appeal for an lbw or caught behind is always quietly matter of fact. He never remonstrates at a near miss nor celebrates profusely at the taking of a wicket. After a day's play, he will sit in the dressing-room, soaking his feet in a bucket of water, puffing away at endless fags and downing beer after beer, while Trueman will nurse the same pint for hours, pulling on his pipe and yarning his head off.

Trueman stories, told by and about him, are legion. At Trent Bridge on the last afternoon against the West Indies in 1957, May brought Trueman back for a final, all-out burst with the words: 'Come on, Fred – England expects, you know.' To which (in the expurgated version) the already exhausted Trueman replied: 'Oh, do they, skipper, is that why they call her the mother country?' Statham doesn't go in much for banter and byplay, although he has his own dry humour. At the pre-match talk, after Trueman had explained exactly how to dismiss every member of the Australian side, Statham apparently remarked: 'Fred's got all ten, lads. Let's go to the bar and have a drink.' He himself has two main idiosyncrasies: one of which is that he is so supple he can remove his sweater, simply by reaching one hand over his shoulder to the small of his back and pulling the sweater forward over his head.

Statham's action is quite different from Trueman's, much more open-chested, so that he looks towards the batter from inside and under his raised left arm. This means he naturally tends to whip the ball in towards the right-hander, though he can also seam it away. His stamina is legendary, as is his accuracy. ('If they miss, I hit' is his motto.) After more than ten years of grind on the county and Test circuits, neither he nor Trueman are as quick as they once were; but they know that on a wicket like this, potentially offering movement both ways, line and length are the key.

Statham, too, starts with a moment of bathos. His other idiosyncrasy is that he crosses his feet over just before his delivery stride, and, if his rhythm isn't quite right, this sometimes leads to a tumble. He tumbles now, second ball, slipping over at the crease and collapsing in a slither of tangled feet. But, after a single to Lawry, he strikes. Off his fifth delivery, Simpson, having already played and missed outside the off stump, flicks again at one that moves away. *He's caught at the wicket. Simpson caught Murray bowled Statham for 4. Australia 8 for one.* Simpson leaves, his face a puzzle, the breeze lifting a lock of his hair. The crowd applauds. Game on.

Next in is Harvey, with one ball to face. Two left-handers at the crease. Most consider Harvey the greatest Australian batter since the Second World War. A little below medium height, quick on his feet, he has all the shots and is notoriously hard to pin down. He scored a memorable 100 in the Test here eight years ago, but bagged a pair three years later in 'Laker's Match'. Statham bowls a rising delivery around off stump. Harvey goes back, nudges it into the covers, and calls Lawry through. *And there's Dexter. Oh, a good, short run there. Harvey off the mark.* Australia 9 for one off two overs.

Trueman and Statham continue in tandem for seven overs, which produce 28 runs. There are few false strokes and no further alarums for Australia: Harvey leg-glances Statham for four; Lawry comes down the wicket – the height of effrontery to a fast bowler – and drives Trueman to the long-off boundary. At this, the crowd claps, and the sun briefly appears. The field becomes more defensive. Statham, after three overs, gives way to the Test debutant Flavell.

At thirty-two, he is a year older than Statham and two years older than Trueman. Solidly built, he has a shortish, pounding run-up and, as he delivers the ball, his left forearm is clenched in front of his face like a crossbar. His first ball is right on a length, and Harvey can only defend; Flavell goes on to bowl a maiden, the first of the innings. Lawry takes four fours off Trueman's next two overs, and, a little under par, the latter is rested (six overs, none for 29). Lawry faces Flavell. *That's a better one. Played square. Pullar running round from third man, and they've taken two runs. Nice return* (to Murray straight in over the bails).

Statham returns at the Stretford end, now with the wind at his back. *Statham to Harvey. Nicely turned round. There's a long leg there. Just the one run. That's the fifty up.* The Australian fifty has come in forty-six minutes off seventy-three balls, excellent going for the first hour of the first morning of a Test. But then Statham finds the edge of Harvey's bat, and Subba Row at second slip clings on to the fast, ankle-high snick. Harvey pauses, checks with Subba Row that it's a fair catch, gets the nod and departs. Australia 51 for two. Harvey 19. Statham two for 16.

O'Neill replaces Harvey. Three years ago, he was being touted as the new Bradman, and, in the recent series against the West Indies, he was Australia's premier batter (522 runs at an average of 52). He is particularly strong off the back foot. Today, as Arlott notes in his journal, he bats 'like a man on edge. Again and again he moves across his stumps, square with the line of the ball, and attempts to play it on the on-side. This is not "business" cricket' – particularly with Statham and Flavell, spurred on by the juicy pitch, really turning the screw. Lawry plays and misses twice in succession off Flavell, but manages to drive Statham straight. *And that'll come down for four, down to the sightscreen. Peter May just making a token chase.*

Flavell is now making the ball lift awkwardly, and he proceeds to rough O'Neill up, as day-in day-out he roughs up any average county player. He hits O'Neill in and around the upper thigh area three times in an over. On the third occasion, O'Neill requires treatment. He inserts a new thigh pad. Statham then hits him again, the ball deflecting off the inside edge into exactly the same region. O'Neill staggers, moves away from the wicket, drops his bat, and bends forward in agony, surrounded by sympathetic English fielders. *There was a heartless laugh all round the field*, vouchsafe the fruity tones of Jim Swanton, now at the microphone. *And that went, as you can see, off the bat onto the ... groin.* O'Neill throws up on a neighbouring pitch, but staunchly declines May's suggestion that he should retire.

After further treatment, including a drink and a replacement box, he plays on. Statham pitches the next ball up on the off stump, perhaps hoping O'Neill will hang back. He does hang back, but nevertheless strikes the ball cleanly to the long-off boundary rope. *I wonder what was in that drink*, ponders fellow-commentator Jack Fingleton. At the boundary rope, a gaggle of small boys excitedly squabble over the ball before one of them throws it back to the pursuing fielder. Lawry at the other end, now on 46, drives at Flavell, but the edge doesn't quite carry to second slip.

With half an hour to go until lunch, a more threatening Trueman takes over from Statham and soon jams Lawry's fingers painfully against the handle of his bat. Meanwhile, Dexter has replaced Flavell. Flavell's impressive spell of ten overs has gone unrewarded, but has cost only 14 runs. At both ends, small trenches outside the right-hander's leg stump, created by the bowlers' follow-through stride, are becoming plainly visible. Dexter, tall, floppy dark hair, easy approach and action, is faster than he looks. He often takes useful wickets, but, compared to Statham and Flavell, is not a notably tight bowler. It is typical of his more cavalier approach to cricket that, as he now prepares to bowl, he doesn't bother to remove his long-sleeved sweater. He soon delivers an over-pitched ball outside the off stump to Lawry, who drives it fluently for four through extra cover. Swanton: *That's gone through, and there's his fifty*. Lawry's hard-won, but never stodgy, half-century has been made out of eighty-nine and taken an hour and three-quarters. He raises his bat to prolonged applause from the crowd, gives the congratulating O'Neill a pat on the back, before flicking a bit of dirt off the wicket. He touches the peak of his cap, settles again over his bat. Fingleton: *That's a splendid fifty, that one by Lawry. Good batting, plenty of courage.*

Dexter retaliates with a sharper, shorter one which jumps on Lawry. Swanton: *Notice that he takes that bottom hand off the bat a great deal. Perhaps he's ... perhaps he's jarred it. Rather looks like that, doesn't it?* Fingleton: *It's a habit Ken Mackay has got too, isn't it? I should think Lawry's fingers are pretty sore there from those hits he got from Trueman.* The next delivery from Dexter is fuller again and well wide of the off stump, perhaps inviting another drive, but Lawry, deliberately playing well inside the line, lets the ball fly through to Murray.

Trueman, faced with O'Neill, inevitably unleashes a bouncer. It's quick, and O'Neill shapes to hook, then sensibly decides the shot is not on. Still perhaps a little unsteady, he loses his balance and falls over in trying to get out of the way. The ball hits him on the forearm and flies to Barrington at first slip. There's an appeal for a catch, which Phillipson turns down. In falling, though, O'Neill has dislodged the bails. Allen and Subba Row approach the wicket and stare down questioningly at the disturbed stumps. Swanton: *And he's bowled him. Or has he knocked his wicket over? Anyway, he can only be out, can't he?* Allen, Subba Row and O'Neill, still dazed and half-lying down, all turn their eyes towards the square-leg umpire, Langridge. As he ponders, the crowd seems to hold its collective breath.

This is one of those decisions which divides opinion. Has O'Neill or has he not completed his stroke before the stumps are broken? If he has completed his stroke, then the laws say he should be given not out. Some watchers instantly recall a comparable instance in 1948 at Trent Bridge, when Denis Compton was given out, going for a hook off Keith Miller. Struck on the head, he reeled back, involuntarily kicking the stumps. Compton hit wicket Miller 184. Langridge, who has had a clear view, evidently thinks the shot (or, in effect, the evasive non-shot) was still in progress and gives O'Neill out, hit wicket. O'Neill, far from gruntled, picks himself up and, still in obvious pain, slowly makes his way back to the pavilion. Fingleton: *Yes, he's given him out, the only possible decision.* Australia 89 for three. O'Neill 11.

Trueman, roused by the dismissal, tries more short stuff on Burge, the next man in. The burly Burge's favourite shots are the cut and the hook, and he duly dishes out one of each. Statham, unusually, is fielding at short leg; he ducks, the hook nearly taking his head off. At 1.30 and lunch, Australia are 99 for three, with Lawry 50* and Burge 10*. It has been a tense, enthralling morning session, watched by a crowd that has swelled to 20,000. Bar a couple of false shots, Lawry has looked security itself; but, after the first hour, the fast bowlers have held the upper hand.

LUNCH INTERVAL

John (Jack) Flavell has already amply justified his selection. Like a number of professional English quick bowlers, he has had to queue up for a decade behind the same handful of well-established figures: initially, the masterly Alec Bedser (Surrey) and, briefly, the electrifying Frank 'Typhoon' Tyson (Northamptonshire); more recently and consistently, Statham and Trueman, with the amateur all-rounder Trevor Bailey (Essex) occasionally also taking the new ball. Some of those in the queue have from time to time had a chance to show their quality. For instance, Peter Loader (Surrey) has played in thirteen Tests and taken 39 wickets. He even claimed a hat-trick against the West Indies in 1957 and toured both South Africa and Australia (twice); but he has never commanded a regular place, perhaps because, in this era of hyper-awareness about throwing, his action (especially his bouncer) has raised suspicion. So, too, does the action of Harold Rhodes (Derbyshire), who took nine wickets in two Tests against India in 1959.

There are no such queries about the persevering Alan Moss (Middlesex), but he has been picked only nine times and been little more than steady. A few others have been even less lucky: Derek Shackleton (Hampshire), three Tests since 1950, despite taking over 100 wickets every season for the previous twelve years; Les Jackson, praised by Bradman, but only selected once (against New Zealand in 1949) before his admirable, short-lived, return at Headingley; while Terry Spencer (Leicestershire), despite being handy enough to bowl May, Compton, Reg Simpson and Bailey in the 1953 Test Trial, has never been picked for a Test.

Nor, of course, has Flavell until now. In fact, Flavell's cricketing career almost never happened at all. As a teenager, he was also a promising footballer and briefly played full-back as a professional for West Bromwich Albion and Walsall. While on National Service, he took part in the 1948 Army Cup Final at Aldershot. The match was abandoned after a bolt of lightning struck the stadium, killed two players and caused other injuries, including burning off Flavell's hair and eyebrows.

Since 1949, he has toiled away for unfashionable Worcestershire. In his early years, he was a tearaway fast bowler, which together with his mop of crinkly red hair earned him the nickname 'Mad Jack'. Initially, in and out of the side, he played apprentice to the evergreen Reg Perks, who had opened the bowling for England in the 'Timeless Test' at Durban before the Second World War. When a back injury prompted Flavell to shorten his run, he found, like other fast bowlers (Tyson, for one), that added control and accuracy can lead to equal hostility and greater reward. When Perks finally retired in 1955, Flavell took on his mantle, and in a couple of years he and the newly signed Len Coldwell developed into the most challenging opening attack on the county circuit. The pair complement each other perfectly. Flavell is an enforcer. Hitting the seam, he bowls a 'heavy ball', has twice taken nine wickets in an innings, and can keep going for long periods. Coldwell, not as quick, bowls big, late in-duckers, which he varies with a well-disguised slower ball. Flavell has taken well over 100 first-class wickets this season, but it is undoubtedly that clinking spell in the recent Gentlemen v Players match which has at last forced the Test selectors' hand.

AFTERNOON SESSION

At 2.10, the weather still overcast, Flavell and Trueman resume the attack. A quarter of an hour later, Flavell gains his first Test wicket. Burge drives impetuously at an in-swinging yorker and loses his leg stump. Australia 106 for four, last man 15. Booth, tall, balanced, comes to the crease to face his first ball in Test cricket. Flavell now really has his tail up. *Another nasty one which just gets him in the midriff. But Brian Booth, a physical fitness expert, doesn't seem to mind a bit*, comments Brian Johnston, now back at the microphone. Perhaps he did mind the blow a bit; he certainly gives the spot a quick rub. *Flavell to Booth. Ooh, he nearly got through with that.* This ball is not quite as short as the previous one and is heading for the stumps. *He just got his bat down. Flavell to Booth.* A little too straight this time, and Booth glances the ball to fine leg. *And that's his first run. And there are four of them there for him. Four, his first scoring stroke in Test cricket. Booth now not out 4.* At the other end, Trueman tries to bounce Lawry, is hooked to the boundary, and goes for 10 in the over. Then, at 2.40, after half an hour's play, the rain starts to lash down, forcing the players off the field. Australia 124 for four. Lawry 64*, Booth 6*. The current regulations in England say that the pitch must remain uncovered until play is definitively abandoned for the day.

STOPPAGE FOR RAIN

'I didn't expect to be selected. I am twenty-seven,' Brian Booth told the journalist who phoned him at Narwee

Boys' High School with the advance news that he had been picked for the tour to England. If thirty-two is old for an English cricketer (like Flavell) to make their debut, twenty-seven is equally old for an Australian. Booth, a modest, devout schoolteacher, is good at several sports, representing his country at hockey at the 1956 Melbourne Olympics. His first-class debut for New South Wales against the MCC tourists in 1955, in which he scored a praiseworthy 74* against Tyson, Bedser & co., suggested a bright future awaited him, but New South Wales was stocked with batting talent and he struggled to hold a regular place.

His fortunes looked to be changing last December when he made 87 against Worrell's touring West Indies, and Worrell himself said to Booth, 'I'll see you in England.' But, despite making 548 runs at an average of 60 in the Sheffield Shield, Booth was not chosen for any of the Tests. His elegant, wristy play had finally been noticed, however, and he was one of the tour party on the *Himalaya* when it sailed for England. Like the other members of the seventeen-man squad, he is being paid £1,200 for the trip. At a farewell at his school, he was presented with a 'Travel Diary' to chronicle his progress.

In the opening match on a slow, soggy pitch at Worcester, he got off the dreaded nought with a single and heard the friendly voice of Graveney from the covers: 'Well done, Brian, congratulations on your first run on English soil.' He went on to score an encouraging 37 out of a first-innings total of 177. His form remained solid, with hundreds against Cambridge University and Somerset, and he was twelfth man for the first two Tests. In the second match against Lancashire, he made 99 before being caught behind off his leg-spinning namesake: B. C. Booth caught G. Clayton bowled B. Booth. The humour of the situation struck him at once, and Benaud remarked in the dressing-room that it was the only time he'd seen a batter burst out laughing when dismissed on that score. In due course, Booth received a tie from the 99 Club, the key number repeated nine times in Roman numerals: XCIX. Now, McDonald's injury has finally given Booth his chance and, so far, he is taking it.

*

Later in the afternoon there is one attempt to restart the game; but the heavens open again before a ball can be bowled, and play for the day is finally called off at six o'clock.

*

The English team are staying at a country club out of town, the Australians at the prestigious Midland Hotel in the city centre. After a day's play, Booth likes to go to the 'flicks'. Last night, it was John Ford's edgy Western, *Two Rode Together*, starring James Stewart and Richard Widmark; tonight, it's Walt Disney's more wholesomely exciting *Swiss Family Robinson*. Of his team-mates, the honours so far belong to Lawry, who has again lived up to his nickname, 'the Phantom'. It derives from a comic-strip character the opener enjoys, but is apt in a cricketing sense, since he seems to acquire his runs without the spectator quite being sure how he has done it. Hutton, in his *Evening News* column syndicated to the Manchester and Birmingham evening papers, has been, for him, fulsome: 'He is not a batsman you get tired of watching, so sound in his defence and so methodical in his attack.' It was an observation often made of Hutton himself in his prime. Looking ahead, an X-ray has revealed a broken blood vessel in O'Neill's forearm; but he has been cleared to field and will bat in the second innings.

5

Day Two: Friday 28 July

The weather looks encouraging. The rain has blown through; the Pennines are visible. Although cloudy and windy, there are odd glimmers of sun. Benaud is one of those at Old Trafford early to check on the state of the pitch, and is reassured to find it firm and hard, and relatively unaffected by yesterday's downpour. A crowd of 15,000 is already inside the ground, and long lines snake away outside the gates.

Many of the spectators, like those at home preparing to listen to the radio coverage or follow the action on TV, will – in what is still the age of print – have been devouring the reports of yesterday's play in the morning papers. For English supporters, these make heartening reading, with their widespread assumption that England are in command. Some of the headlines are simply variations of one another: 'Lawry Alone Defies England's Heavy Artillery' claims the *Guardian*; 'Lawry Stands Firm As Fast Bowlers Strike' maintains the *Daily Telegraph*. For Australian supporters, the *Age* carries a similar message: 'Bill Lawry Again Australia's Test Match Hero'.

In the reports themselves, Lawry is praised by Rowbotham in the *Guardian* for 'another superbly cool, disciplined innings'. Woodcock in *The Times* is equally admiring: Lawry 'stood firm while others of greater renown fell around him ... He gets rigidly in line, is unfailingly watchful, and yesterday was driving with unwonted freedom'; so, too, is Percy Beames in the *Age*: Lawry 'was the only Australian to really get on top of a hostile England attack on a good, true wicket'. Praise also goes to Flavell for his accuracy and persistent hostility, with even Swanton, who would probably have preferred Lock's inclusion and rarely deigns to notice players from counties as far from the metropolis as Worcestershire, admitting in the *Telegraph* that Flavell bowled 'extremely well'. O'Neill's unfortunate dismissal is much discussed. No one in the English press thinks him hard done by, but the *Canberra Times* notes that although Benaud has made no comment, he is 'obviously upset about O'Neill's dismissal'.

After breakfast, Booth and other team-mates pay a visit to the huge warehouse in Oxford Street of the Manchester clothing company Tootal. A delay getting back is presumably the reason why there's a transport kerfuffle at the Midland Hotel, and some of the Australian team only just reach the ground by the start of play.

MORNING SESSION

The overnight batters, Lawry (64*) and Booth (6*), resume at 124 for four. Flavell, from the Warwick Road end, has four balls of his unfinished over to complete. Booth is facing. At first, the wicket seems less responsive than yesterday, as Booth, with easy wrists, turns a shortish ball from Flavell into the leg side. *They'll take possibly two runs there*, suggests Brian Johnston. *Pullar after it to midwicket. They go for a second, Pullar running a little bit gingerly on this turf which must be still a little bit damp.* Pullar wheels and, half off-balance, sends in a meticulous, bail-high return to Murray.

Statham, from the Stretford end, continues the attack to Lawry. He flows up to the wicket, the blustery wind over his left shoulder helping his natural movement away from the left-hander. Lawry comes forward to a well-pitched-up ball and punches it through the offside. *Nice drive there. It's beaten cover. Dexter chasing it down. They've taken two runs. Lawry goes up to 66.*

It is soon clear that Flavell, bowling into the wind, is struggling to maintain line and length. Yesterday, his 14.2 overs cost a miserly 23 runs; now, 11 come in a single over, as Booth flicks and cuts and hooks him. At the other end, it's a different story with Statham his usual probing, economical self, always there or thereabouts. Booth, who cannot have often faced him, soon discovers that the fast bowler also possesses a leg-cutter and can move the ball away from, as well as into, the right-hander. Booth, groping, is beaten three times in quick succession.

Australia 149 for four. Booth jumps a little in the crease to Statham as he deflects the ball down onto the leg side. *And that was uppish again but quite safe, wide of Trueman, down to long leg.* Lawry, now on strike, plays another crisp shot out into the covers for no run. Statham moves in again. This time the ball is a leg-cutter. It comes back a shade into Lawry, catches him on the crease, defeats his hasty jab and raps him on the pads. Statham appeals. Phillipson's finger immediately goes up. Johnston gives a yelp of excitement: *He's out lbw! Lawry lbw, bowled Statham for 74! Australia 150 for five.* Lawry turns and slowly walks away. *First blow of the morning to England. He was in for 176 minutes, hit 11 fours.* In context, it's been an exemplary innings, both patient and enterprising when enterprise has been possible. Lawry is one of those batters who has seven or eight scoring strokes, but mostly confines himself to four: the drive, the hook, the glance and the push. He rarely pulls or cuts. Booth 22*.

Ken Mackay, like Lawry a left-hander, comes to the wicket, as usual gum-chewing away. Arlott in his cricket diary notes that Mackay's initial batting is 'unorthodoxly capable'. This is exactly how he tends to play in Tests, nudging and nurdling, fully living up to his ironic nickname of 'Slasher'. For years now, he has been exasperating international bowlers almost as much as England's Trevor 'Barnacle' Bailey used to. In certain circumstances, of course, such dour defensiveness can be invaluable. In the second innings of the 1956 Lord's Test, Mackay ground out 31 in four hours twenty-five minutes, and it was his seventh-wicket, 117-run partnership with Benaud which decisively turned the match in Australia's favour. Outside of Tests, Mackay can play in much less inhibited fashion and has all the shots, as he showed in the recent game against Middlesex. But today, his job is simply to stick around as long as possible. He pushes his first ball from Flavell safely into the covers, then cuts him neatly to third man for a single.

The scoring rate this morning has been sprightly enough: fifty up in fifty minutes. May belatedly rests Flavell after 7.4 overs for 38, a little too expensive, as things stand. Statham, after a brief exchange with his captain, soldiers on and for once is off target, the ball going down the leg side. Mackay offers a flicker of a leg glance. There is a concerted appeal. Johnston yelps again. *He's out, caught at the wicket by Murray. Mackay caught Murray bowled Statham for 11. Australia 174 for six, Statham's fourth wicket. Just got the faintest touch there on the leg side.* Mackay, not waiting for the umpire's decision, is already on his way, cap pushed up, gloves pulled off, bat tucked under arm, still assiduously chewing. Booth 35*.

At the other end, Trueman would seem the obvious replacement for Flavell. Instead, May brings on Dexter, today in a short-sleeved Cambridge sweater. He may be hoping that, into the wind, the slower Dexter will achieve some swing. (Perhaps, too, he is aware that yesterday, in bowler-friendly conditions, Fiery Fred failed to make the best use of them.) Dexter promptly overpitches to Booth. *That's a nice on-drive. Four runs, beautifully timed in between mid-on and midwicket.* Ripples of applause. Statham keeps plugging away. Dexter moves in once more to the newly arrived Davidson (another left-hander). *This is Dexter's first ball to Davidson and jolly nearly his last,* comments Johnston, as the delivery does indeed swing. In fact, it swings back inside Davidson's attempted stroke and almost bowls him. Davidson, as everyone knows, is more than handy with the bat and, even at this stage, is perfectly capable of resuscitating the innings.

Statham again to Booth. Booth, with another of his assured but this time slightly uppish deflections, gets the ball away on the leg side for two. Close, running back from short leg, returns it to Murray. Statham pitches further up, almost in the blockhole. Booth jams the bat down, turning the face as he does so and sending the ball a foot or two above the ground into the on side. Swanton at the microphone now: *He's out, caught at short leg by Close for 46. A good innings by the New South Welshman.* Good, indeed: 46 on debut in bowler-friendly conditions in eighty-five minutes, five fours. Compact, time to spare, Booth has definitely looked the part. *And now it's Australia's captain coming in at 185 for seven.* Benaud was out for a pair at Headingley and has been short of runs all tour, just one fifty in late May against Gloucestershire. Booth passes Benaud on his way to the pavilion and, characteristically, apologises for getting out. The crowd is tense now, intent.

Dexter goes a little wider on the crease to angle the ball across Davidson; it catches the flailing edge and flies fast and low just to Barrington's right at first slip. He falls to the ground, clasping the ball in both hands like a precious jewel. Players and crowd burst into excited applause. *Davidson caught Barrington bowled Dexter 0.* 185 for eight. Grout now. He is bare-headed; the other Australians have worn the traditional baggy green cap, Booth's the baggiest of them all. Grout can be an effective late-order batter, likes to play off the back foot; the hook and cut are his favourite strokes.

Grout and Benaud add four runs – Benaud gratefully off the mark with a two. Close drops Grout, but it's an inexpensive miss. Grout attempts a cut off Dexter. It's too close to him and doesn't rise as much as expected; there's a snick on the under edge of the bat; Murray catches the ball neatly and joyfully throws it up. 189 for nine. The last man is McKenzie. He is no mug with the bat, either, sometimes appearing in the middle order for Western Australia, and indeed in this series has already batted well at both Lord's and Headingley. Here, however, there are no last-wicket heroics. One run and a few balls later, Benaud lashes out at Dexter and is bowled neck-and-crop. Australia, 190 all out, have lost six for 66 in ninety minutes. Dexter three for 16; Statham five for 53.

This morning, Statham has bowled unchanged for twelve overs – a Herculean effort. He retrieves his sweater from Phillipson and the other players fan aside to let him lead them off to concerted home-ground applause. This morning May has had the Midas touch. His decision to persist with Statham has paid off handsomely, as has his gamble to bowl Dexter rather than Trueman. At the start of play, few England supporters could have dreamed of Australia being out for so modest a total. But then batting collapses have been a feature of the series so far, particularly by the side batting first.

England's first pair, the left-handers Pullar and Subba Row, have twenty minutes to negotiate until lunch. These short, intense fragments of time before an interval or the close of play are often the openers' lot, and often not a happy one. There is no time to become really settled. You are usually facing the fastest bowlers, fresh and prepared to give it everything in the few overs available. The field is up, waiting for you to make a mistake. It is as much a test of nerve as of technique, as the unforgiving minute hand on the pavilion clock seems to freeze. Then, at last, the umpires remove the bails and, with a gasp of relief, you're safe.

Davidson opens from Statham's end, with the wind. He is immediately at top pace. Pullar tries to run the fourth ball through the populous slip cordon; Benaud, diving, prevents an almost certain boundary. Subba Row takes two off a full toss from McKenzie; then, facing Davidson, he is undone by a delivery which initially angles in, then swings out. The ball is one he has to play, but he merely succeeds in edging it to Simpson at first slip. Like Harvey's catch to Subba Row yesterday, the ball travels fast and low; but Simpson is already acknowledged as one of the finest slip fielders in the world, and he almost nonchalantly scoops up the chance. England 3 for one. Dexter, replacing Subba Row, simply tries to survive and barely does so against Davidson. Then, for the final over before lunch, Benaud (inventive as ever) brings on Mackay's sometimes deceptive medium pace. Pullar, however, is not deceived and glances and drives the last two balls for reassuring fours. England 17 for one. Pullar 14*. Dexter 0*.

LUNCH INTERVAL

John Murray, nicknamed 'JT' after his first two initials, is having a good match. Yesterday, he caught Simpson to produce the initial breakthrough, and this morning he has taken two further catches to remove the potentially aggravating Mackay and the potentially pugnacious Grout. As usual, his collection of returns has been immaculate, even making a number of the throwing-ins look rather better than they really were. Some keepers are effective stoppers, but look as if they are wearing iron gloves. JT always brings an air of unruffled calm and unostentatious elegance to his performance.

Like Flavell, Murray has had to wait for his opportunity. Again, like Flavell, he showed early promise as a footballer. (At seventeen, he played as wing-half for the Brentford youth team, losing semi-finalists in 1952–53 to Manchester United's 'Busby Babes' in the inaugural FA Youth Cup. He was later signed by Arsenal as an amateur and offered terms as a professional by Brentford.) He became a wicketkeeper almost by accident, taking over in a Boys' Club competition final when the regular keeper broke his finger. He first kept for Middlesex as substitute for Leslie Compton (brother of the great Denis) in a losing match against Leicestershire in May 1952. He took a catch, scored 3 in his only innings, and conceded 14 and 15 byes respectively. He was only just seventeen.

In 1956, after National Service in the RAF and Leslie Compton's retirement, Murray became Middlesex's first-choice keeper. That year he clocked up the most wicket-keeping dismissals in the county championship (63 caught, 14 stumped) and made useful runs. The following season, he really blossomed and performed the wicketkeeper's double of 1,000 runs and 100 dismissals. He was only the second keeper ever to achieve this feat – Leslie Ames, who managed it an astonishing three times, being the first. That year Murray was chosen for the MCC match against the visiting West Indies and later for their game against L. E. G. Ames's XI, during which he achieved another 'double', taking four catches and making four stumpings. At twenty-two, he was suddenly in the frame.

But, for a few seasons, in the frame is where he stayed. The flamboyant Godfrey Evans was still the resident Test keeper, as he had been for the previous decade. When Evans was finally dropped after a poor game against India in 1959, Murray looked a strong contender to succeed him. Instead, the no more experienced Roy Swetman of Surrey was preferred, with mixed results, followed in turn by Jim Parks of Sussex, a swashbuckling batter who had recently taken up the gloves. Parks, after an undefeated century against the West Indies in Port of Spain, March 1960, kept for the entire 1960 Test series against South Africa, catching reliably standing back to the quicker bowlers, but never seriously troubling the scorers with the bat.

At the start of the 1961 season, Parks was thus the incumbent. However, as Arlott noted, discussing the English team for the first Test, what probably sank Parks, as much as a current lack of runs, was 'mishandl[ing] some leg-breaks from Barrington' on the Saturday of the MCC match at Lord's against the Australians. That left the wicket-keeping position 'wide open' and 'John Murray, a good team man, a tidy wicket-keeper and a serviceable batsman, steps into the English team after several seasons on the threshold'. The first three Tests have seen Murray live up to Arlott's carefully worded approval, the highlight to date being his lightning stumping of McDonald off Lock at Headingley.

AFTERNOON SESSION

Pullar and Dexter resume after lunch against Davidson and McKenzie. Pullar's nickname is 'Noddy', not from any marked resemblance to the Enid Blyton character and his distinguishing characteristic, but because, in the changing-room, Pullar quite often simply nods off. After that brief pre-prandial flurry, his progress now is so slow that the members of the still swelling crowd on this increasingly warm afternoon could be excused for thinking that Pullar is merely sleep-batting at the wicket, while being in danger of nodding off themselves. A more tolerant view might argue that, with the early fall of Subba Row, Pullar sees his role as that of sheet anchor and is batting accordingly.

If Pullar is patience personified, Dexter, like all natural stroke-makers, hates to be confined. Benaud's own instincts as player and captain are also to attack, but he knows, too, when to contain, and how defence can sometimes be the best form of attack. Davidson, McKenzie and, when he is introduced, the wrist-cocked, trundling Mackay keep Dexter subdued with their accuracy and length. He occasionally, momentarily, flares out: there's a mighty drive through the covers off Davidson; a hook for a further boundary off McKenzie; but these are rare flashes of his true quality. Another (mishit) hook off Davidson falls clear of any fielders. Then – Dexter on 16, the score 42 – seeming disaster: he top-edges Mackay. The ball rises and describes a slow, descending parabola between midwicket and mid-on. O'Neill, one of the finest fielders in a team of fine fielders, moves a few yards to his left, positions himself underneath the ball. And, to the crowd's palpable shock and relief, drops it.

That's two narrow escapes within a couple of minutes. Surely now Dexter will take stock, try at least to keep the ball on the ground. But no. McKenzie replaces Davidson with the wind behind him. The Australians have talked about Dexter's penchant for the hook, how he doesn't always correctly gauge the pace of the shorter ball along the line of the body. (In the second innings at Lord's, he was out in just this fashion, trying to hook a short delivery from McKenzie which struck him around the hip and, as he swivelled, rebounded onto the stumps.) McKenzie, with his short, relaxed approach to the wicket and his powerful shoulder action, is often a yard or two faster than he looks. The ball is short; Dexter goes to hook; it's on him quicker than he expects. Dexter caught at midwicket by Davidson, bowled McKenzie 16. England 43 for two.

May walks to the crease, the innings – perhaps the match – in the balance. The crowd senses this. If he's out early, 190 might look a reasonable score. But, if he can only settle and exert his old mastery, a substantial lead is a definite possibility. It soon seems that this will indeed be May's day. McKenzie bowls to him. It's a full toss outside the off stump, curving away slightly. Exactly the gimme May might have hoped to receive. He drives it confidently off the back foot through the offside. *That's a nice stroke for four*, purrs Johnston. *Should get through. Booth chasing it, won't catch it.* Soon afterwards, May clips McKenzie through square leg with a turn of his wrists. *Nicely kept down, all along the ground. Lawry running round from long leg. And that's the fifty up.* The fifty has taken sixty-five minutes – not bad going, given Pullar's virtual immobility since lunch.

Benaud, keen to remove May before he can establish himself, shuffles his bowlers. Davidson alternates with McKenzie with the wind behind them, while at the other end Mackay begins an attritional spell of eleven overs for

16 runs. The pitch seems finally to have flattened out. From time to time, Mackay bemuses Pullar with his seam movement, but he never really looks like losing his wicket; nor does May, rapidly catching up with the opener. So far in this series, he has had starts – 17, 22, 26, 8* – but nothing significant. This is the moment to play a captain's innings, a match-determining innings.

At 80, Benaud brings himself on. A calculated move, but a decisive one? His arm is moving freely; he (like May) is almost back to his best, having against Middlesex revealed much of the old nip, as well as that beguiling, dipping flight. In the past, May hasn't always picked Benaud's googly, but he picks it now and slams it through mid-on for four. At 3.50, when he reaches 33, he overtakes Pullar, who has proved more fallible against Davidson, twice edging him into the slips, the ball not quite carrying. Benaud deliberately bowls a shortish ball to May, on 35, which he pulls for two. The next delivery is also on the short side, but it's the 'flipper', the one that doesn't turn but hurries on. May pulls again, misses. The ball bounces a little more than usual and passes a fraction over the top of off stump.

At tea, England are 105 for two with May 43* and Pullar 42*. The crowd, now up to 27,000, has had an absorbing afternoon, a tight contest between bat and ball. England have lost only one wicket – good – but, in considerably easier batting conditions, have had to work hard for their 88 runs. Of these, May has scored almost half and, apart from that flipper and a couple of air shots against Davidson, has looked reassuringly untroubled. Pullar, too, has been solid in his fashion. His only real rushes of blood have been an uppish cut for four against McKenzie which Benaud, diving in the gully, almost reached, and, the very next ball, a slash for another four high above the slips. Rotating his bowlers, Benaud has kept up the attack from one end and kept things quiet at the other. Although he hasn't himself taken a wicket, his own bowling has, as they say, constantly asked questions.

TEA INTERVAL

Through the long, warm afternoon, standing back or standing up, Wally Grout has kept with his usual composure and supreme competence. No sniff of a chance has yet come his way, but no one doubts that, when it does, he will take it without fuss.

It's a cricketing truism that it's hard to get picked for Australia, but, once picked, even harder to get dropped. Both Grout and his much younger, long-term understudy, Barry Jarman, can attest to the truth of the maxim. When the two were selected, uncapped, as the keepers for the 1957–58 tour of South Africa, Grout was already thirty, Jarman only twenty-one. Grout kept in all five Tests. Since then – except for a single Test on the 1959–60 tour of India and Pakistan when Grout was injured and Jarman deputised – this is how it has remained, although Benaud makes sure that Jarman has his fair share of games outside the Tests.

Grout first got hooked on cricket at the age of seven, watching the then teenage, later legendary, wicketkeeper Don Tallon. Grout (who also enjoyed Aussie Rules and rugby union) showed early promise with the gloves in Queensland school and grade teams, but tended to be picked instead as an opening bat. From his late teens until his mid-twenties, he hovered on the fringes of the Queensland Sheffield Shield side. A string of disappointments followed. The first was when a supposedly better batter, Douglas Siggs, was preferred to keep for Queensland in 1947–48 when Tallon was away on Test duty. A second came, on Tallon's retirement, when Grout had finally established himself as the regular Queensland keeper, but was not considered for any of the Tests against Len Hutton's triumphant 1954–55 England touring side. Probably an even sharper disappointment was being entirely ignored for the 1956 touring party going to England.

At this point, Grout's Queensland team-mate and friend Mackay told him in no uncertain terms that he had to improve his fitness. He acted on the advice, and, together with Jarman, was duly chosen to go to South Africa. Early in the tour, Grout sustained a hairline fracture of the thumb, but, desperate to play, declared himself fit for the first Test, at Johannesburg. In Australia's first innings, he helped Benaud (122) put on a vital 89 for the eighth wicket and in South Africa's second innings took six catches, a world record in Tests. He had at last arrived and went on to snap up nineteen Test dismissals in the series.

It was in South Africa that Grout acquired his alliterative nickname 'Griz'. Harvey is said to have coined it as a teasing response to Grout's habitual grousing at less than pinpoint returns. When Australia regained the Ashes from England in 1958–59, Grout's twenty 'victims' were a major contributing factor, besides equalling his former idol Tallon's record for an Ashes series. In February 1960, his eight catches in Western Australia's first innings set another world record. The tied

Test against the West Indies the following December saw Grout take seven catches, and he was one of those at the crease during the heart-stopping, pressure-cooker final over. First, he was dropped when Wes Hall, determined to catch a sitter off his own bowling, collided with Rohan Kanhai and spilled the chance. Then, with the scores level and going for a third run that would have won the game, he was magnificently thrown out by Conrad Hunte from the midwicket boundary. Grout ended the series with twenty-three dismissals, an integral factor in Australia's 2–1 victory. So far in the current series he has accounted for thirteen batters, twelve caught and one stumped. At thirty-four, he is unquestionably the best keeper in the world.

EVENING SESSION

May and Pullar; Benaud and Davidson. At 4.55, May is on 49 and facing Benaud. He drives a well-pitched-up ball through the covers for a single to Brian Johnston's evident delight: *And there's his fifty.* Pullar claps his glove against his bat. May smooths back his hair with his right hand, raises his bat with his left to acknowledge the spectators' prolonged applause. He must feel even more relieved than they do, must have wondered in the year or so he was out of the game whether he would ever again have a moment like this. His fifty has taken 106 minutes, and he's hit eight fours.

Five minutes later, at 121 for two, it's Pullar's turn. He square-cuts Benaud. *He's hit that very firm*, remarks Denis Compton, then after a slight pause – *oh, it's been misfielded by Lawry, and it's going down for two runs. And that's*

Pullar's fifty. Both batters now start to score more freely, even off the parsimonious Mackay, May punching him wide of mid-on and Pullar driving him uninhibitedly through the covers. The hundred stand comes up in two hours twenty-five minutes, the previous fifty in just over the hour. But, at a quarter to six, Pullar plays across the line, trying to force a rare full toss from Davidson into his favoured leg side and is bowled: 154 for three. Last man 63 (in 218 minutes). The partnership between Pullar and May has, note sharp-eyed observers instantly aware of the resonance, been worth 111 runs.

Cricketers (at all levels) and fans are notoriously superstitious. Some players always put the same sock and boot on first; others will wear a 'lucky' piece of clothing or a charm. The South African off-spinner Hugh Tayfield is nicknamed 'Toey' because of his superstitious habit when batting of forever tapping his toecap on the ground before each delivery. 'Nelson' (111 and its multiples) is probably the best-known English cricketing superstition, applying alike to individual and team totals. It is often claimed that it derives from the inauspicious image of the three stumps left without the bails on; more colourfully, it recalls the famous English admiral during the Napoleonic Wars who, latterly, had only one eye, one arm and one leg (though, since he never lost a leg, another part of the anatomy is sometimes substituted for it). A particularly Australian superstition involves the number 87 (or 187, 287 etc.), again both on the individual and team level. This is because 87 is 13 off a hundred, that most coveted of scores.

Pullar trudges off, with forty minutes to go, to be replaced by Close. Cricket is made of a succession of moments, seemingly small in themselves, but capable of starting an avalanche. Everyone on the field and almost all the northern crowd will be well aware of Close's situation: that he hasn't played in a Test for four years and that, at MCC headquarters and among at least some of the more highbrow cricketing press, he has a reputation for unreliability, for letting the occasion get to him. If he falls quickly, it might cause a late rockfall of wickets. Benaud immediately rings Close around with close fielders. But if he's nervous, it doesn't show. He confidently tucks a full pitch off his legs away for one four; he hits Benaud for another; and, generally, he looks far more at home than Pullar did. May, for his part, is clearly content to play for stumps, although he does twice on-drive McKenzie to the boundary and straight-drives Davidson. A different kind of player (Dexter, Harvey, O'Neill – Benaud, say) would almost certainly press for his century and the innings lead by the close. May, however, learned his Test cricket under the cautious tutelage of Len Hutton and seems happy for tomorrow to be another day. The crowd is happy, too, and cheers him off with England 187 for three; May 90*, Close 14*.

*

It has undoubtedly been a great day for England and especially for May. Australia have been bundled out for 190; England are now only 3 runs behind with seven wickets in hand; and May himself is on the verge of another Test hundred. For his part, Benaud probably takes some heart from keeping England to under 200 in the two and a bit sessions, but would have hoped for more wickets on a pitch that Statham and Dexter exploited so well. Or as Hutton has already put it in his regular daily reflection, as usual sent off to the printers soon after lunch, 'a wicket like this one with a little moisture in it brings out the best in English bowlers', whereas 'Australian bowlers' tendency to bowl short means that they sacrifice all that such a wicket as this possesses'. Benaud can also take a degree of heart from his own constraining performance, just 34 runs conceded from twenty overs.

That evening, Booth for once does not go to the cinema, but sees 'the Little Favourite', Johnny Martin. Martin bowls left-arm, back-of-the-hand spinners and was chosen for three Tests against the West Indies. Not making the tour party, he is nonetheless over in England, playing for Colne in the Lancashire League, where among those also taking a hatful of wickets this summer are Accrington's Wes Hall, Burnley's Lance Gibbs, Nelson's Johnny Wardle and Todmorden's Frank Tyson; while in the rival Central Lancashire League, the all-round virtuosity of Radcliffe's Garry Sobers is making them the runaway leaders – though the top run-scorer is a still relatively little-known 'coloured' South African, Middleton's Basil D'Oliveira.

6

Day Three: Saturday 29 July

England's promising position is enough to make some of the national newspaper headlines superstitiously cautious. 'May and Pullar Give England the Chance to Take Command', claims the *Guardian*, reserving any patriotic upsurge for the sub-heading: 'Statham shocks Australians'. *The Times* is similarly hesitant, couched in a more liturgical register – 'May and Pullar Add 111 at Time of Need' – complemented by the quasi-biblical sub-heading: 'Statham chastens Australia before his own people'. By contrast, the *Daily Telegraph* is more confident, more plainly factual: 'May Shows Limitations of Australian Attack', succeeded by 'England Three Behind With Seven Wickets Left: Statham 5–53'.

Naturally in the English reports it is Statham and May who receive most of the plaudits. 'Wonderfully enough, he seems to be bowling as well as ever,' murmurs Woodcock of Statham, while casting May as a kind of latter-day Horatius from Macaulay's *Lays of Ancient Rome*: 'Understandably, May came off through the shadows and a cheering crowd wearing a smile of pleasure and relief.' Pullar and Close, too, are given their due: the former for his unflappable adhesiveness and the latter for his steadiness and enterprise. Even Swanton gives Close two restrained cheers: 'There were three-quarters of an hour to go when Close arrived, and one can only say that on his return to Test cricket he has so far given no cause whatever for anxiety.' As for Australian reactions, the *Canberra Times* claims that 'May was the batsman Australia knew years ago', whereas by contrast Percy Beames reckons that, apart from Booth and Lawry, 'Australia's batting prestige has never been lower', full of 'weak strokes and lack of concentration'.

The sky may be grey, but local excitement and expectation run high. Before the start of play, the ground is filling up so fast that the Lancashire secretary, Geoffrey Howard, advises those queuing outside the gates that 'conditions inside will be pretty uncomfortable. You will be able to get a view of the game but only from seats on the grass.' Indeed, so great is the press of attendance that both captains agree to spectators on the grass sitting right up to the boundary rope – as they do, the legs of numerous small boys even trespassing onto the field of play.

MORNING SESSION

Close (14*) and May (90*) make their way to the wicket. The ground has acquired an atmosphere of gripped anticipation. As the knowledgeable are aware, the new ball is due in a couple of overs; its effectiveness (or not) could be decisive. Close takes strike to the Australian captain. *And Benaud runs in to bowl the first ball to Close*, says the hard-to-recognise Australian commentator, not Fingleton.

Two captains, one winner: Benaud and May after Australia regain the Ashes at Adelaide, February 1959.

Benaud and his men with Birmingham schoolboys, 7 June 1961.

FIXTURES AT LORD'S ,1961

APRIL
Sat. 29   M.C.C. v. Yorkshire, 3 days

MAY
Wed. 3   M.C.C. v. Surrey, 3 days
Sat. 6   Middlesex v. Northants., 3 days
Wed. 10 †M.C.C. v. R.M.A.Sandhurst, 1 day
Thur. 11 †M.C.C. v. Club Cricket Conference, 2 days
Sat. 13   M.C.C. v. Gloucestershire, 3 days
Wed. 17   Middlesex v. Essex, 3 days
Sat. 20   Middlesex v. Sussex, 3 days
Wed. 24 †M.C.C. Young Profs. v. London Fed. of Boys' Clubs, 1 day
Sat. 27 *M.C.C. v. Australians, 3 days
Wed. 31   Middlesex v. Lancashire, 3 days

JUNE
Sat. 3   Middlesex v. Warwickshire, 3 days
Wed. 7   Middlesex v. Kent, 3 days
Sat. 10   Middlesex v. Somerset, 3 days
Wed. 14   M.C.C. v. Oxford Univ., 3 days
Sat. 17 †M.C.C. v. Bermuda, 1 day
Thur. 22 *ENGLAND v. AUSTRALIA, 5 days
Wed. 28   Middlesex v. Hampshire, 3 days

JULY
Sat. 1   Middlesex v. Glamorgan, 3 days
Fri. 7 *Eton v. Harrow, 2 days
Mon. 10 †R.A. v. R.E., 2 days
Wed. 12   M.C.C. v. Cambridge Univ., 3 days
Sat. 15 *Oxford v. Cambridge, 3 days
Wed. 19   Gentlemen v. Players, 3 days
Sat. 22 *Middlesex v. Australians, 3 days
Wed. 26   Middlesex v. Derbyshire, 3 days
Sat. 29 *Beaumont v. Oratory, 1 day
Mon. 31 †Clifton v. Tonbridge, 2 days

AUGUST
Wed. 2 †Rugby v. Marlborough, 2 days
Fri. 4 †Cheltenham v. Haileybury & I.S.C., 2 days
Mon. 7 †Southern Schools v. The Rest, 2 days
Wed. 9 †Combined Services v. Public Schools, 2 days
Fri. 11 †M.C.C. v. Denmark, 1 day
Sat. 12   Middlesex v. Surrey, 3 days
Wed. 16 †Royal Navy v. Army, 2 days
Fri. 18 †R.N. v. R.A.F., 2 days
Mon. 21 †Middlesex II v. Hants. II, 2 days
Wed. 23   Middlesex v. Worcs., 3 days
Sat. 26   Middlesex v. Yorkshire, 3 days
Wed. 30   Gentlemen of England v. Australians, 3 days

SEPTEMBER
Sat. 2   Middlesex v. Glos., 3 days
Wed. 6 *M.C.C. Young Professionals v. English Schools Cricket Association, 1 day
Thur. 7 †H. S. Altham's Public Schools XI v. English Schools Cricket Association, 1 day
Fri. 8 †M.C.C. Young Profs. v. Young Amateurs of Middlesex, 1 day
Mon. 11   Cross Arrows C.C. match every week-day (Saturdays included) until Saturday, 30 September.

*Rover tickets issued for these Matches only
†Members may introduce personally two friends into the pavilion during these matches.

MCC membership card, and Lord's fixture list, 1961.

Day Two: May hits out; Simpson and Grout look on.

Day Three: Subba Row drops Lawry on 25 off Trueman;
Murray and Barrington watch.

Day Five: Benaud goes round the wicket.

Day Five: Benaud has Dexter caught behind – the breakthrough.

Day Five: Simpson catches Allen off Benaud.

Day Five: Davidson cleans up Statham to win the match.

Day Five: May b Benaud 0 – the defining moment.

Twenty Years Later: May as MCC President, March 1981.

In Memory of Richie: Sydney, January 2018.

It's outside the off stump and he comes back and drives it through the covers. He'll take one, probably two for this. It's being chased by Burge. They come back for the second. Close at once looks in good touch, back in the groove.

Yesterday, May glanced the last ball of the final over for four. Now he only needs ten for his fourteenth Test century; he hasn't scored one since the first Test against India in June 1959. He faces Davidson, who bowls the second over. Davidson is below full pace, just limbering up prior to taking the new ball. May pushes a quick single into the off side, running in that rather ungainly, laboured way he has. Other singles follow. He inches towards his goal with careful control: 92, 93, 94, 95.

Close, meanwhile, is purposeful, apparently quite at ease. Facing Davidson, he takes what looks like a leg-stump guard, even slightly outside leg, so that the bowler has a clear view of all three stumps. His bat is tucked so far behind his pads he seems to be deliberately hiding it from the bowler. Benaud sets the field meticulously, giving Davidson two short legs, Harvey and Booth, one in front of square and one behind. Close clips an overpitched ball confidently off his pads, and they take another single. Benaud to Close, with the mystery Australian still at the microphone. *Plenty of air and it's hit high back over the bowler's head and it's six, I think. Yes, six. Close 23. Three for 197. What a lovely shot! He was to it, picked it up on the rise and hit it high over towards the sight board.* This is what the crowd, giving a tremendous roar, wants: England in the box seat, driving home their advantage.

Davidson takes the new ball after four overs. At once there are demons in the wicket and in the air. Close almost edges what to him are two outswingers and then does edge a rising ball off the shoulder of his bat down to third man for a single. McKenzie bowls a wide, and later in the over a full toss. Close wristily flicks the full toss off his legs for four; riskily nicks Davidson for another four between second slip and gully; smoothly works a single down to fine leg. That's 24 runs in the first half-hour, of which Close has scored 19.

In the same Davidson over, now with a mystery English commentator describing the action, May, who had seemed so secure, reaches for an outswinger. *Ooh and he's edged it. Is he caught? Is he caught? He's caught, yes; a double-handed conjuring trick, and May is out for 95, deflected by Grout to Simpson at first slip off the bowling of Davidson and England are 212 for four.* What has happened is that May has snicked the ball fast and low to Simpson's right ankle, but Grout, believing the catch his, has dived across. He can't properly reach the ball, but has knocked it up (whether by luck or good judgement) and Simpson has safely gathered it. May is known to be vulnerable to the new ball, which is perhaps why he latterly prefers to bat four rather than three; and now the new ball has again done the trick. May leaves, jerking his head back in irritation, pulls off his batting gloves and walks in to sympathetic applause. The Australian fielders are cock-a-hoop. This is the wicket Benaud really wanted. With its fall, the whole match takes a pronounced tilt.

Almost immediately, it tilts further. A bare-headed Barrington faces one ball, and at the other end McKenzie continues. His first over presented few problems: too wide, too full, too short. The first ball of this new over, however, is on a good length and quicker than Close expects. He plays back and across the line. The ball defeats his stroke; it hits his pads; the appeal goes up and so, instantly, does Langridge's finger. Close is reluctant to leave, looking pointedly at Langridge, then at his pads, before turning from the crease. Close lbw McKenzie 33. England 212 for five. In three balls, England have slipped from riches to incipient rags. The lead is 22; the ball is still fresh; two new batters, Barrington and Murray, are at the crease; the nearby dock hooters are booming out twelve o'clock and the end of the Saturday shift; and there's still an hour and a half until the lunch break.

Few in the crowd can doubt how Barrington will confront this crisis. He began his career with Surrey in 1953, quickly establishing a reputation as a free-scoring player, particularly off the front foot. Two years later, he was picked for the first Test against the visiting South Africans. He made a duck in his only innings. In the first innings of the second Test, he top-scored with a slow, painstaking 34, but, according to *Wisden*, 'never looked comfortable'; and that, and 18 in the second innings, led to him being dropped. Over the next four years, he completely refashioned his game. He adopted a more front-on, two-eyed stance and became a grand accumulator, a back-foot player proficient in cut, hook, glance and nudges to the leg side. He now tends to give a little hop while making his defensive shots against quicker bowlers, but this nervous tic is misleading: he's still almost always solidly behind the ball. (He does get nervous, however: waiting to bat, he will sit, drumming his fingers and smoking cigarette after cigarette.) Possessing as he does a keen – even quixotic – sense of humour, he likes to reach a milestone like a fifty or a hundred with a six. He was recalled to the Test side in 1959, withstood a battering from Wes Hall and Chester Watson in the West Indies that winter, and has been a middle-order fixture ever since. Shoring up and rebuilding fragmented innings are his forte, and that is what he and Murray prepare to do now.

The score freezes on 212 for five for a quarter of an hour. Then Barrington and Murray both open their account with singles to relieved cheers from the crowd. Mackay, his right calf heavily strapped, comes on; Barrington strikes a long hop to the extra-cover boundary. Murray lofts a straight drive back over Mackay's head and hooks McKenzie for another four, but these are oases of aggression in a desert of obdurate defence. Nine runs in thirty-five minutes, 27 in an hour: this is post-war professional batting at its most rationed and abstemious. The increasingly frustrated crowd claps the sun when it makes an appearance and slow handclaps Barrington and Murray.

Benaud comes on and after one delivery tries unsuccessfully to persuade the umpires to change the ball. He shrugs his shoulders and continues to point to a spot on the ball. The scoring rate perks up a little. Benaud bowls a tempting, wider delivery, and Murray elegantly late cuts it: *Oh, that's a nice stroke*, exclaims Brian Johnston, *and it's gone for four. I think it just hit Simpson's left boot. Murray got well on top of it. It's his fourth four in his innings of 22. Both batsmen on 22 now, and England leading by 68, 258 for five.* The crowd is packed tight against the boundary rope and is beginning to constitute a problem on the relatively rare occasions fielders have to chase the ball to the edge.

When Benaud bowls a faster, even wider one (perhaps a 'flipper' gone wrong), Barrington is galvanised out of his shell and lunges, cutting compulsively. Johnston again: *Oh my goodness, nearly a wide, but anyhow he got it, and it's four runs.* England at lunch are 268 for five. Barrington 28*, Murray 24*. Eighty-one runs have been compiled during the session in thirty-five overs for the loss of those two early wickets. The see-saw balance of the match seems to be shifting again with England, now 78 runs ahead and five wickets in hand, starting to look the more dominant. And, indeed, the seldom-glass-half-full Hutton feels sufficiently confident by about this time to tell his amanuensis that 'the truth of the matter is that the Australians lack the bowling resources to press home any advantages they may get'. 'On such a wicket as this,' he adds, 'they have only one bowler, Davidson.'

LUNCH INTERVAL

When, after the disastrous 1958–59 Ashes tour, the great off-spinner Jim Laker retired from Test cricket, it was always going to be hard to find his successor. Martin Horton, John Mortimore and Ray Illingworth were all tried during the 1959 series against a weakish Indian side. Horton and Mortimore were discarded, but Illingworth was retained for the winter's tour of the West Indies. Also picked was the uncapped David Allen.

Allen, a bus driver's son from Bristol, has played off and on for Gloucestershire since 1953, but his progress was initially thwarted by the county's strong cohort of spinners – 'Sam' Cook (left-arm orthodox); 'Bomber' Wells and Mortimore (both right-arm off-break) – and Allen often missed out. In the early months of the 1959 season, he regularly batted at seven but until early July hardly bowled. Then, in a sudden burst, he took forty-three wickets in eight matches and shot to second place in the first-class averages. This led to his selection for the fifth Test against India, although in the event he dislocated a knuckle in a Sunday exhibition game and had to withdraw. Nonetheless he gained a place in the England squad to go to the Caribbean.

With the leg-spinner Tommy Greenhough as well as Illingworth in the party, Allen left with no great expectations. These were not increased by the manager, R. W. V. Robins, informing him: 'You're not going to be playing much cricket on the tour. And I'll have a lot of speeches to make. So I'd like you to look after my briefcase. That'll keep you busy.' In fact, Allen ended up playing in all five Tests. On the hard, mostly unrelenting pitches, his and Illingworth's role was to keep things tight for long periods, while the main strike force, Trueman and Statham, rested. Often, according to Swanton in *West Indies Revisited*, bowling to a slip, an off-side ring and only three on the leg side, Allen and Illingworth between them sent down nearly 400 overs, only going for a blink over two runs per over. This was against a West Indies team that boasted Garry Sobers, Rohan Kanhai and Frank Worrell, some of the world's most attacking stroke-makers. The two off-spinners took only thirteen wickets between them (Allen nine, Illingworth four), but they were integral to England winning the series 1–0. Allen's batting also proved an asset, prompting Alan Ross in his tour book to reflect at the end that 'in Allen, picked as an apprentice off-spinner, we had fished up a genuine Test all-rounder'.

This verdict proved a little premature. Allen played in just two of the Tests against South Africa in 1960 and hasn't been a certainty in the present series, though he has consistently taken wickets on the county circuit. But here he is the sole front-line England spinner and so far hasn't bowled a ball. He probably received the nod over Lock on account of the number of left-handers in the Australian side and his own superior batting. He has made a number of fifties for Gloucestershire this season, batting at seven, and only a week ago against Nottinghamshire notched up his maiden first-class century, decisively changing the course of the game.

Allen takes a shorter run-up than most off-spinners (though not as short as that of his former team-mate Wells, who claims to have once got through an over while the clock of Worcester Cathedral was striking twelve). Allen has a quick convulsion of an action with a hint of windmill about it, can adroitly vary his spin, pace and flight, and can bowl equally well over or round the wicket. He is no Laker yet, but he is potentially on the way.

AFTERNOON SESSION

Allen's batting prowess and nerve are soon being tested. Murray, without adding to his score, stretches forward to the hobbling Mackay; the ball wobbles that vital inch or two, brushes the edge of his bat, and Grout does the rest. How often a wicket falls after an interval or a break in play. England are 272 for six and, with a substantial tail, back under the pump.

The bowling perceptibly tightens; the fielding becomes even sharper. Initially, Allen, wearing a cap, looks a little out of his depth and has trouble finding the middle of his bat. Two streaky strokes run away past slip and gully for four. At the other end, Barrington takes 9 off one wayward McKenzie over, but is otherwise the embodiment of concentration; this is his sort of game and he relishes every moment. The consequence is not quite stalemate, but at times feels like it, as 44 runs are inexorably ground out in five minutes short of an hour and a half. Mackay limps gamely on, at intervals bowling from wide on the crease to vary his angle of delivery. Davidson, rolling his shoulders, puts in a Job-like spell of nine overs for 7 runs. He pitches the ball up to Allen, who is reluctant to drive, and pitches it just short of a length to Barrington, who as a result can neither drive nor pull with safety. The restive crowd slow-handclaps again. The sun checks up on the progress of play. It stays to watch Barrington hit a Benaud long hop for four and reach an indispensable, if soporific, fifty in a little over two and a half hours. At this point, Benaud, feeling perhaps that anything is better than this snail-slow accretion – or perhaps out of simple necessity – brings on Simpson to bowl in tandem with himself.

Leg-spin at all is a reasonably unusual sight in English cricket nowadays, but to have it operating at both ends … though India did sometimes play two leg-spinners on their 1959 tour. Pre-war, most county sides could boast at least one leg-break bowler, and immediately after the war Doug Wright, Eric Hollies and Roly Jenkins all played intermittently for England with some success. Then, in county cricket, in-swing bowling to a strong leg-side field became all the go, backed up by parsimonious finger-spin in preference to the more unpredictable wrist-spin; while in Tests, both Hutton and May used the left-arm Johnny Wardle mainly in his orthodox finger-spinning mode rather than risk his 'Chinamen' and googlies, even in circumstances where wrist-spin might well have proved a match winner. It's true that, over the previous two years, Tommy Greenhough and Bob Barber have appeared in the odd Test, but neither has been entirely convincing. Although Simpson is not yet in Benaud's class as a leg-spinner, he is, with his captain's example and encouragement, becoming distinctly useful, with a well-disguised googly.

At first, there's little change in the batters' approach; and, as Barrington once more plays back defensively to Simpson, even the usually cheerful Johnston echoes the crowd's mounting impatience: *One feels that England should be pushing the score along, but somehow batsmen just don't seem to be going for their shots. The crowd are getting pretty restless. We've got a very large crowd here, estimated 33,000, which must be near record for Old Trafford, and it's an awful pity that they've got to put up with this.*

Allen is plainly bewildered by Benaud, but not Barrington, no mean purveyor of leg-breaks himself. He hits Benaud over mid-on for four and then cuts him for another. Allen takes heart and, with Benaud and Simpson pitching shorter, puts both away to the cover boundary, and swings the unusually expensive Benaud to long leg. From virtual inertia, the scoreboard suddenly hiccups into overdrive: 46 runs are made in a little over half an hour, taking the Barrington–Allen stand to 86 in 105 minutes. But just as famine turns to feast, and the haven of the tea interval is in sight, Simpson (having switched to the other end) pitches up to the now more aggressive Allen. Allen sweeps against the spin. He slightly misjudges the length, and the ball soars off the top edge towards Booth at square leg. Davidson at midwicket also moves across, and hovers hopefully. There's almost a moment of slapstick and pratfall, as the distracted Booth juggles and nearly drops the ball, before clasping it at the second attempt. Three hundred and fifty-eight for seven: Allen caught Booth bowled Simpson 42.

With Allen's dismissal, the shutters go up again, and Barrington and Trueman block their way to tea. England 361 for seven with a lead of 171. Barrington 78*.

TEA INTERVAL

His team-mates call the twenty-year-old fast bowler Graham McKenzie 'Garth' after the muscly hero of the *Daily Mirror* strip cartoon. He is a recently qualified Phys Ed teacher and, like Booth, is an accomplished hockey player, as well as playing Australian Rules football. He works at a high school in Perth and heard of his selection for the tour during the break after his very first class. He was in the playground, when he spotted some expectant-looking reporters, and it was they who told him the news. Some say he was extremely fortunate to be picked – having only in the last season become a regular member of the Western Australian side.

What helped to gain him selection was almost certainly his role in Western Australia's 94-run victory over the West Indies in the tourists' opening match the previous October.

He took four for 41 in the visitors' second innings and greatly impressed Frank Worrell, who publicly praised his attitude and zip off the wicket. This and other commendations eventually led to the Test selector Jack Ryder flying across the country specifically to see him bowl. McKenzie hadn't played a Test before boarding the boat for England and hadn't even met several of his future team-mates. He was presumably chosen more as an investment than a likely starter in the major matches; yet this is already his third Test.

Ron Gaunt and Frank Misson, both of whom had at least some Test experience, were expected to compete to share the new ball with Davidson. On tour, however, injury can disrupt all expectations. Gaunt took useful wickets in the opening match against Worcestershire, including twice dismissing Tom Graveney, but soon sustained a troublesome side strain. Misson pressed his claims with six for 75 against Sussex and was picked for the drawn first Test. He kept his place for the second Test at Lord's, but, with Benaud unable to play, Australia (wisely? unavoidably?) played McKenzie as a third seamer. His debut was a triumph with bat (34) as well as ball (six wickets), before at Headingley he again showed his quality in both disciplines, despite his team's heavy defeat.

Even so, McKenzie, like Allen, remains very much a tyro at Test level. His line and length are still often inconsistent; yet, as he showed at Lord's and yesterday with Dexter and this morning with Close, he can produce deliveries that defeat good batters, even when they seem reasonably established. For all his shortish, leisurely approach to the wicket, he's appreciably quicker than Davidson and probably at times as quick as Statham and Trueman.

EVENING SESSION

When Barrington and Trueman resume after tea, it is obvious that they are under instructions to hit out or get out. They achieve the second of these objectives with the minimum fuss to themselves and the maximum satisfaction to Simpson, who claims all three remaining wickets at the cost of 2 runs. In the opening over, Barrington mishits Simpson to O'Neill at extra cover (361 for eight). Soon afterwards, with Trueman facing, Swanton describes the final two balls, his exasperation palpable: *Now, then, that one goes very high in the air but he's going to be caught by Harvey at cover point. A very disappointing stroke and a very disappointing innings. Trueman caught Harvey bowled Simpson for 3. Total 367 for nine. England 177 runs on. Simpson now to Statham and he hits that up in the air and that's caught in the covers. And that's the end of the innings. Mackay the catcher, Simpson the bowler. Four, I can only say, extremely cheap wickets to Simpson, and England are all out for 367.* Simpson has four for 23; Benaud, unfairly, none for 80; and Davidson, even more unfairly, three for 70 off thirty-nine overs. Flavell, who (like Statham) bowls right-handed but bats left, troops off without having faced a ball.

A lead of 177 looks overwhelming. All the same, the long-suffering crowd might well have preferred to see Barrington and the tail stretch the lead up to and over the psychological 200-run mark. In that scenario, England's pace bowlers could have launched an all-out assault for the final thirty or forty minutes. As it is, the post-tea self-immolation does seem rather odd after all those hours of hard, patient graft.

The pitch is playing more easily, and there's still just over eighty minutes' batting until stumps. Which means that the Australian openers, instead of having simple survival on their minds, can concentrate on seeing off the new ball and giving the innings a solid foundation for Monday: a very different proposition.

This, in good light, is precisely what Lawry and Simpson proceed to do. Trueman and Statham, as usual, open the bowling – with a third man and long leg at both ends, a far less attacking field than Benaud would have set in the circumstances. Both bowlers press for a breakthrough, but there's little movement in the air, and the wicket now holds no terrors. When Trueman overpitches, Lawry drives him for four. When he tries a bouncer, he hooks him. Once Statham, with a near yorker, catches Simpson on the crease and appeals confidently. *Very close, I think*, reckons Johnston. *Very adjacent.* Then with palpable disappointment: *Umpire Langridge says no.* 'A loud appeal for lbw against Simpson,' agrees Arlott in his diary record, 'clearly found the batsman apprehensive, and probably represented a hair's breadth umpiring decision.' On such a hair's breadth can a Test match hang.

On dropped catches, too. Flavell takes over from Statham, inducing a false stroke or two, and Trueman takes a turn downwind. The score is 38, Lawry 25. Lawry goes for another drive to a Trueman delivery outside the off stump; he flashes hard; the ball takes a thick edge and flies, chest-high, fast and straight to second slip. Simpson would surely hold it. Cowdrey would surely hold it. Subba Row took a harder catch there in the first innings, but not this time. He sights the ball too late, fumbles, clutches, falls, fumbles again; the ball drops to the ground. Lawry carries on phlegmatically; Simpson, his morale no doubt buoyed by his catching of May and his bag of late wickets, looks increasingly secure.

Around ten past six, Allen comes on for his first spell of the match. The score is 49. The left-handed Lawry is facing. Allen's first ball lands in the ever-deepening footmarks created by the fast bowlers. The ball kicks and fizzes past Lawry's bat, past Murray's raised gloves, is taken by first slip. Later in the over, Lawry plays and misses again. Allen bowls four maidens on the trot, also beating Simpson, and looking far more dangerous than the faster bowlers. Simpson's wickets don't look quite so cheap now that the wicket is clearly taking spin. By the close of play, Australia have scored 63 runs in a little less than an hour and a half, not quick but a more enterprising rate than England managed for most of the day. Lawry 33*, Simpson 29* leave the field to deserved applause. Australia 114 behind with all their wickets standing.

*

No cinema this evening for Booth, who has an 'early night'. But for TV viewers, there is not only episode 25 of *The Valiant Years* (based on Winston Churchill's Second World War memoirs) and a helping of *Perry Mason* ('The Case of the Green-Eyed Sister'), but also the latest instalment of Rupert Davies as *Maigret*, in which a man acting suspiciously in a café arouses the French detective's curiosity and leads him to investigate the lives of three apparently respectable citizens.

SUNDAY INTERLUDE

Sunday, as ever, is rest day – a day for taking stock, not always happily. In 1937, in the Lord's Test, it fell after England's debutant opener Len Hutton had been castled for a duck by New Zealand's Jack Cowie, only for the other batters to make hay. Most of the home team on that Sunday went golfing, but the twenty-one-year-old Yorkshireman opted for a lonely, introspective wander across town, finishing up at Charing Cross station. There, the news cinema's half-hour show, repeated on a loop, included highlights of the previous day's play. Miserable yet transfixed, Hutton could not help himself sitting through it at least five times, imagining each time at the fatal moment disapproving tut-tuts from the audience. But a year later, during England's 1938 Oval Test against Australia, a much happier rest day: Hutton midway through his record-breaking 364, a thirteen-hour epic; he and Hedley Verity, his fellow Yorkshireman, driving down to Bognor Regis; a wealthy Yorkshire supporter, who lived there, giving them a slap-up Sunday roast. 'And do you know what Hedley and I did after lunch?' Hutton many years later would rhetorically ask Frank Keating, before providing the reply. 'Unnoticed, we played cricket on the beach.'

No beach cricket on 30 July 1961 for Brian Booth. Instead, he goes to church in the morning, writes letters in the afternoon, and in the evening goes again to church, where he gives testimony. His more secular team-mates perhaps plump for a movie: *One Hundred and One Dalmatians* (premiered in the spring, but only just reaching Manchester) is showing at the Odeon. There's *Ben-Hur* at the New Oxford and *Spartacus* at the Gaumont. The England team, staying more luxuriously at the Mere Country Club, near Knutsford (Elizabeth Gaskell's 'Cranford'), have other options. Films not too far away include *The Sins of Rachel Cade* (wartime drama, set in the Belgian Congo, with Angie Dickinson torn between Peter Finch and Roger Moore) and the promising-sounding *The Taste of Ashes*. The latter, in fact, is a made-for-TV American number, part of a private detective series called *Bourbon Street Beat*, and absolutely nothing to do with the only ashes that matter at this particular moment.

It is perhaps this same evening that Benaud, with his highly developed sense of public relations and the common touch, attends to an affecting request. He has just been sent a copy of his *Way of Cricket*, asking him to autograph it for a friend of the sender who is ill in hospital. Benaud signs the book himself – and has the entire touring party add their autographs as well. Not only that, the promptly returned copy includes a get-well card with the inscription: 'Wishing you a speedy recovery to Health and Happiness – Richie Benaud.'

Elsewhere on this warm, fairly unremarkable English Sunday in the high summer, with train specials, charabanc coaches and seaside resorts all suitably crowded, the prime minister, Harold Macmillan, is at home in Sussex preparing to announce to the Commons the next day his government's intention to apply for membership of the European Economic Community, aka the Common Market; a much younger Conservative, Nigel Lawson, reflects in the *Sunday Telegraph* that the chancellor, Selwyn Lloyd, has through his recent restrictive measures 'shown himself to be yet another adherent of that strangely masochistic belief that if the medicine tastes nasty enough it must do us good'; the same paper reports with tacit satisfaction that British naval forces East of Suez are to be modernised and strengthened over the next eighteen months; Field-Marshal Viscount Montgomery, addressing 2,000 Combined Cadet Force members after a drumhead service at Tweseldown Racecourse near Aldershot, urges cadets and politicians alike to learn, as a crucial life lesson, the need 'to reach a decision and do something'; the police hunt two escapees from Birmingham's Winson Green Prison, both of them with heavily tattooed arms; a lorry driver dies after a collision with a steam train at Pitsea in Essex; Prince Philip plays polo at Windsor before arriving for Cowes Week on HMS *Britannia*; an obscure, leather-jacketed Liverpool group are due to play in the city's Walton district, but John and George, following a row the previous night over payment, bunk off instead to the pictures; an interview on BBC television with Aldous Huxley prompts one admiring viewer (the *Guardian*'s Mary Crozier) to observe that 'it was like seeing someone hurl a ball at a magic batsman who connected with it and then multiplied the ball and executed six perfect delightful strokes all at once'; a leading Manchester doctor, Hugh Selbourne, prefers to watch 'discussion of the Eichmann Trial'; and one of us enjoys his tenth birthday confident in the expectation of an England win at Old Trafford.

7

Day Four: Monday 31 July

Cricket columnists in the Sunday and Monday morning papers in England and Australia have had much to ponder. Is a 177-run lead really enough? Should the England middle order have pushed on faster and/or for longer? Will the squandering of those cheap wickets after tea turn out to be significant? Will dropping Lawry prove decisive? Has Lawry and Simpson's unbroken opening stand restored Australian morale? Which team, if either, holds the advantage? What price a draw?

The headlines offer up a smorgasbord of responses. 'Australians Set Stage for Grand Finale', the *Observer* boldly proclaims, while the *Sunday Times* fronts with 'Australia Fight Back in Test', followed by the more patriotic sub-heading: 'But odds still on England'. The *Sunday Telegraph* plays a very straight bat: 'Lawry and Simpson Cut Back England Lead to 114', as does Monday's *Canberra Times* with 'AUSTRALIA FIGHTS BACK; 114 BEHIND', and Monday's *Age*: 'OUR BATSMEN MUST FIGHT BACK IF TEST IS TO BE *SAVED*'. Meanwhile, Monday's *Times, Guardian* and *Daily Telegraph* all highlight a slackening of England's grip.

The accounts themselves, while registering some sympathy with the crowd's impatience, mostly tend to exonerate the slowness of the Barrington–Murray and Barrington–Allen partnerships. The consensus is that a policy of risk-free accumulation became virtually inevitable after the early dismissals of May and Close, and given the naturally defensive mindset of the later middle order. J. M. Kilburn in the *Yorkshire Post* is representative. He acknowledges the homespun nature of Barrington's and Allen's batting ('entirely without flourish or adventure'), but commends the pair for being 'always in full understanding of their obligations'. Like others, he is also deeply perturbed by the loss of those last three wickets 'by woeful mis-hitting of the surprised and rejoicing Simpson', so that 'England's lead was suddenly and altogether irrationally limited to 177'. The *Canberra Times*, while applauding the 'solid' Lawry–Simpson stand 'in the tense and crucial 83 minutes before stumps', is more generous than some English pundits in its praise of 'the stocky hawk-nosed' Barrington, who 'played a grand game for England'. Tom Goodman in Sydney's *Sun-Herald* goes even further, claiming that the England batters 'flayed the Australian bowlers to take a match-winning lead' and that only rain can 'save Australia from defeat in the two remaining days'. Percy Beames for his part pins any hopes for a serious Australian fightback on the mercurial Harvey, the obdurate Lawry, 'the talented if unreliable Norm O'Neill' and 'the phlegmatic Mackay'.

The docility of the wicket and the relative innocuousness of the Australian attack are again routinely mentioned in passing, but only Jack Fingleton and John Woodcock really remonstrate about the pace of the England scoring.

Fingleton, a rare, abrasive, Australian voice in the quality press, is especially forthright in his *Sunday Times* piece. After blaming the 'utilitarianism' of the English batting for delivering 'the cause of Test cricket ... a bit of a jolt', he puts the boot in: 'The trudge from noon to tea suggested there were gremlins in the pitch, and the Australian bowling a combination of Miller, Lindwall, charitable O'Reilly and Grimmett.' Similarly, Woodcock in *The Times* does not mince his words. Barrington & co., he says, 'made heavy weather' of their task, and adds damningly: 'The spirit of adventure so widely pronounced before the series was not expressed, a tally of 243 runs from six hours' play on a good wicket was ... poor entertainment.' Behind such protestations about brighter cricket, the exhilarating glamour of the Australia–West Indies series still looms large. Why isn't the current Test more like that?

Swanton is less critical of the English approach per se, but is clearly bothered about its possible consequences. His opening sentence in Monday's *Daily Telegraph* is positively Henry Jamesian in its parenthetical sidle up to his point of concern: 'Looking back at the third day of the Test match, and gazing warily into the future, as is the occupational habit of cricket writers, one cannot help wondering whether England may not have loosened their grip on a golden chance.' Swanton assumes a draw the most probable outcome, as does Woodcock: 'Obviously the most unlikely result is that England will lose, although whether they can press home their advantage may depend upon the weather and its influence on the pitch.' Denys Rowbotham in the *Guardian* is of the same mind: 'Unless ... rain assists one side or the other, neither will find it easy to force victory in the twelve hours that remain.' Ray Lindwall, providing the expert analysis for the *Daily Herald*, is of an altogether different mind, claiming that England's position is 'almost impregnable' and that if Australia are to escape defeat: 'THEN O'NEILL HAS GOT TO SCORE A CENTURY OR MORE'.

As for Fingleton and Kilburn, for all their differences they sign off with a similar thought. 'How strange that Benaud didn't get a wicket and Simpson got four,' muses the Australian. 'Perhaps it will be Benaud's turn in the second innings …' And Kilburn (with perhaps Allen as much as Benaud in mind): 'Simpson need not be the only rewarded spinner before this match is over.'

The weather this Monday morning is fine with high cloud, just a touch humid after the dry weekend. There's little or no discernible breeze to assist any swing. The wicket looks brown and unyielding; at both ends the deep footmarks outside the left-hander's off stump remain pronounced. Another bumper crowd is pouring through the gates.

MORNING SESSION

May starts, sensibly enough, with Allen and Statham to Lawry and Simpson. In yesterday's *Sunday Telegraph*, J. J. Warr imagined how a favourite comedian might describe Lawry's batting: 'Tony Hancock would sum up Lawry's success on this tour by saying that his "hooter" is always over the ball.' His 'hooter' is at once over the ball again, as he blocks out a maiden from Allen, who has two slips and a short leg. After playing and missing on Saturday evening, Lawry is careful to leave alone any balls Allen tosses up invitingly into those footmarks outside his off stump. Simpson opens the scoring, pushing Statham off the back foot wide of cover for a quick single. He and Lawry have a good understanding between the wickets and, like Hornby and Barlow, the 'run-stealers' in Francis Thompson's famous poem, they 'flicker to and fro', as England's lead is whittled away.

Allen is economy itself, and Lawry is clearly not comfortable against him; yet somehow he doesn't look like taking a wicket. Statham, less economical than usual in his opening spell (six overs for 22), nonetheless does pose problems. Early on, Simpson snicks him for a boundary and is then beaten outside the off stump three times in an over. As Allen wheels on, Flavell (rather than Trueman) takes over from the Stretford end. The gates are now closed, the crowd for the first four days estimated at over 107,000, a record for an Old Trafford Test. The score stands at 90 for no wicket. Whatever humidity there is evaporates fast as the clouds disperse.

Flavell overpitches, and Lawry (like an unfolding pelican) leans into a drive. *Good stroke!* observes Swanton appreciatively. *No, he needn't chase that. Allen loses his cap and Australia score four. Lawry one off his half-century.* Which he duly completes with an easy flick down to long leg. Lawry raises his bat, doffs his cap. There is generous applause. Flavell pitches up to Simpson along the line of middle and off. Swanton again: *A good straight drive for four. There's his fifty.* Simpson swings his bat, twitches his pad, nibbles his glove. More applause. *Very good innings. No chance.* Australia 113 for none. Lawry 57, Simpson 51. Flavell pounds in again. Simpson slashes at a shorter ball that leaves him. The ball catches the under edge and flies, dipping, towards first slip. Murray dives across. *And a catch behind, next ball. Finely taken by Murray, too.* Australia 113 for one. Last man 51. This is the first century opening stand in the series by either side. In fifty-five minutes this morning, Simpson and Lawry have put on fifty: an enterprising rate in the circumstances.

Harvey comes in to join Lawry. With two left-handers in, May rather surprisingly replaces Allen with Trueman, but it is Flavell, with his tail up, who almost makes another breakthrough. Harvey, on 2, swings, edges, and at second slip the normally safe Close puts down a straightforward chance. Harvey celebrates with a couple of twos. From then until lunch, he varies flashes of brilliance with regular air shots, driving Trueman in particular into histrionics of despair. Lawry 'hooters' staunchly on. Lawry (74*) and Harvey (21*) leave the field with Australia 150 for one, now only 27 in arrears. They have scored 87 in the session, and England, to their credit, have bowled thirty-eight overs. The crowd is estimated at 34,000.

Among those in the press box starting to get their thoughts in order for the evening papers are not only Hutton, but also the *Manchester Evening News*'s John Kay. The former, reflecting on the morning's play, notes that 'the wicket has never played easier' and that Murray's catch to dismiss Simpson was 'in the Evans class'. He returns again to Lawry's qualities: 'Again he was hitting every half volley that came his way with a certainty that I have not seen in a batsman recently – with the exception of Cowdrey and Harvey. He has, too, a remarkable facility for finding gaps in the field.' Where he may be fallible, Hutton feels, 'is against slow bowling. He was often at sea against Allen, not moving his feet to him as I would expect a batsman of his apparent class to do.' Hutton has doubts, too, about his hooking: 'Lawry's luck with the hook shot continues. He often plays this stroke only to see the ball travel the shortest of distances ... and it always falls wide of a fieldsman.' All true enough, but he's still there.

As for Kay, he has no doubt where the crux lies. 'All the talk during lunch,' he will be telling his readers, 'was on the fact that England's two dropped catches had been at second slip ... the place where Colin Cowdrey fields ... first Subba Row had boobed and now Close.' Also true enough.

LUNCH INTERVAL

Bobby Simpson, after his failure in Australia's first innings, is having an excellent match. In the England innings he took two exceptional slip catches to account for Subba Row and, vitally, May. (How he shows up Cowdrey's absence in this department.) He then went on to pocket those four late wickets before and after tea on Saturday, and, that evening and this morning, he has shared with Lawry in a crucial 100-run opening stand, as Australia begin to haul themselves back into the contest.

Simpson is still relatively young (twenty-five), but has nonetheless taken his time to establish himself at the highest level. As a youngster, he showed talent at various sports and might well have become a top professional golfer. Whatever the sport, his intense competitiveness has always been apparent. In an early club match against one of his older brothers, he apparently appealed vociferously for lbw despite a very obvious edge onto the pad. (The appeal was granted.)

He had his first game for New South Wales in January 1953 at only sixteen. At first, he was predominantly a batter, but steadily worked on his leg-spin. In those days, he was in and out of the state side and usually fielded away from the bat. This changed when, coming on as sub against Victoria in early 1954, Keith Miller sent him to first slip. He took two brilliant catches and subsequently, when picked, made the position his own. Less admirably, that fierce competitiveness of his could get out of hand, as it did in a state match a couple of years later, when the Victorian opener John Shaw ducked into a Pat Crawford bouncer and was hit on the head. While Simpson's concerned team-mates rushed to check on Shaw, Simpson himself was vehemently appealing for lbw. Mixed success for New South Wales and a switch in career from accounting to journalism took Simpson, still only twenty, to Perth, where he gained a regular place in the Western Australia side and eventually the captaincy.

He was selected for the 1957–58 Australian tour of South Africa, one of eight up-and-comers in Ian Craig's new-look squad. He batted in the lower middle order in all five Tests, making few runs and probably only holding his place on the strength of his impressive slip-catching (thirteen catches in the series). In his single Test against England in 1958–59, he made a duck and was not retained. The end of that series did, however, mark a turning point. Jim Burke, for some years Colin McDonald's regular Test opening partner, announced his retirement. This led to Harvey encouraging Simpson to open for Western Australia with a view to eventually filling the gap in the Test side. Simpson did so with immediate success in Sheffield Shield matches the following summer, scoring 902 runs in six innings at an average of 300.66.

Nineteen fifty-nine was also the year that Simpson spent a season as the professional for Accrington in the Lancashire League, for which he was paid £950. It was here that he radically refined his technique, getting much more side-on as he played his shots and switching from a light, long-handled bat to the heavier, chunkier, short-handled model favoured by many of the taller players. His 1,444 runs at an average of 103.14 compared more than favourably with the record of West Indian stars Conrad Hunte and, playing in the Central Lancashire League, Garry Sobers. In the match against Enfield, Hunte's club, Simpson was given out caught and bowled off a bump ball and refused to go. On Hunte supporting his refusal, the umpire was forced to rescind his decision.

Hunte and Sobers were commanding performers during the West Indies' recent tour of Australia, so it is fitting that this was the series which seemed finally to have established Simpson as a Test player. Temperament and technique had come together: he could bat for long periods and had all the shots, though rarely hooking or pulling. He played in all five Tests, sharing a number of useful opening stands with McDonald against the fiery pace of Wes Hall, and finishing the series with 445 runs at 49.44 (plus another thirteen catches).

And yet. On the current tour, Simpson has once again found himself battling for his opening spot. Games against the counties have seen alternating permutations of McDonald, Lawry and himself open the innings. In the Tests until now, Lawry's extraordinarily consistent form has meant that he (not Simpson) has been preferred as McDonald's opening partner, with Simpson largely failing lower down the order (76, 0, 15, 2, 3). McDonald's injury has allowed Simpson to reassert his right to open. It is an opportunity which, like his slip catches, he is grasping with both hands.

AFTERNOON SESSION

Dexter, from the Warwick Road end, begins the afternoon with a wide. It's soon clear, however, as Lawry slices him for four at catchable height between first and second slip, that he's getting more out of the wicket than the faster bowlers. Harvey continues in his pre-lunch vein: a liquorice-allsorts of air shots and expansive strokes. In Dexter's second over, he flashes at the ball, edges. Barrington, at slip, muffs the 'sitter', shakes his head. Usually giving Harvey one life, let alone two, leads to tribulation, but not today. After a couple more boundaries, and with the partnership with Lawry worth 62, he cuts at Dexter; this time the edge is thinner. Murray throws up the ball, his second catch of the innings. *And he's caught behind the wicket*, barks Swanton. Harvey leaves the crease. Australia 175 for two, last man 35.

O'Neill comes in, his team still two runs in arrears. His first ball from Dexter is invitingly wide on the off, he slashes at it and, luckily, misses. He was badly roughed up in the first innings, particularly by Flavell, and the obvious move now would be to bring on the Worcestershire enforcer. Instead, May quickly shuffles a combination of Dexter, Allen and Statham, while Lawry mainly shields O'Neill from the strike. There is one moment of near disaster when Lawry cracks a delivery from Dexter to wide mid-off and calls O'Neill through. Flavell is not the most agile of fielders – long leg and third man are his usual haunts – but he moves quickly, gathers cleanly and throws down the wicket at the bowler's end, as Lawry lunges, lunges, for the crease. *Very nearly a run-out*, exclaims an excited Swanton. *He's very, very nearly out. Fine bit of fielding by Flavell. There can't have been a whisker in it.* Flavell is now bowling, and, as Lawry leaves a ball outside the off stump, Swanton's co-commentator, Denis Compton, a famously poor judge of a run, continues to reflect on that closest of close calls: *If the same thing had happened to me, Jim, I think I'd have been about four yards out.* Swanton in response initially contents himself with *Well, he needed to skedaddle down there pretty sharp, didn't he?*, before adding, *I dare say in your footballing days ...*

Then, to widespread surprise, May throws the ball to Close – but only after first trying Trueman, who responds decisively enough with a 'Piss off, skipper. Let Closey bowl, I'm fucking knackered.' In fact, it is not a completely irrational move. Close bowls regularly for Yorkshire, both medium-pace seam-up and off-spin, and there was his five for 23 in the recent Gentlemen and Players match. Still, he is not a front-line bowler, even for Yorkshire, and normally needs an over or two to adjust his radar. Now his length and direction are inconsistent, and, as Arlott wryly notes in his journal, a released O'Neill hits 'three rattling fours which put him on terms with himself'. Would Benaud have risked a bowler like Close at such a juncture? It seems unlikely. He would surely have put maximum pressure on the unsettled new batter.

Soon afterwards, Lawry pulls a rare long hop from Allen for four. *And there he is with his hundred*, observes Swanton, as though he had been predicting it all along. Lawry raises his bat in modest, well-deserved triumph; he's batted for over four and a half hours, and it's his second century in his first Ashes series – a unique achievement. But, just as breaks in play can disturb a batter's concentration, so can reaching landmarks like fifty or a hundred. In the same over, perhaps not quite back in the zone, Lawry pushes forward, misreads Allen's arm-ball for an off-break, and Trueman, at short leg, dives to pull off a brilliant reflex catch inches from the ground. Lawry leaves, shaking his head in disbelief or disgust, and returns to the pavilion to sustained applause. Australia 210 for three, last man 102. The lead is now 33.

Burge is next in. The new ball is due. As most captains would, May promptly takes it, though there must be a case for giving Allen an over or two at Burge. After all, he had him lbw for 0 at Headingley, and Burge proved particularly susceptible to Laker's off-spin five years ago. May, like Hutton before him, prefers to put his trust in pace, and brings on the old firm of Statham and Trueman. O'Neill, however, has now settled and promptly square-cuts and drives Statham for four. Trueman, no doubt remembering O'Neill's first-innings problems, gives him an early bouncer. O'Neill of course goes for a hook and, in Arlott's words, is hit 'a thundering blow'. After a short respite for repairs, he faces up again. Fast bowler's logic says the next ball will be either another bouncer or a yorker. It's a yorker, which O'Neill jams down on and keeps out. The next ball, as he must have anticipated, is the bouncer. Some batters, expecting this, would duck. O'Neill, by contrast, relishes a challenge, hooks hard, and the ball is soon rocketing to the square-leg boundary.

Two further fours high over the slips, and the total is racing along. In fact, the new ball goes for 36 off eight overs, so that at tea Australia have scored 102 runs in the session and reached 252 for three, 75 runs ahead. O'Neill, having routed any demons, is 47*. The balance of the game is tilting once more.

TEA INTERVAL

Unlike Simpson, Raman Subba Row is not up to now having a good match. Davidson was again too good for him in the first innings, having now taken his wicket four times in the series. And although he caught a good catch in the slips on the first day, he has already missed a much easier one off the obdurate Lawry in Australia's second innings.

Subba Row's name perhaps conjures up certain cricketing expectations. Indian batters are rightly known for their elegant drives, wristy cuts and immaculate leg glances: in a word, they are thought of as stylish. Subba Row's batting has many excellent qualities, but stylishness is not one of them. His watchword is patience; he wears the bowling down. He is a pusher, a nurdler, an accumulator par excellence, although, when set, he can also drive and cut with power.

Born in 1932 to an Indian father and English mother, he grew up in Surrey, attended Whitgift School and was in the First XI for four years as (like Simpson) a leg-spinning all-rounder. At Cambridge, he gained a Blue in his first year (his team-mates included May, David Sheppard, J. J. Warr and Robin Marlar) and took five for 21 in Oxford's second innings of the Varsity match. This was probably the high point of his bowling career, but, as his bowling began to decline, his middle-order batting continued to develop. In his last year at Cambridge (1953), he headed the university's averages and played half a season for Surrey, finishing fifth in the first-class averages with 1,823 runs at an average of 50.63.

Subba Row moved from Surrey to Northamptonshire in 1955, did two years' National Service in the RAF, and returned to Northants as captain in 1958. Another triumphant season with the bat led to selection for England against New Zealand in the fourth Test. He scored 9 and lost his place for the last Test, but was picked to tour Australia that winter. Here he would almost certainly have been chosen for the first Test (having notched up several fifties), had he not, fielding in the gully, broken a bone at the base of his thumb. This injury more or less ruled him out of serious contention for the rest of the series, though May's tour report also suggests other drawbacks: 'The bounce of the leg spinners was always a great problem to his batting ... He is rather laboured in the field, though he is a safe catcher near the wicket.'

He was back for the final Test against India the following summer, now as opener. As with Simpson, the switch did the trick, and he scored a painstaking 94, made in something over five hours. 'Subba Row is not exciting to watch: he is not even truly correct in his stroke-play,' conceded Arlott in his cricket diary. 'But he has a good eye, infinite patience and courage, and he never parts easily with his wicket. He has been opening the innings for Northants for only three weeks. Now here he was, going in first for England. He obviously did not regard the affair as fun, but he proposed to succeed in the task he had accepted.' That innings, and nearly 2,000 runs for the season, secured his place on the winter tour to the West Indies.

Here, once again, his brittle hands threatened to let him down. He was left out of the first three Tests, but on May having to return to England for further treatment of his abscess, Subba Row regained his place. Pullar and Cowdrey now had first claim on the opening berth, so he slotted in at three. He scored 27 in the first innings, chipping a bone in his knuckle. In the second innings, with a heavily bandaged hand, he compiled a very slow but invaluable hundred. Woodcock offered a similar appraisal to Arlott's: 'Subba Row is one of the great stickers in English cricket, however unconvincing he may sometimes appear ... nudging and cutting and pushing and scotching, his shoulders hunched, his stance open, his stride between wickets long and loping.'

During the continued absence of May last summer, Subba Row held his place against the touring South Africans and again scored valuable runs in the top order. Then, in the fourth Test, he dropped a fast slip catch and, in the process, broke his thumb in almost the same place as he had in Australia. That put him out of action for the rest of the season. This year, he and Pullar have been automatic choices at the top of the order in the Tests. One or the other has usually dug in, although so far they have only managed a couple of fifty partnerships. Of the two, Subba Row in his ungainly, sub-Lawry fashion, has looked the more adhesive. Moreover, in the drawn first Test at Edgbaston, he had the distinction of scoring a match-saving hundred in his first Test against Australia.[*] Woodcock characteristically dubbed Subba Row's hundred 'an achievement as much of temperament as technique'. Subba Row will no doubt need all that temperament, that stickability, in the second innings here.

EVENING SESSION

Statham may have bowled less demandingly than usual today, but he is still May's go-to bowler when play resumes. O'Neill at once cracks him through extra cover. *Lovely stroke*, says Brian Johnston. *I don't think it will quite go for four. Dexter might catch that one. They've taken two runs and they're going for a third. And what a lovely throw! So that's O'Neill's fifty. O'Neill fifty in 104 minutes.* Statham, however, in tandem with Flavell and Dexter at the other end, is soon back to his taxing best, and reels off a heroic ten-over spell. Inevitably perhaps, it is the more unpredictable Dexter who takes the next wicket. Burge has been looking eminently safe, but now slashes at a short delivery that lifts a bit outside the off stump and Murray swallows the catch. Australia 274 for four; Burge 23. Booth joins O'Neill.

More drama follows not long after. O'Neill glances hard at Dexter. Trueman at backward short leg leaps to his left, shoots out his left hand. The ball sticks, comes unstuck. He twists, tries to recapture it with his right hand; the ball falls to the ground. It would have been a miracle catch. O'Neill,

[*]Subba Row thus became the fourth England player of Indian extraction in a row to score a hundred in his first Test against Australia, following Ranjitsinhji, Duleepsinhji and the senior Nawab of Pataudi.

attacking boldly, is still treating Statham with respect. He goes back, checking a punch into the covers. Johnston momentarily breaks off his discussion with Fingleton about Australia's progress, then picks it up again: *Dexter fields it. Yes, I must say, Jack, they've done extremely well. The run-getting about sort of forty-seven runs an hour, but they've really been getting out of an awkward position. Now it'll be interesting to see if in this last hour they can put on the pressure and get a fairly good lead tonight.* Fingleton agrees: *I think we can say that they've lived up to Benaud's promise that they wouldn't let the game die.*

Then, commentator's curse: after making two balls seam into O'Neill, Statham gets one to move away slightly. O'Neill flicks at it, without moving his feet: *Oooh, he's caught him! He's out! O'Neill is out. Murray's fourth catch.* Several England fielders actually jump for joy. Australia 290 for five. O'Neill 67. Mackay chews his way to the wicket. He has faced many crises before: most recently, in January, he and number 11 Lindsay Kline hung on for an hour and fifty minutes to save the Fourth Test against the West Indies. He knows his role. The lead is 113. As with that second dropped catch off Harvey, England haven't been made to pay for Trueman's near-blinder off O'Neill. The luck and the momentum are coursing England's way. Booth is trying to keep up the run rate, but goes back when he should have gone forward and is lbw to Dexter. Australia 296 for six. Last batter 9. The lead is 119 with nearly an hour to go. Davidson joins Mackay.

Two left-handers. Another wicket now, and England can really begin to hope. May finally turns to Allen, who bowls containingly but not especially threateningly, while Flavell and Trueman take turns at the other end. It's Trueman – a bit out of sorts so far in this Test – who should have raised English hopes even higher. He goes round the wicket to create a different angle. Mackay, on 11, slices him at catchable height just to the right of Subba Row at gully. Subba Row is slow to react, dives too late, doesn't lay a hand on it; the chance is gone. Close – off-spin at both ends – is given two overs before stumps. Davidson works him neatly to fine leg for four. Davidson and Mackay, both on 18, walk in, having put on 35. Australia 331 for six are 154 ahead, a handy but not decisive lead. It is, as Arlott concludes his diary entry for the day, 'an absorbing situation from which any result is possible, but an English win seems as probable as any'.

*

After the players have left the field, and the vast crowd has dispersed, Benaud strolls out to examine the wicket. Stylishly casual as ever, he is wearing a pair of blue suede shoes. *Blue suede shoes*. It is probably fanciful to suppose that Benaud bought the shoes, is wearing them now, in a deliberate nod to Elvis's mega-hit a few years ago with the Carl Perkins song, but he just conceivably might – that's the thing with Benaud: he preserves a degree of enigma behind the public persona. It is impossible to imagine his opposite number, May, wearing suede shoes at all, let alone blue ones.

Benaud pays particular attention to those rutted footmarks outside the left-hander's off stump. Pullar, Subba Row, Close, Statham, Flavell: almost half the England team is made up of left-handers. He recalls a match on England's 1958–59 tour when Lock bowled successfully into churned-up rough left by Trueman in his follow-through. A daring idea starts to form in his mind. Back in the pavilion, he tries the idea out on his canny old team-mate Ray Lindwall. What if the next day he were to bowl his leg-breaks round the wicket into the rough to both left-handers *and* right-handers? 'Is it worth the risk?' he asks. Lindwall's first reaction is that, if he misses the spot, he'll be easy to hit. Eventually, however, he thinks the idea worth a shot.

Publicly, Benaud keeps his idea to himself, although one comment to a journalist perhaps contains an oblique hint: 'The match is still in a very interesting stage. We want runs, of course, and as much as I dislike setting targets, another hundred tomorrow would be handy. The wicket is still quite good except for the rubbish near the stumps kicked up by the bowlers.'

Booth, probably reflecting the more general mood in the Australian camp, notes in his diary: 'Looks like Test is definitely lost.' He takes himself off to see the heart-warming *One Hundred and One Dalmatians*. Which means that he probably missed the crowd of locals that apparently packed the foyer of the Midland Hotel eager for a glimpse of members of the Australian side. No prospect of seeing Benaud, who has retreated to his hotel bedroom, where he listens to his Gilbert and Sullivan tapes.

8

Day Five: Tuesday 1 August

Play starts half an hour earlier today, at 11 a.m., and will finish by or at 6 p.m. (with for once full-day BBC TV coverage except for a quarter of an hour of *Watch with Mother* after lunch). The weather this first day of August looks promising: fine, with no prospect of rain, little if any breeze. The pitch, except for those footmarks, seems to be holding together remarkably well. Benaud, who (as captain of the side currently batting) has the choice, has opted for the heavy roller. Perhaps, thinking of the initial overs, he hopes to squeeze out any residual overnight moisture. Perhaps, too, anticipating a later Australian push for victory, he hopes the heavy roller might help, just a bit, to break up that now unresponsive surface. Roller-effect remains an inexact science.

Some newspaper headlines offer contrasting, Janus-faced perspectives of the state of play. 'LAWRY AND O'NEILL EARN AUSTRALIA 154 LEAD' announces the *Daily Telegraph*, before wagging its finger at those dropped catches: 'Splendid England Bowling Receives Poor Support in Field'. In marked contrast, *The Times* looks forward to the day ahead with anxiously mixed emotions: 'TREMBLING HANDS FOR LAST DAY OF TEST: THRILLING FINISH IN PROSPECT', while the *Canberra Times* again bluntly states the position from the Australian perspective: 'Fight by Aust. to Save Test'.

Swanton begins his account in the *Telegraph* with all the superstitious wariness of the diehard England supporter: one who still dares to hope England will win, but knows that to proclaim this hope aloud is invariably to invite hubris. Day four has been, for him, 'infinitely the best of the series' and – how tiptoeingly he proceeds – 'has paved the way for what might be an even more dramatic one'. He briefly sketches different scenarios. With Australia currently in possession of the Ashes, Benaud is hardly likely to 'indulge in a quixotic declaration'. However, were England to dismiss Australia for, say, another 50 runs by or before 12.30, that would mean a chase of around 200 at considerably less than a run a minute. At which, in case he's allowed himself a hope too far, he pulls back: 'There are the possibilities of great deeds to come, though, to be honest, the end might be anti-climax if the task on hand is beyond England's capabilities.'

Rowbotham in the *Guardian* doesn't seem to contemplate any result other than a draw or an England win, and his report ends in upbeat fashion: 'So England must break through early this morning to achieve victory. Excitement there can scarcely fail to be.' In *The Times*, Woodcock agrees that the previous day has been 'the best day's cricket of the series', 'full of thrust and counterthrust, of good bowling and challenging batting, of disappointment and elation'. For all this yo-yoing, and England's lapses, he still reckons that, on balance, the present match position leaves England 'with a chance of victory'. And from the other end of the political spectrum, in the *Daily Worker*, Philip Sheridan takes a similar view – but with the crucial rider that 'if England fail to take the remaining Australian wickets in the first hour ... the Australian total will be too big in the time left and Australian captain Richie Benaud with his leg-breaks should enjoy himself on a pitch which is getting dusty'.

'Maybe, but probably not' appears to be the view held by Mancunian cricket-lovers. Most seemingly anticipate a draw, with Australia batting until early afternoon and setting England a steepish run chase which they won't attempt. Which, if so, would explain why, after the huge crowds of the first four days, under 15,000 show up to see the two left-handers Mackay and Davidson make their way to the wicket.

*

In a small village outside Worcester, an eleven-year-old boy leans forward in a blue wing-backed chair, staring tensely at the black-and-white screen.

MORNING SESSION

Allen opens the bowling, round the wicket, to Mackay. Quite quick and flat, he's obviously aiming for the rim of the rough outside the left-handers' off stump so as to threaten either edge of the bat while keeping things tight. His first ball, anti-climactically, is a wide. His next two are on target. Mackay prods forward in smothering defence. The fourth ball, pitching in the same area, turns a little more sharply. Mackay prods forward again. *He's caught!* Swanton's voice is at least an octave higher than usual. Excited applause breaks out from the crowd. Close at very short second slip seemed almost to pluck the ball straight off the bat. He now clasps it to his chest, rubs it in his hands as if to make absolutely sure it's really there. *Mackay caught Close bowled Allen.* Australia 332 for seven.

Davidson and Benaud together: two of Australia's greatest all-rounders. Their bold, hard-hitting partnership so very nearly won the tied Test against the West Indies. Bowling in tandem with Allen, Statham is steadiness personified. The score clicks on by two. Allen to Benaud. He's switched to over the wicket for the right-hander. Neither forward nor back, Benaud plays a nothing defensive shot. *An appeal*, Swanton's voice rises again, *and he's lbw! To an off-break, which did quite a little bit, I think!* Benaud pulls off his right batting glove, turns towards the pavilion. As usual, the top few buttons of his shirt are undone; his face is impassive. Murray, gloves clapping, advances towards Allen, who almost diffidently puts his left hand in his pocket, then withdraws it, and not quite casually places it on his hip. *Benaud lbw bowled Allen for 1*. Australia 334 for eight.

Grout survives a couple of deliveries; then *Oh, he hits him hard and high and it's going to be caught. Grout caught Statham bowled Allen. A very wild mishit against the spin of the ball and, believe it or not, Australia have lost three wickets for 3 runs.* The small boy agog in the blue wing-backed chair certainly can't believe it. Australia 334 for nine. Only 157 ahead with one wicket left and all but twenty minutes of the day still to go. Allen has bowled fifteen balls this morning and taken three for 0, a Laker-like achievement. This is the stuff that dreams are made on and Allen thinks to himself: 'Our luck's in. We're going to win this.'

The tumble of wickets means that the Australian changing-room is, understandably, in some disarray. This is not helped by McKenzie, whose leg has become increasingly painful after his long bowl in the first innings, being just back from a session with the physio. Now he has to scramble to put on his pads and, to the muttered 'good luck' of his team-mates, hurry out onto the field. Davidson meets him with a 'Just play straight down the line and we'll see what we can do'. If ever a last-wicket stand were needed, it is now.

Davidson takes 7 off Statham's next over. Then, in a bubble of expectation, almost nothing happens. Davidson, shielding McKenzie, sets up camp at the Stretford end where Allen has been causing such havoc. He isn't finding the off-spinner any easier than Mackay, Benaud or Grout did, but (with a mixture of long reach and judicious leaving alone) he manages to keep him out. This is when having Lock to bowl at the other end really would have been useful. He, too, could have used the rough and could have helped to peg Davidson down, while Allen had a go at McKenzie.

In fact, it is another quarter of an hour before Allen concedes his first run of the day. Meanwhile Statham toils on, but those long spells earlier in the match are beginning to take their toll of even his remarkable stamina, and he just can't extract any significant movement or lift out of the pitch. He resorts instead to the occasional yorker. When he misses his length, he is driven or worked away by McKenzie, who seems increasingly at home on this essentially flat track. Forty minutes after coming to the crease, he is still there and has still hardly faced a ball from Allen.

At this point, May simply has to give Statham a breather and again has his ear bent by Trueman: 'Why don't you try Closey? He's got a knack of getting wickets when you want them.' The suggestion makes a kind of sense. It will at least present McKenzie with off-spin at both ends. Perhaps, like Grout, he will hole out.

The gamble didn't pay off yesterday: O'Neill simply tucked into Close's buffet of loose deliveries and grew in confidence. Nor does it pay off today. McKenzie and Davidson likewise tuck into two overs of full tosses and half-volleys (to the tune of 15 runs), and, when Dexter replaces Close, their partnership is firmly established. The crowd, quieter, senses a shift. Davidson, now on 36, senses it, too, and takes his own gamble.

A leg bye off Dexter sees Davidson back at Allen's end. At this point, the latter has conceded only 2 runs this morning in nine overs and, in the innings overall, has taken four for 38 from thirty-seven overs. As the field changes over and Davidson once more prepares to take guard, May approaches the bowling crease. 'Let's encourage him to play a shot or two at your end,' he says to Allen, indicating Davidson. 'Yes, right,' Allen replies. He admires May, and May is the captain.

He wheels in, this time flighting the ball more invitingly. Davidson advances. *Oh, and he's hit him high into the outfield – for six!* exclaims an impressed Swanton. *Over extra cover. Beautiful hit, with the spin … Three hundred and five minutes left to play.* Allen, obeying instructions, continues to toss it up. Davidson is again down the track. *And he hits that one very hard indeed for four runs between the bowler and long-off.* Two more balls in the over. May brings the field in to prevent Davidson farming the strike. That's obviously not on his mind, however: *I don't think he worries so much about McKenzie at that far end but I see that the off-side field is coming all in now to save one … but they may not save four.* Shortish ball, faithfully dealt with. *There it is, Davidson's fifty.* His fifty has come in 112 minutes.

Davidson isn't finished yet. When Allen again tosses the ball up, he drives him for an even bigger six, a towering hit sailing high over long-off and right over the terraces and rebounding from the brick wall by the railway yards at the back of the ground. That makes 20 in the over. The last wicket has put on 50 in only thirty-nine minutes. The lead has jumped to 200, and the runs/time equation is narrowing. Arlott describes Davidson's onslaught with thoughtful precision: 'These were not wild, slogger's swings, but superbly made measured strokes of immense power and perfect timing.' It is an act of nerve, daring and skill. It threatens to alter the whole psychological weather of the match.

How will May respond? A more instinctively attacking skipper – Benaud, say – would challenge Davidson to do it again, confident that such aggressive play against the turning ball cannot last. He would give Allen at least one more over to see if he can entice Davidson into a fatal mishit. The all-conquering May of 1956 – had Miller, Harvey, Davidson or Benaud mounted such an attack during one of Laker's mesmerising spells – would almost certainly have kept the off-spinner on. Or would he? He wasn't prepared to risk Wardle's back-of-the-hand stuff in the third, drawn, momentum-tilting Test against South Africa in January

1957. And this is an older, more besieged, more doubt-ridden May: one still finding his way back after illness and a year and a half out of the game; one desperate to recover the Ashes after being trounced in the previous series; one only just starting to regain his old mastery with the bat. At this moment of nice judgement, he reacts as his mentor Hutton would undoubtedly have done. 'Thank you, David,' he says, 'that will do', and he reverts to pace.

But there's no stopping the partnership now, even when a weary Statham and a frustrated Trueman take the new ball. As Arlott notes, Davidson and McKenzie are by this stage batting 'more like an opening pair than tail-enders' and are clearly aware that time is quite as important as runs. It's true that Trueman has McKenzie dropped (a hard chance) by Dexter at forward short leg and also beats him a couple of times, but the runs keep piling up. The two have added almost a hundred when, to the relief of the agonised small boy in the blue wing-back chair, Flavell is belatedly introduced for his first bowl of the day. In his second over, at one o'clock with the Australian total on 432, he thuds in once more. The ball to McKenzie is pitched up on middle-and-off; McKenzie tries to work it to the leg side. *And he's clean bowled him*, exclaims Swanton with relief. *Flavell bowls McKenzie. And now we know exactly what the proposition is.*

The proposition is that England have to make 256 in around 230 minutes, or at a rate of a smidgen over 67 runs an hour. Davidson (77*) and McKenzie (32) leave the field to the cheers of the crowd. For the last wicket, the pair have put on 98 runs in 102 minutes, the third-highest such stand for Australia against England, and none more crucial. In the

Australian changing-room, Benaud makes a special point of congratulating McKenzie, while a grinning Davidson, after tossing his bat into a corner with the words, 'We'll do these jokers, Rich', unbuckles his pads as his team-mates thump him on the back. Allen, so nearly the hero of the hour, has final figures of 38 overs, 25 maidens, four wickets for 58 runs (20 of these in that hectic final over).

Having saved their side and given England a demanding total to chase, Davidson and McKenzie now open the bowling. For Pullar and Subba Row, this is another of those awkwardly short passages of play before an interval, but they see it through without mishap. What is more, with nudges and deflections and even an on-drive, they manage to keep in touch with the required run rate. England at lunch 20 without loss.

LUNCH INTERVAL

The most recent *Wisden* has canonised Ted Dexter as one of its 'Five Cricketers of the Year' (1960). 'No English cricketer bred since the war', trumpets R. G. M. (Sussex amateur Robin Marlar) in his opening paragraph, 'has so captured the imagination of those inside, outside and far from, the boundary ropes of our big cricket grounds.' Few would disagree, although Dexter's form in the current Test series has not always lived up to this billing.

In common with other top-class cricketers of his generation, Dexter (born in Milan in 1935) is multi-talented at sport and, like Simpson, seriously considered golf as a career. His cricketing prowess revealed itself early. Picked for the Radley College XI at fifteen as an all-rounder, he was in the team for four years and captain in his last. National Service, following school, sent him to Malaya, where he took to the matting wickets and quickened his pace.

At Cambridge, he gained a Blue as a freshman in 1956, his attacking strokeplay to the fore, but only occasionally turning his arm over. The next year saw him eighteenth in the first-class averages with an aggregate of 1,511 runs, including a fifty in one of his three innings for Sussex. His pacey swing-bowling, too, began to attract attention, notably a headline-attracting five for 8 in his first Gentlemen v Players match. By then, the combination of his adventurous batting, high, rhythmic action and sustained follow-through were encouraging some to see him as an English Keith Miller in the making. Cambridge captain in 1958, Dexter jumped seven places in the averages, again scoring over 1,500 runs. With forty-four wickets at 24.72, he could now be classed as a genuine all-rounder.

That season he was widely touted for Test selection and was eventually picked for the fourth Test against the visiting New Zealanders. New Zealand batted first on an easy wicket, and, with rain restricting play, Dexter, at six, did not come to the crease until the Monday afternoon. The previous day the seventeen-strong touring party for the upcoming Ashes series in Australia had been announced. Dexter's name was not on the list. He proceeded to score a thunderous 52 in quick time and, as Arlott's journal recorded, it was 'an ironic thought – but a reasonable one – that, if he had played this innings on Saturday instead of Monday, Dexter must almost certainly have been among the players selected for Australia.' Other cricketing pundits were more openly aghast. R. C. Robertson-Glasgow ('Crusoe') considered it 'the biggest clanger I have ever known selectors anywhere commit ... a child of six who'd played one season's cricket on the lawn with his mother could surely have seen Dexter's genius ... He is a possible Trumper or Macartney.'

In the event, the England side was from the start beset with injuries, and Dexter was flown out as a replacement after the first Test. Short of practice, unused to Australian conditions, he made little impression (apart from his mimed golf-swings and lackadaisical fielding). However, on the New Zealand leg he gave a taste of what he might have achieved, had he been originally selected, scoring a commanding century in the first of the two Tests. Two Tests against India in 1959 produced little, but over 2,000 first-class runs and fifty-nine wickets for Sussex booked him a place on the tour to the West Indies that winter.

There, against the fiery pace of Hall and Watson, Dexter suddenly and explosively became the player his admirers had proclaimed. He finished top of the Test averages with 526 runs at 65.75. Swanton waxed lyrical. Dexter's 'forcing off the back foot into the covers and past mid-off', during a masterful 136* in the opening Test, 'reminded the older school of Walter Hammond': than which, from the seasoned campaigner, there could be no higher praise. Alan Ross, summing up the series, was equally enthusiastic: 'In Dexter, who would never have come as a batsman alone, we had looked for an all-rounder; instead we had found a successor to the luckless Peter May.'

The tabloids by this time had taken to referring to Dexter as 'Lord Ted'. The doubly apt nickname has stuck. The flair of his strokeplay does have a Regency dash about it, while his air of privileged aloofness carries more than a sniff of the *Beano*'s 'Lord Snooty'.

Cricket, as its devotees endlessly enjoy reminding themselves, is a great leveller. Dexter's Caribbean triumph was followed, last summer, by a modest series against the South Africans: no hundreds, two fifties, 241 runs at 26.77; five wickets. The great South African off-spinner 'Toey' Tayfield was expected, if anyone, to trouble Dexter (still thought in some quarters to be vulnerable to spin). In fact, Tayfield took his wicket only once in the Tests; it was the South African quick, Neil Adcock, who most often dismissed him, usually after a useful but unconverted start. For all that, Dexter again scored over 2,000 first-class runs in the season, took forty-six wickets and was now a highly proficient cover fielder.

May's return to Test cricket and the captaincy have, for England supporters, been this year's major talking point – together with the condition of Benaud's right shoulder. Consequently, how 'Lord Ted' might fare against the old enemy on home pitches has commanded fewer column inches. All the same, despite his match-saving, five-and-three-quarter-hour 180 in the first Test, there have been doubters and, had Cowdrey been fit, it might well have been Dexter who made way for him. So far in the current game, it has been his nippy, penetrative bowling (three wickets in each innings) which has justified his selection; doubters have not been slow to write off his first innings as yet another start only flattering to deceive.

For Benaud, however, the threat of Dexter running amok is second only to that of the recovering May.

*

During the lunch break, journalists and former players have been chewing over the morning's events. Hutton voices a characteristic position. He thinks May 'might have brought on the fast bowlers sooner than he did. It would have been a bold move to take Allen off in view of his striking success, but I believe fast bowlers are the men for tail-end batsmen.' Others understandably focus more on the chances, or not, of an English victory. Frank Worrell reckons that 'the runs can be got *if* England is prepared to lose'. Swanton thinks England will initially go for the runs, but, failing to keep up with the clock, will settle for a draw. John Woodcock takes a dimmer view: 'We will lose three or four chasing them, and then come to grief against Richie.' For Arlott – one who in his own phrase 'suffers their cricket' – the game is now so taut with 'emotion and tension' that 'the pattern of runs-wickets-time' approximates to something akin to 'the ingredients of Greek tragedy'.

AFTERNOON SESSION

Pullar and Subba Row resume on 20 without loss. England require 236 runs in the two remaining sessions (approximately 210 minutes); Australia require ten wickets. At this stage, and on past performance, Swanton's prediction seems the most likely to be realised.

Davidson bowls a maiden to Pullar. Benaud brings himself on at the Stretford end. Initially, he bowls over the wicket to both left-handers, but soon changes to round. Australia's best two bowlers, but also, with Mackay and McKenzie carrying injuries, the two fittest bowlers.

England's approach soon shows positive intent. Subba Row, a natural sheet anchor, is clearly to stand firm while Pullar (usually something of a sheet anchor himself) goes for his shots. Benaud at once starts to drop the ball in and around those deep footmarks outside the two left-handers' off stump, but initially to no effect, 6 being taken off his first over. When, a little later, Davidson bowls a slower one to Pullar, he straight drives it for four. That's 40 in forty-two minutes; the crowd cheers every run. Davidson's next ball is shorter, quicker, and on to Pullar sooner than he expects. He tries to hook. The ball spoons up to O'Neill at midwicket: 40 for one, last man 26.

Dexter makes his entrance: 216 to make and a match to win. The boy in the blue wing-backed chair looks across at his father who has joined him in front of the box. Their hushed excitement is palpable.

And Dexter doesn't disappoint. After a quick look at the bowling, he's straight onto the attack. He drives Davidson, forces Benaud (over the wicket to him) through the covers, cuts and drives Davidson again. He's on 14 already, the same score as Subba Row. Soon the total is 60. To Subba Row, Benaud (back round the wicket) continues to land in those footmarks, but the left-hander keeps him out. Now Davidson, too, is bowling spinners to Subba Row. He, undismayed, comes out of his shell and lofts two on-drives to the boundary, so that Davidson (eleven overs on the trot since lunch) concedes 16 in two overs before he is given a well-deserved break. An hour after lunch, England are 76 for one, then in a twinkling 86 for one. At this point (3.15), Benaud calls for drinks. The crowd, sensing more than an element of gamesmanship, boos Ian Quick as he bears the refreshments out to the middle. This is after all the first such break either captain has called for in the match. Similarly placed, however, mightn't May have done the same? If he had, the crowd would no doubt have applauded.

In any case, the drink only seems to spur Dexter to greater heights. McKenzie, who replaces Davidson, is noticeably limping and goes for 13 in an over, including two wides. Subba Row faces Benaud, cuts him behind square. *Single*, Swanton pauses slightly, *brings up the hundred in an hour and a half, just a tiny bit over.* Subba Row has 31, Dexter 40. Benaud has a brief exchange with his vice-captain. 'We've had it as far as saving this, Ninna,' he says to Harvey. 'The only way we'll get out of it is to win.' Harvey grins. 'Get into it then,' he replies. 'I'm with you.'

Benaud's response is to replace McKenzie with Simpson rather than his other injured bowler, the thrifty but hobbling Mackay. It's another attacking move: another wrist-spinner will encourage the batters to keep playing shots and will speed up the over rate. Simpson, like Benaud, sometimes flummoxes Subba Row, but holds no mystery for the now rapacious Dexter who strikes him for four imperious fours in two overs. *That's gone through*, purrs Swanton, as the third of these – another force off the back foot – rockets to the boundary, *and there's his fifty*. Round after round of applause rings out. Subba Row claps his bat in appreciation. Dexter nonchalantly half-raises his bat in acknowledgement of the applause, takes off his cap, sweeps back his hair, readjusts his cap, briefly touches the peak as the ovation continues. *He's hit ten fours in that and he's been batting two minutes over the hour.* England 119 for one. Despite the power of Dexter's strokes, Benaud is maintaining a ring of five in the covers. Anything hit directly at the fielder is stopped with wringing hands, but to either side is a certain boundary.

Dexter studiously blocks the next delivery to some amused catcalls and wolf whistles. Simpson pitches shorter and wider. Dexter leans across, head over the ball, bat scything down. *Square cut, beautiful shot. Four more. One doesn't often see Dexter square cut, but he is a very good cutter, as a matter of fact, which makes his armoury all the more powerful, of course; because the natural thing with such a strong driver is for the bowler to drop them a little short to him. Fifty-seven.* Simpson pitches it up this time. As if to chasten Swanton, the ball, a big leg-break, lands around leg stump, spins across to the off, evades Dexter's twitching blade and is collected and returned by Grout. Dexter, head down, pats the last delivery almost reverentially back to Simpson.

This is turning into exactly the kind of innings Swanton most relishes but nowadays all too rarely sees: an English amateur of impeccable credentials ruthlessly putting Australia to the sword. A barely concealed I-told-you-so lurks within his next comment: *I wonder whether any of you viewers can search your hearts and say that you weren't wondering whether Dexter ought to have played in this Test match.*

Benaud does at last turn to Mackay. Dexter drives him straight for four. England are halfway to their target. Benaud now plays his last card. He goes round the wicket to both the left-handed Subba Row and to the right-handed Dexter. The luck, however, definitely seems to be running England's way. Subba Row drives at Benaud. *Off the edge by Subba Row*, chuckles Swanton, *but it gets him into the forties.* Dexter cover-drives Benaud and lofts him into the outfield. Mackay, he continues to treat like a net bowler. A short ball is banished for four. Mackay hobbles in again off his five-pace run, wrist cocked, and bowls from the extreme edge of the crease. The ball is a half-volley on the stumps. *Ooh*, Swanton in ecstasies now, *he's hit him into the crowd there. A magnificent shot over long-on. Superb stroke!* Dexter confidently flicks another well-pitched-up ball into the leg side. *A single brings up the 150.* Dexter is on 76, Subba Row 45. Arlott notes down: 'This latest burst saw the 150 up in 123 minutes and the hundred partnership in seventy-nine minutes with the last fifty coming in less than half an hour.'

After Benaud moves a fielder from off side to leg side, Grout asks him what the plan is. To a laugh from his keeper, he replies, 'We've got to get them out … it's our only chance.' And though so far he is wicketless in the match, and indeed has taken only five wickets in the series, Benaud clearly intends to go on bowling himself in pursuit of that objective. His plan at this stage seems to be to try to frustrate Dexter for most of an over and then tempt him with something to drive or force. So, for five balls, he bowls leg-breaks on and around the footmarks outside Dexter's leg stump. No runs accrue. The sixth ball is slightly shorter and a little quicker, just outside Dexter's off stump. It is perhaps intended as a top-spinner. Whether it is or not, the angle at which Benaud is bowling (from the extreme edge of the return crease) carries the ball away further to the off side. Dexter, from the back foot, chases it, aims to cut. The ball seems to bounce a fraction more than he expects. Grout gleefully throws up the nicked catch: 150 for two. Dexter departs instantly, pulling off his batting gloves and doffing his cap. *And the Australians applauding him in. Magnificent innings. The whole crowd standing.* He's scored 76 in eighty-four minutes: it's been a knock for the ages. Dexter leaves the game, jots down Arlott, 'lying like an emperor's gift in England's hands'.

A bare-headed May comes to the wicket. He has a quick word with Subba Row and watches the opener play out a maiden from Mackay. Then May, taking a leg-stump guard, faces Benaud. The first ball is aimed at the footmarks, but pitches too short, too straight, and May calmly flicks it into the leg side, looks for a non-existent single, and is sent back. Swanton and Compton mull over Benaud's virtues as a bowler. *He can almost pitch the ball really, Jim, on a sixpence*, remarks Compton. *That's one of his great assets.* May taps his bat in the crease, a light breeze floats a strand of hair across his forehead. He taps again. Benaud's next delivery bears out Compton's point. It is deliberately further up, deliberately landing right in the footmarks well outside May's leg stump – a clear invitation to take what looks like a free hit into the mostly untenanted spaces on the leg side. With the ball pitched there, May can't be lbw. The obvious option is simply to cover his wicket with his pads and allow the ball to cannon harmlessly away. Alternatively, he can cover his wicket and attempt a sweep (Compton's own favourite stroke). He does neither. Without really moving his feet, he aims a strange, stiff-armed swing at the ball as it passes him and misses completely. The ball grips in the footmarks, spins back sharply. *He's bowled May behind his legs, has he?* Swanton's voice is edgy with anxiety. May, frozen in the crease, looks behind him almost guiltily, like a model schoolboy surprised in some childish misdemeanour.

He is so incredulous, in fact, that he even checks with Grout that it is the ball, not the wicketkeeper's gloves, which has clipped the leg bail. *Yes, he's out, bowled behind his legs*, confirms Swanton crisply. Benaud lets out a yell of triumph and leaps in the air. The rest of the Australian team are leaping, too, and capering about. The great May walks slowly away: 150 for three. Last man 0. The crowd, buzzing with elation one moment, buzzes with apprehension the next. The small boy and his father are stunned into silence. Neither needs Swanton's bleak summary: *And the picture changes with a vengeance.*

The father tries to reassure the boy that, with seven wickets left and time in hand, an England win is still entirely possible. But the boy, who witnessed disaster from the non-striker's end in a school match earlier in the summer, has passed beyond comfort.

The left-handed Close, also bare-headed, takes strike. Benaud lands the ball again exactly in the footmarks outside what is his off stump. Close, down on his left knee, takes a huge heave across the line. *He sweeps at that one and it goes most riskily* [nervous laugh] *for two runs and Grout in his excitement knocks the wicket over.* The ball has caught the top edge of Close's bat or possibly even the back of the bat, sailed high into the air and fallen safely out of reach of the limping Mackay at square leg. Close sweeps again at another ball in the footmarks and misses, the ball bouncing off his pads into the off side. Two further failed sweeps in the same over bring a *Well, words fail me* from Swanton. Close leaves the final ball. Subba Row plays out another maiden from Mackay. Benaud replaces Mackay with the more mobile O'Neill behind square on the leg side.

Benaud to Close once more. He blocks the first ball, then, wonderfully, comes down the wicket to the second, swinging through the line. *And now he's hit him for six*, bursts out a bemused, exasperated Swanton, as the ball drops into the crowd beyond long-on. *Yes, it's gone for six.* Benaud, tempting that premeditated sweep shot, shrewdly pitches the ball wider and wider of the off stump so that to sweep him Close has to fetch it from further and further outside his eyeline. Close heaves across the line: once, twice without connection. Swanton maintains an appalled silence. The fifth ball, closer in, is driven wristily into the covers for no score. At the sixth, wider again, Close heaves once more. *And he's caught behind square leg. Almost inevitable. O'Neill the catcher off the shoulder of the bat. Well, I think there's not much to be said about that. It just speaks for itself.* Not much to be said ... As Close leaves the crease, the former England and Yorkshire captain Norman Yardley is on the radio, declaring that he should never play for England again, before adding the ultimate condemnation: *Close's innings ... was a disgrace, really ... for a Yorkshireman.* 158-4, last batter 8.

Barrington, capless as usual, joins Subba Row. Subba Row hits Mackay for four. It's now the last over before tea. Benaud to bowl it. He has bowled all afternoon, probing, canny, absolutely relentless. Barrington takes a single to get off the mark. Subba Row, on 49, has four balls to face. He nudges the first into the leg side. The second, he leaves. The third, he blocks, lumbering rather awkwardly onto the front foot. Benaud could just bowl another one into the rough, which Subba Row could safely leave. An English spinner probably would. But Benaud is intent on winning the game. He gives the final ball much more air. It is tossed up on the stumps, tempting the apparently untemptable Subba Row. And Subba Row, who has done such a solid job all afternoon, can't resist. He drives, perhaps losing the flight in the sun behind Benaud at the Stretford end. *He's clean bowled! Subba Row bowled by the last ball before tea, trying to play it on the on-side, as you can see, for his fifty.* One hundred and sixty-three for five. Last man 49.

In the last twenty minutes or so, Benaud has taken four wickets for 9 runs and created the fourth volte-face of the day. First, Allen had Australia down and out; second, Davidson and McKenzie's last-wicket stand hauled Australia back from the brink; third, Dexter's innings vaulted England back into the box seat; and now, Benaud's nerve, tactical daring and consummate skill have wrested back control for Australia.

England need 93 in eighty-five minutes with five wickets remaining. It is still just about doable.

TEA INTERVAL

Aquiline features, crinkly hair, Alan Davidson began as a wrist-spinning all-rounder, but at seventeen switched to pace. It happened suddenly, as these things often do. At practice one day, a team-mate who was also his uncle asked him to bowl faster than usual in preparation for their Hunter Valley John Bull Shield match the next day. Davidson did so, clean-bowled him, and the following day his uncle handed him the new ball. After a return of four for 39, there was no turning back, although Davidson does still sometimes revert to spinners or slow cutters when conditions demand it, as he did this afternoon and, more lengthily, in the previous Test at Headingley.

Playing for New South Wales under Keith Miller made almost as deep an impression on Davidson as it did on Benaud. Off the field, he bore absolutely no resemblance to the ex-fighter pilot, flutter-loving Miller – Davidson worked for a bank, was a committed Christian and model citizen – but on the field he was fired by Miller's all-round panache as a player and his willingness as captain to take risks to keep matches alive. This morning's sudden, clean-striking onslaught on Allen was absolutely in the Miller mould. So, too, was his second-over burst at the start of the second Test of the 1958–59 series. With his first ball he had Peter Richardson caught behind; with his fifth, he bowled Willie Watson; with his sixth, he had Tom Graveney lbw with a late in-swinging yorker to which the batter had shouldered arms. That burst more or less determined the match.

But all this has taken years to achieve. Davidson first played for New South Wales at the age of twenty in December 1949 against South Australia. Opening the bowling, he took a wicket with his second ball (another late in-ducker) and finished the innings with four for 32. Batting eight, he scored 34. (Benaud had a rather less successful game.) Davidson gained his opportunity due to Miller's belated summons as a replacement for Bill Johnston on the current Australian tour of South Africa. By the end of the season, he had taken twenty-six wickets and become more or less a regular in the New South Wales side.

His Test career began on the 1953 tour of England where he played in all five Tests. His overall figures were not impressive, but a much-praised 76 in the second Test at Lord's, including a huge six into the Mound Stand, helped to turn an innings unravelling into a competitive total. It was during England's 1954–55 tour that he acquired the nickname 'the Claw', after taking several prehensile catches close to the wicket. Nonetheless, for all his notable flashes, he only came into his own as a Test bowler with the retirement of Miller in 1956 and the more gradual fading of Lindwall. It says much for the Australian selectors that, as with Benaud, they took the long view and continued to pick Davidson on a regular basis.

The breakthrough and final attainment of mastery occurred on the triumphant 1957–58 tour of South Africa. Under Ian Craig's captaincy, Davidson, like Benaud, flourished. If Benaud was the brightest all-round star, Davidson was close behind him. Thereafter, in successive series against England, Pakistan, India and the West Indies, he would stand out as the pre-eminent opening bowler on either side, as he has been in the current series. The relative weakness and inexperience of the Australian attack (together with Benaud's troublesome shoulder) has meant that, as his stamina-draining spell this afternoon attests, he has had to be stock- as well as shock-bowler. For a player not backward in complaining about aches and niggles, this has pushed his endurance, mettle and great ability to the limit.

Six foot, fourteen stone, fifteen-pace run-up, classical action: does he still have one last kick in him?

EVENING SESSION

Back in the English changing-room, what has been said over cups of tea? Is there a plan? What instructions, if any, has May given his remaining batters? 'Have a look and give it a go, if you can'? Or is he too shell-shocked by the abrupt shift in fortune and the disaster of his own dismissal to give any instructions at all? It is an irony that, had Dexter not put England in a winning position with his dashing innings, they would probably have dug in and now be well on the way to a draw. But now? Whatever the others may be thinking, Barrington, at least, is still full of hope. He sees himself as about to make cricketing history.

Over their tea, Benaud has asked Mackay if, despite his injury, he can summon up another spell. Mackay asks if he means into the wind, such as it is. That is exactly what Benaud means. 'We're going to get this crowd out,' he assures Mackay. Mackay gamely trundles up to deliver the first ball to Barrington (now with a cap), who turns it to McKenzie at backward square leg. No run. There's the sound of planes passing overhead. Brian Johnston is at the microphone: *Perfect evening and the crowd have had a wonderful afternoon.* The next ball is a half-volley outside the off stump. Barrington, without any noticeable movement of the feet, reaches for it. *That's a lovely stroke. It's four! As good an off-drive as we've seen and that's saying something when one remembers some of Dexter's this afternoon.*

Murray takes guard to Benaud, still coming round the wicket, to a slip and backward short leg. *Murray hasn't had a ball yet. That's a friendly full-pitch; it's four runs!* A boy in shirt sleeves crosses the boundary rope, stops the ball and enthusiastically throws it in. Benaud moistens his fingers, as he often does, wheels round and bowls again. Murray defends off the back foot. Johnston runs quickly through the fall of the English wickets. *A sensational collapse*, he reflects. *And, if the runs come, then I suppose we shall see some forcing cricket towards the end, but I think they'll have a good look at it.* Murray does seem to be having a good look. He twirls his bat, touches his cap in a familiar gesture, settles once more. The next few balls, he props forward, stunning them effectively enough. But then Benaud lands one on his leg stump; it turns quite sharply. Murray only gets half-forward, the face of his bat half closed. There's a snick. Simpson, standing rather wide at slip, leans quickly to his left. *Yes, he's caught by Simpson at slip. Murray caught Simpson bowled Benaud. Benaud's now taken five for ... 53; five for 53, and England really in a bad mess now: 171 for six.* Last batter 6. Allen replaces Murray.

In his next over, Mackay manages from somewhere to put in a bit extra, and Barrington, deceived, plays across the line and is given out lbw. 171-7. Out for 5, his dream of heroics over, Barrington turns to the pavilion. He is the last specialist batter, and his dismissal signals, in effect, a point of no return. While he was there, anything (even victory) remained possible, but not now. Trueman joins Allen. Benaud whips off Mackay who has more than done his job, and brings on Simpson to tempt Trueman. The instructions for Allen and the tail, with seventy-odd minutes still to go till stumps, are now presumably to play for a draw; nonetheless, Allen cuts and sweeps Benaud for fours. When, more temperately, he starts to cover up and ignore anything pitched outside his leg stump, Benaud reverts to over the wicket. The ball is up; Allen is lured forward into a firm drive; Simpson is a blur as he leaps low to his left almost behind Grout. *Oh, magnificent catch by Simpson! What a fine catch. Left-handed there. He's a fine slip fieldsman. So that's Allen out, caught Simpson bowled Benaud for 10. England 189 for eight. Benaud now six wickets.* The Australians, cock-a-hoop, cluster round a jubilant and grinning Simpson. The catch to dismiss Murray was sharp (would any of the English slips have caught it?), but this one is a stunner, a wonderful reflex effort. Allen leaves. Statham appears.

Neither Trueman nor Statham take their batting too seriously, though Trueman likes to claim he can pick Benaud's googly (or 'bosie', as Australians still call it in honour of its inventor, B. J. T. Bosanquet). The quick 39 the two put on at Lord's in what Arlott described as 'a stop-or-swing operation' is really their forte – not holding out surrounded by close fielders. The two restrain themselves and restrain themselves against the wiles of Benaud and Simpson; but, with thirty-five minutes left, Trueman can no longer resist taking a swing, and the faint edge carries to slip. Johnston still: *Caught Benaud bowled Simpson for 8. England 193 for nine and I don't think that this new ball will be needed or not for very long. Thirty-five minutes left for this last-wicket stand. It'll be between Flavell and Statham. Silly point, two forward short legs, a leg slip and slip close. Simpson to Flavell.*

Flavell didn't face in the first innings, so this is his first ball in Test cricket. He survives it, and for a while the two left-handers keep Benaud and Simpson at bay. Five minutes pass. Then ten minutes. Davidson and McKenzie batted for ten times that length of time this morning. Flavell (normally another slogger) mostly employs his pads and doesn't trouble the scorers. Statham whacks Benaud straight for a couple of fours past mid-off which mean nothing in themselves except that they bring Statham and the crowd momentary relief and eat up precious seconds. Benaud bowls on. He's bowled thirty-two overs in succession, broken only by the tea break, and taken six for 70 (after his figures at one stage were none for 40 off seventeen overs).

Almost fifteen minutes have passed; there are just over twenty minutes still to survive if England are to salvage a draw. Harvey has the ball. He beckons Benaud to a midwicket conference. He seems to be remonstrating with his captain, even threatening to hurl the ball towards the boundary. (It was noticeable that he made little apparent effort to stop those two fours from Statham which went pretty close to him at mid-off. Was he trying to register a protest?) What he wants becomes clear, as Benaud takes himself off and hands the ball (still the old one) to Davidson. Statham keeps out the first three deliveries. To the fourth, he prods forward, bat crooked. *Clean bowled!* exclaims Johnston. Statham's head slumps. The small boy wants to cry. Australian fielders caper, cheering, slapping backs. *Australia have won and they've kept the Ashes. They've won by 54 runs. Congratulations to Australia, to Richie Benaud and his men. A really surprising victory after the turn of fortune today. I don't think anyone would have backed them when England were 150 for one. Well, hats off to them.* 'At twenty to six,' notes Arlott, 'Davidson, returning, bowled Statham with the air of a firm parent stopping the children's game.'

Benaud's first action after the wicket falls is to run to Harvey. The two hug each other, jumping up and down and yelling 'We've done it!' before, arm-in-arm, they lead their triumphant team off the field. *And there's Richie Benaud looking as happy as any man has a right to be.* The crowd, bitterly disappointed but instinctively generous, applauds and applauds. It has witnessed, in Arlott's words, 'in the stand of Davidson and McKenzie, the batting of Dexter and the bowling of Benaud, three of the truly historic performances in cricket history'.

Once the players have left the field, the now thoroughly deflated spectators quickly disperse and the ground is soon empty.

Hearing the result on his car radio, the chairman of selectors, Gubby Allen – who left early, confident of an English victory – is so shocked he almost swerves off the road.

In the English changing-room, Barrington sits with a beer staring out at the empty field, repeating to himself: 'Isn't it bloody marvellous?'

On the train to Pontypridd where Gloucestershire are to play Glamorgan the following day, David Allen sits on his own. It's a five-hour journey, and the weight of disappointment will increase, hour by hour.

In the Australian changing-room, Benaud simply sits down and laughs.

ENGLAND v AUSTRALIA (4th Test)

At Old Trafford, Manchester, on 27, 28, 29, 31 July, 1 August 1961.
Toss: Australia. Result: **AUSTRALIA** won by 54 runs.
Debuts: England – J.A.Flavell; Australia – B.C.Booth.

AUSTRALIA

W.M.Lawry	lbw b Statham	74	c Trueman b Allen	102
R.B.Simpson	c Murray b Statham	4	c Murray b Flavell	51
R.N.Harvey	c Subba Row b Statham	19	c Murray b Dexter	35
N.C.L.O'Neill	hit wkt b Trueman	11	c Murray b Statham	67
P.J.P.Burge	b Flavell	15	c Murray b Dexter	23
B.C.Booth	c Close b Statham	46	lbw b Dexter	9
K.D.Mackay	c Murray b Statham	11	c Close b Allen	18
A.K.Davidson	c Barrington b Dexter	0	not out	77
*R.Benaud	b Dexter	2	lbw b Allen	1
†A.T.W.Grout	c Murray b Dexter	2	c Statham b Allen	0
G.D.McKenzie	not out	1	b Flavell	32
Extras	(B 4, LB 1)	5	(B 6, LB 9, W 2)	17
Total	(63.4 overs)	190	(171.4 overs)	432

ENGLAND

G.Pullar	b Davidson	63	c O'Neill b Davidson	26
R.Subba Row	c Simpson b Davidson	2	b Benaud	49
E.R.Dexter	c Davidson b McKenzie	16	c Grout b Benaud	76
*P.B.H.May	c Simpson b Davidson	95	b Benaud	0
D.B.Close	lbw b McKenzie	33	c O'Neill b Benaud	8
K.F.Barrington	c O'Neill b Simpson	78	lbw b Mackay	5
†J.T.Murray	c Grout b Mackay	24	c Simpson b Benaud	4
D.A.Allen	c Booth b Simpson	42	c Simpson b Benaud	10
F.S.Trueman	c Harvey b Simpson	3	c Benaud b Simpson	8
J.B.Statham	c Mackay b Simpson	4	b Davidson	8
J.A.Flavell	not out	0	not out	0
Extras	(B 2, LB 4, W 1)	7	(B 5, W 2)	7
Total	(163.4 overs)	367	(71.4 overs)	201

ENGLAND	O	M	R	W		O	M	R	W
Trueman	14	1	55	1		32	6	92	0
Statham	21	3	53	5		44	9	106	1
Flavell	22	8	61	1		29.4	4	65	2
Dexter	6.4	2	16	3	(5) 20	4	61	3
Allen					(4) 38	25	58	4
Close					8	1	33	0

AUSTRALIA	O	M	R	W		O	M	R	W
Davidson	39	11	70	3		14.4	1	50	2
McKenzie	38	11	106	2		4	1	20	0
Mackay	40	9	81	1	(5) 13	7	33	1
Benaud	35	15	80	0	(3) 32	11	70	6
Simpson	11.4	4	23	4	(4) 8	4	21	1

FALL OF WICKETS

	A	E	A	E
Wkt	1st	1st	2nd	2nd
1st	8	4	113	40
2nd	51	43	175	150
3rd	89	154	210	150
4th	106	212	274	158
5th	150	212	290	163
6th	174	272	296	171
7th	185	358	332	171
8th	185	362	334	189
9th	189	367	334	193
10th	190	367	432	201

Umpires: J.G.Langridge and W.E.Phillipson.

Close of Play – Day 1: A(1) 124-4; Day 2: E(1) 187-3; Day 3: A(2) 63-0; Day 4: A(2) 331-6.

PART THREE

9

Aftermath

How had it all gone so horribly wrong? How on this truly dramatic final day had England somehow managed to snatch defeat from those tantalising jaws of victory? 'ASHES GOODBYE' (*Daily Sketch*); 'ENGLAND, YOU THREW IT AWAY!' (*Daily Express*); 'ENGLAND JUST CHUCKED IT AWAY' (*Daily Mirror*) – the popular press did not hold back on Wednesday morning about what was indisputably a national disaster.

Nor did most of its reporters. For Crawford White in the *Mail*, the really vexing thing was that England had blown it against 'the weakest Australian team seen in this country since the war'. Who was to blame? Here there was an inconsistency. Almost inevitably he focused on Close, who had 'committed suicide' in 'what must be his last innings for England'; yet, added White, 'the only redeeming feature of England's collapse was that Dexter, May and Subba Row [i.e. the three amateur batters], at least, died swinging hard for the runs'. For the *Daily Worker*'s Philip Sheridan, Australia's 'show of courage and determination when their backs were to the wall' made them worthy winners; the *Express*'s Frank Rostron highlighted Close's innings as 'one of the most grotesque batting displays I have ever seen in a Test match'; while the *Sketch*'s Brian Scovell put the weight on the Davidson–McKenzie partnership, when not only 'the bowlers bowled badly', but 'Peter May used the wrong ones on at the wrong time'.

Perhaps the greatest vitriol came from the *Mirror*'s pair, Brian Chapman and Peter Wilson. 'Our sawdust champions ... no side so pusillanimous deserved to win ... dropped catches ... slipshod bowling ... shocking batting flop ... the auto-da-fe procession of victims ...' – Chapman confessed to 'not a scrap of comfort from the fact that I tipped Australia to win, and warned that Benaud would be the acid that bit fatally into England's vitals'. As for Wilson, 'Alas! I have to record that never have I seen a more spineless, spiritless and senseless piece of sporting suicide in all my born days.' By contrast, 'the Australians still believed in their star', even when Dexter was flaying them, and 'no possible praise can be too high for Benaud, who was a snake charmer achieving the Indian rope trick'. In sum: 'With all praise to the Australians – and how they deserve it – this will go down as the Test England SHOULD have won, COULD at least have drawn – AND DID IN FACT LOSE MOST IGNOBLY.'

Of course, that morning over their toast and Frank Cooper's Oxford marmalade, most discerning cricket-lovers looked elsewhere: some no doubt to the *Guardian*'s Denys Rowbotham – who emphasised how Benaud's 'relentless accuracy into the rough' had reduced England's left-handers to either strokelessness or suicide, thereby placing too much pressure on the team's right-handers – but above all to the two great oracles: Swanton and Woodcock. Duly acknowledging that it had been 'fine bowling' on Benaud's part, as well as 'a magnificent game of cricket', the *Telegraph* man let the England captain off relatively mildly: bringing on Close for Statham soon after McKenzie had come in deemed 'a reasonable change'; no opinion either way about removing Allen immediately after the Davidson assault; May's ignominious duck merely a technical failure in leaving the leg stump uncovered. As for how 'the England tactics after tea left some doubt in the mind as to the objects of the exercise', Swanton forbore to mention the captain's name. Instead, his greatest ire was directed entirely predictably. 'To describe Close's innings taxes charity beyond endurance, as indeed it taxed credibility to behold' began his account of nothing less than a 'nightmare'. Woodcock was little kinder – an innings 'best talked about in whispers' – while more generally, in a dignified report by an observer as hugely disappointed as anyone, he portrayed England's failure as one of 'temperament', brought on by 'their inability to play spin bowling, particularly leg breaks, of the highest class'.

What about the Australian perspective? 'It is neither reasonable nor fair that after five days of keenly fought cricket the technique adopted by one man during a period during which he received only ten balls should be blamed for the result of the game,' insisted Lindsay Hassett in the *Evening Standard*, though he did not deny that Close had 'played badly' and 'risked an unsound technique which failed and at the same time looked clumsy'. But after all: 'If Close can be blamed, why not May? ... May's off-balance swing against the turn without covering his stumps with his pads was just as faulty in technique as the strokes Close attempted.' Tom Goodman in the *Sydney Morning Herald* – which bore the headline 'Australia Wins Test After Thrilling Battle Against Time' – was unsurprisingly more interested in Australian heroics than in English technical failures: the 'great recovery partnership' between Davidson and McKenzie, and the raw facts of Benaud's remarkable spell: 'Benaud broke the back of the English batting, dismissing Dexter 76, May 0, Close 8, Subba Row 49, Murray 4, in less than 30 minutes.'

'BOLD BENAUD IS MY HERO' was the headline for Keith Miller's piece in the *Express*, where, though he did not forbear from criticising the English team ('chicken-hearted batting that a junior school would have bettered'), his admiration was unstinting for the Australian captain who 'never for a moment lost his grip or clear thinking'. So, too, the *Age*'s Percy Beames, who in his retrospective overview for Thursday's issue did not hesitate to declare that 'there was a stage when Benaud alone believed the seemingly impossible was possible' and that 'had Peter May used Benaud's confidence and boldness in his tactics the result might have been different'. He was particularly critical of May's decision on the last morning to take off Allen, which he equated to 'the hoisting of the "white flag"'. Beames also took the opportunity to look ahead, especially given that both teams on show at Old Trafford had been on the elderly side, with few ready-made replacements in immediate view. 'It could be,' he predicted, 'that the Ashes will yet take some prising away from Australia.'

These were all public thoughts, but for the moment Arlott's meditations – his written ones anyway – remained private. His journal account of the final day (a day which 'will be recounted, mulled over, and disputed as long as anyone who saw it – and many who did not – are alive to talk cricket') offered, like Swanton, no view on May's decision about Allen; reckoned that the disconcerting rough outside the left-handed batsmen's off stump had been 'produced largely by Trueman'; found May doubly guilty in his execution of the fateful sort-of-sweep ('he neglected to put his leg in line, his stroke was crooked'); employed adjectives like 'grotesque' and 'hideous' to describe Close's innings; and found in England's batting tactics after tea 'no indication' of whether they were trying to win or save the game.*

Arlott also reflected on how, in the series as a whole, the Australians had as usual performed 'in a more enterprising, even attacking, manner' than their English opposition, who as ever had played 'more cannily, even defensively'. Was that why Benaud and his men had come out on top? Here, Arlott was instinctively reluctant to concede the larger point. 'It is not true to say,' he insisted, 'that attacking cricket is always more successful than the "tight" method.' And, added this staunch defender of English cricket's tradition of honest if not always inspiring craftsmanship: 'The Ashes, we can now see, turned, in the final analysis, on two catches dropped – off Lawry and Harvey – at Old Trafford. They were dropped by fieldsmen who would have held them three times out of four.'

The inquests and speculations continued the following weekend. For the *Sunday Telegraph*'s Michael Melford, the biggest 'if' was not the widely held assumption that England would have won if only Cowdrey had been available to add stability to the batting and certainty in the slips, given

---

*Several writers at the time and since have described May's fatal stroke as a 'sweep'. The YouTube footage shows this to be a misnomer. The only sweep-like feature about the shot was that May played across the line.

that – argued Melford – 'if Cowdrey had played Dexter would have been left out', and England would have badly missed his fine all-round contribution. Rather:

> A more subtle 'if' concerns the stand of Davidson and McKenzie on Tuesday morning. Their scoring rate, it will be remembered, declined almost to nothing after an hour and Davidson made no effort to attack the new ball though it did not look a particularly formidable weapon.
>
> If they had gone on for a few minutes at the rate which had previously brought them 50 runs in half an hour, they would, of course, have left England with a target too distant to contemplate, and some of the strokes perpetrated later would have mercifully stayed as a mischievous twinkle in the batsman's eye.
>
> As it was, 256 had to be attempted, though only two sides in the whole history of Test cricket in this country had ever made 200 or over in the last innings and won.

Ian Peebles in the *Sunday Times* nobly overcame partisanship – 'it was, in its violent fluctuations, dashing feats and accidents, a great cricket match and this, to real lovers of the game, transcended any disappointment on the home front' – but Alan Ross struggled in the *Observer*. 'I must, at once, declare my interest,' he began. 'I hate to see England lose, especially to Australia.' In fact he did with a poet's eye pay due tribute to the victors – 'Lawry's craggy, rugged defiance; Davidson's sudden summoning of the old sweet masteries, a half-crocked, tired Neptunian figure, hair-flecked with foam but magically regenerated as if by some Faustian potion; McKenzie, brash and unabashed when resistance seemed all but pointless;

O'Neill, living for the moment as immediately as any paid-off cane cutter; Benaud, mercurial, buoyant, tigerishly lazy of movement' – but his strongest emotions were reserved for the defeated: how England 'failed to move with the tide on Saturday morning'; how 'the slip fielders, first, then the bowlers, at vital points, lost their sense of urgency (something the Australians, no matter how unpromising the context, never did)'; above all, how, 'with victory sniffable, there was a loss of nerve among the middle and later batsmen of a kind one can even now scarcely credit'.

Was May ultimately to blame? Not according to Ross, who wondered 'whether any captain could have curbed the cretinous excesses of the batting when only a run a minute was needed'. Tom Goodman in that day's *Sun-Herald* disagreed, declaring that over the series as a whole Benaud had been the 'superior' captain to either May or Cowdrey, especially when it came to man management, with May 'more assured than when in Australia, but still does not always get the best out of the material available'. One way and another, questions, questions; and next day Swanton in his regular 'Monday Cricket Commentary' noted that his 'every friend and acquaintance' was continuing to fire them at him. 'What came over our batsmen? Why did May play that shot? What were their instructions? Why did Trueman throw his wicket away? Above all, why did Close go completely mad?'

The England selectors dropped two players for the final Test, starting at The Oval on 17 August. One of the decisions was entirely predictable – prompting Woodcock to reflect that 'the last has probably been seen of Close as an international cricketer, the last and nothing like the best' – but the other, so soon after his Headingley heroics, was much less so.

'Nothing short of an astonishment,' declared the *Yorkshire Post*'s J. M. Kilburn about the omission of Trueman; but on the grounds of a below-par performance at Old Trafford, allied to the way his follow-through had created a helpful rough for Benaud, neither Swanton nor Woodcock was inclined to quarrel with it. Even so, noted Swanton, 'the fact is Trueman is widely accepted at his own valuation as a symbol of pugnacity, indeed almost its epitome, and many, especially in the North, will find his exclusion hard to bear'.

The match itself was, perhaps inevitably, something of an anti-climax. England's disappointing first innings of 256 featured a fine 71 from May, seeming to attain mastery over Benaud before holing out to deep point; Australia's reply of 494 was dominated by centuries from O'Neill and Burge; while Subba Row (137) – equalling Lawry's feat of two centuries in his first Ashes series – and Barrington (83) were largely responsible for overcoming the deficit, as England reached 370 for eight. 'At twenty-five past five Harvey came on to bowl a ceremonial maiden, and at half past five the game was given up as drawn without the extra half hour,' recorded a weary, less than enchanted Arlott. 'The Test series of 1961 had ended on the old, grimly defensive note, with the English batsmen demonstrating that they are better at saving Tests than winning them ...'

As the season wound down, though with plenty of cricket still left for the hard-working tourists, two contrasting contests began on Wednesday the 30th: at Lord's, watched by one of us as a first-time spectator there, Gentlemen of England versus the Australians; and at Bournemouth, intently and partisanly watched by Arlott among others, Hampshire v Derbyshire, with the home county poised to win the Championship for the first time in its history. Two days later, the amateurs at Lord's achieved a dullish draw, while on the south coast it was jubilation unrestrained as the visitors were bowled out by the ageless Derek Shackleton. Later in September was festival time, above all at Scarborough, where May and Benaud had their final encounter, albeit in light-hearted mode as T. N. Pearce's XI and the Australians rattled up 1,499 runs in three days, culminating in May's declaration and the visitors scoring 357 in three and a half hours to get home by three wickets. That was the end of the Australians' first-class programme – in which across the thirty-two matches they had largely fulfilled Benaud's promise to try if possible to play attractive, enterprising cricket – but there were still fixtures against the Minor Counties, Scotland and Ireland. Last knockings were at Dublin on the 19th; and Benaud's final victim was M. H. (Mike) Stevenson, who twelve years earlier had played for Cambridge University against Yorkshire in the match that had seen the debut of (in *Wisden*'s immortal words) 'Trueman, a spin bowler'.

Bittersweet memories of Old Trafford were kept alive during the autumn by the publication of not just Arlott's journal (*The Australian Challenge*), but no fewer than five books about the Australian tour.

'What happened on that last day is a story often told already but adequately explained by none,' declared Charles Fortune. 'The one explanation that will not stand up is that Benaud suddenly came out with a burst of brilliant and unplayable bowling. His six wickets owed something to a worn wicket but more still to some strange mystification that overcame England's batsmen.' As for the specific matter of May's 'sweep', this according to Fortune had been a legitimate stroke, given that 'the objective was runs', whereas Close 'played an innings that lasted eight balls and will for ever have taken his name off the England selectors' longest lists'.

For Ray Lindwall, the second author, it had been, bar only the tied Test at Brisbane, 'the best Test match I have ever seen', with Davidson on the final morning playing 'one of the greatest fighting innings in the history of Test cricket'. Even so, he did not spare May for his tactical errors as captain: failing to encourage quicker scoring on the Saturday; giving O'Neill an easy start on the Monday by bowling Close, not one of the fast men, despite the batter's travails in the first innings; the same day, after taking the second new ball, sticking too long with the quicks before turning to Allen; and on Tuesday morning not only mistakenly bringing on Close, but just as mistakenly taking off Allen.

The third book was by Bill Bowes, who much like Fortune largely exonerated May the batter ('the ball pitched so wide of the leg stump that May, quite rightly, went to sweep it'), but charged Close with failing to learn the lesson from his first few balls that 'with the uneven bounce of the ball after dropping in the rough it was dangerous to try this violent cross-bat swing'.

Fourth up was yet another bowler with a well-developed cricket brain, Jim Laker, able here to write in a fuller, more considered way than in his briefish *Daily Sketch* reflections. Deeply unimpressed with the events of the final day, he 'felt certain Allen should have been allowed at least another over' before being taken off; condemned May's shot as 'ill-advised and half-hearted'; described Close's effort as, not in a good way, 'the most extraordinary innings I can ever recall from an accredited batsman in a Test match'; and was still not quite able to believe how England had 'throughout the five days appeared to be in command only to toss away the advantage in the last couple of hours with a disgraceful display of batting'. Even so, he concluded, there was always the bigger picture: 'England brought defeat on their own heads whilst Australia, playing more positive, attacking cricket recorded a great and famous victory. May the game of cricket always work out that way.'

The best of the five books – for style and sympathy as well as insight – was *The Fight for the Ashes* by the *Daily Telegraph*'s R. A. (Ron) Roberts. Take his analysis of the last session on Saturday:

> England were 361 for seven at tea, and their subsequent tactics, I considered, were wrong. This view was out of step with the army of critics demanding a show of aggression with England so far out in front. The pitch was now playing so well, however, that England were surely better employed batting for much of the evening and bowling for no more than forty-five minutes or so. A lead of around 200 with which to contemplate the week-end would have given England a moral advantage as well as a practical one. Instead the remaining three wickets were carelessly surrendered, as though the batsmen were under instructions to quicken up, and thus were Australia given time to close the gap. From a score of 212 for five England had ruggedly raised themselves to 361 for seven. It was wrong to jeopardize so much hard-won ground. Jeopardized it was, however ...

As for May's handling of Allen, Roberts like Lindwall criticised him for tardiness on the Monday, but broke with semi-received opinion by arguing that taking off his spinner the next morning was not 'quite as much a mistake, for Davidson seemed to have the measure of Allen in defence or attack, as the introduction of Close and the holding back of Flavell, the leading wicket-taker in the country'. Turning to May's downfall, he could see arguments on both sides: 'I have seen May sweep a few times, and generally for four runs, but it is not a stroke for which he is recognized, and in any case it was a risky one in those conditions. On the other hand, had he connected Benaud might have had to revise his tactics about bowling round the wicket.'

Roberts was also fair-minded about Close ('no doubt the Yorkshireman could have set the Australians back on their heels with a few well-chosen blows, but the methods he employed were quite extraordinary'), even as overall he left his readers in no doubt about his own 'profound feeling of disappointment' about the match's outcome: 'To surrender one winning hold in a day is, perhaps, understandable; to do so twice is inexcusable. England did not deserve to win: that was what was so hard to swallow.'

What of the Australians, above all their captain? 'If ever there was any doubt as to Benaud's place not only among the great cricketers, but also among the great captains of all time,' declared Roberts, 'surely that last afternoon provided the answer':

There he was, inspiring his team when his personal empire looked to be crumbling at his feet. Benaud said afterwards – and in future it will be quoted of him many times – 'I felt that, while we could not save the game, we might still win it.' Incurable optimist though he is, I cannot think that Richie more than half believed that. If he did, why the stoppage for drinks, why the recourse to Mackay's medium-paced, unpenetrative bowling with Dexter in full spate, why bowl round the wicket to Dexter? These were not attacking gestures, symptomatic of a winning bid.

Yet all that said, Roberts went on, 'the fact that Australia bowled forty overs in the first two hours of the England innings, that Benaud himself bowled on and on, and that he tried Simpson did show that Australia were prepared to look for the winning chance, and were scornful of purely defensive measures'.

Wisden's judgement on Old Trafford awaited the following spring. Its typically sober match report refrained from criticising individuals, while Norman Preston in his 'Notes by the Editor' concentrated on the series as a whole, arguing that England had 'come to grief' through 'pursuing the same defensive methods which contributed to defeat in the last tour of Australia'. Specific examples included Subba Row (valuable runs, but 'in no sense did he shape like a Hobbs or a Washbrook or a Woolley') and Cowdrey ('usually surrendered the initiative to the Australian bowlers'); while 'dilatory running between the wickets – Murray was a notable exception – emphasised England's negative attitude'. In short: 'They did not appear to derive pleasure from the game as did the Australians.'

Elsewhere in the almanack, the retiring chairman of the selectors, Gubby Allen, looked back on 'My Seven Year "Stretch"' in fairly benign mode, though not without insisting that England would be unlikely to regain their Test supremacy without 'a more aggressive approach' in the batting; and Jack Fingleton gave his overview on the previous summer ('An Enjoyable Visit to Britain'). Old Trafford inevitably featured strongly, with May's second-ball dismissal (poor choice of shot, compounded by failure of legs to protect stumps) and Close's barely less brief innings ('vainglorious swishes') naturally highlighted – but not quite as much as how Trueman's footprints, enabling Benaud to bowl round the wicket and aim at them, had left 'their imprint on the sands of cricket time'. Why, wondered Fingleton, had Trueman not been deterred from this dangerous habit of an over-straight follow-through? After all: 'On the evidence, with Benaud the Prosecutor, the series of 1961 turned on his footprints. Millions throughout the United Kingdom this day saw on television or heard on the wireless as this game dropped right out of England's lap. It must have been a depressing business for them. I seemed to detect next day some suggestion of national gloom.'

There was yet one more account to digest. *A Tale of Two Tests* was the neat title of Benaud's book, published in spring 1962 and focusing mainly on the two recent epics at Brisbane and Manchester. His compelling narrative-cum-analysis was careful, with a victor's generosity, to make no explicit criticism of his opposite number; it revealed how after his pitch inspection on the penultimate evening he had become almost obsessed with how he might exploit Trueman's footmarks ('deep holes, not just surface scratches'); and it gave great emphasis to that mid-afternoon moment on the Tuesday when he realised that a draw was no longer in the equation, that therefore the only viable tactic was to go for the win. Over the years, Benaud's would become the canonical account, except perhaps in one respect. 'Let me say quite frankly,' he wrote, 'that I thought the slating of Close was one of the most unjust things I have ever experienced':

> During the afternoon Dexter and Close were the only two players who had me scared. Dexter for obvious reasons, but Close because he could have turned the game in a matter of minutes if some of his attempted sweeps had come off. His ideas were perfect ... sweep with the spin, and then wait for the shorter one to pull, and take as many runs as possible from the other end. His execution was not perfect. I was quite prepared to believe that I would get him out at some stage ... But at what cost? Even twenty runs at this stage could have been disastrous.

Benaud ended his chapter by recalling how, some two hours after it was all over, 'May and his men were kind enough to come in for a drink with us, and tender their congratulations'. 'I know', he added, 'how they must have felt. I've been beaten myself when playing for Australia against England, and it seems as though the end of the world has come. Perhaps that's why this is such a great game ... it is the greatest leveller I know.'

10

Blood on the Tracks

By this time, an era in English cricket was over. 'MAY WILL NOT LEAD ENGLAND AGAIN' had been the *Telegraph* headline at the start of 1962, after his announcement that for business reasons (insurance broking at Lloyd's) he would not be going on any more overseas tours and did not wish to be considered for the captaincy. There remained a hope-cum-expectation that he might yet play for England again; but in the event, after a full season for Surrey in 1962 and a few matches in 1963, May dropped out of first-class cricket for good, barely in his mid-thirties. Would it have been different if England in 1961 had regained the Ashes? Perhaps even more, if he had not been put through the wringer that last traumatic day at Old Trafford? Impossible to know with such an archetypically tight-lipped Englishman, but at the least quite possibly.

Still, that was not on the mind of the selectors (now chaired by another attack-minded amateur, Walter Robins) as in July 1962 they decided on a captain for the winter's tour of Australia. Inevitably, the three prime candidates – Cowdrey, Dexter and David Sheppard – were all privately educated, Oxbridge amateurs; and in the course of the

Gentlemen v Players contest at Lord's they plumped for Dexter – not least because Gubby Allen, present in an 'advisory' capacity, warned them against the political dangers of Sheppard potentially repudiating in public the host country's 'White Australia' policy.

Days later came the even less socially mobile choice of manager for the tour: to widespread astonishment, the Duke of Norfolk. That autumn, in late November, the touring entourage was in Brisbane, preparing for the first Test, when the unexpected news came through from London that the Advisory County Cricket Committee had decided to recommend the abolition of amateur status in English first-class cricket (a recommendation confirmed, however reluctantly, by MCC some two months later). Although Swanton was instantly and predictably appalled – 'not only unnecessary but deplorable' – opinion in the world at large, including probably the cricket world taken as a whole, would not have disagreed with the *Daily Mail*'s satisfaction in seeing at last the end of 'humbug and the need for petty deception, a blot on cricket for years'. No more Gentlemen v Players, no more Gentlemen of England against the tourists ... And, in these palpably more meritocratic and egalitarian times (including a Labour government in the offing), presumably in the near future an end to the young gentlemen of Eton jousting annually at Lord's with the young gentlemen of Harrow.

'DEXTER HOPES TO PLEASE CROWDS' had been *The Times*'s headline earlier in the autumn, as his team flew out from London Airport (prior to catching a boat at Aden). 'We do not want to sit on the fence,' he had promised. 'We will try and keep the score moving at a good pace.' If the assumption was that England now had an attack-minded captain to match Benaud, it did not quite work out like that. The first three Tests were engaging enough – a draw, followed by a win apiece – but then came a defensive stalemate at Adelaide, leaving everything to play for in the fifth Test at Sydney, with England needing to win to regain the Ashes. 'Dexter is determined to attack,' Woodcock reassured his readers, shivering back home in the Big Freeze. 'He sees this as his main chance of victory ...'

Sadly, the first day turned out to be – admittedly on a slow, unsatisfactory pitch – 'a miserable day for England and not deserving of victory', as they slowly compiled 195 for five. A characteristically gritty century by Barrington included only four boundaries, while Dexter's 47 took two and a quarter hours, with Woodcock sighing that 'he seems to have lost the ability to command'; and the match eventually petered out as the tamest of draws, amid protracted booing and slow handclapping. A thoroughly disenchanted Woodcock concluded not only that Benaud as a captain was 'not so much adventurous as occasionally adventurous', but that 'Dexter, involved subconsciously, perhaps, in a personal clash with Benaud, was affected by the air of gravity that surrounds a Test match', with the result that 'the desire not to lose began to haunt him'.

Also less than enamoured was Ray Illingworth, Yorkshire all-rounder and consummate professional. 'There was a lot of southern bias on that tour,' he would recall almost half a century later about the pervasive amateur influence he had encountered. 'Ted was not as bad as some of them. You could speak to him as a man, trust him ... but I didn't trust the others. They said they were going to do one thing, and then went off and did something else.' His particular *bête noire* was the vice-captain: 'Sometimes Cowdrey didn't fancy opening, and he'd pick and choose where he wanted to bat. It used to annoy everyone.' Altogether, argued Illingworth, the series was there for the taking if England had had a more professional approach. While as for the Duke of Norfolk: 'We'd arrive in each state, and he would make a little speech about "The bonding of Commonwealth" – and did absolutely nothing else.'

The 1963 season began with the heady brew of C. L. R. James's *Beyond a Boundary*, published in May and, along with much else, taking in rich reminiscence about his Trinidadian childhood and the West Indian cricketers of his youth, a meditation on W. G. Grace and the Victorian Age, a lengthy essay on the aesthetics of cricket, and a personal account of his role in the campaign to make Frank Worrell the first full-time Black captain of the West Indies team. 'Not Quite What I Call Cricket' was the memorable headline for Swanton's *Sunday Telegraph* review, which to his considerable credit did fully acknowledge – for all their political differences – 'the lucid beauty of the writing, the author's width of vision as well as his depth of learning, and the skill with which he weaves his complicated pattern into an integrated whole'. Over the next few weeks, other reviewers included a somewhat grudging Neville Cardus ('when he escapes from polemics and aesthetics he writes extremely well, especially of the cricketers of his own habitation'), a largely admiring R. C. Robertson-Glasgow (praising James's 'strong observation, loving memory and a dignity that never swells into pomposity'), and a not quite wholly captivated Alan Ross ('a remarkable book, though one marred here and there by a disfiguring militancy'). But the supreme critical moment would come almost a year later, with the 1964 *Wisden*, when Arlott devoted the first page and a half of his annual survey of cricket books to what he acclaimed as 'the finest book written about the game of cricket', indeed the best book about any sport that he had ever read. 'This is not, like most cricket books, a book about cricket in isolation but a book about cricket and life – the life being that of a man who has studied and thought so widely that he can take as his text "What do they know of cricket who only cricket know". To answer that question, the author says, "involves ideas as well as facts".'

All of which was undeniably true – and yet, in retrospect anyway, what seems most striking is that a writer who still broadly considered himself a Marxist offered so little class-based analysis of English cricket in the third quarter of the twentieth century. 'A romantic traditionalist ... in thrall to the Victorian public-school ideology' would be Francis Wheen's crisp characterisation of James, while a recent assessment by Abbie Rhodes, marking the book's sixtieth anniversary, sternly finds him guilty of 'expressing deference to the English cricketing establishment and its traditions while failing to go far enough in criticising their origins'. Even so, in that summer of the Profumo Affair, revealing the rotten and hypocritical core of the British establishment as a whole, what *Beyond a Boundary* did unmistakably mark was precisely what the title said: however hard it might try, a world game that was still run from inside the thick protective walls of Lord's could no longer ignore what went on in places and societies very far and very different from London NW8.

The timing of James's book could hardly have been more serendipitous, as later in the summer England and West Indies contested a compelling series. It featured, from an English point of view, a major turn-up and an hour of rare splendour. The turn-up was Close's recall to the colours, playing all five matches, including a heroically bruised and battered 70 at Lord's, an innings of true redemption, as England came within a whisker of winning (albeit also losing). Earlier in that thrilling draw, the splendour had come from Dexter, as he took on Wes Hall and Charlie Griffith, meeting fire with fire in his own 70 at almost a run a ball. 'The magisterially defiant cameo represented the last sneering fling of Empire,' remembered Frank Keating. 'Crack! went Dexter's blade. Crackle! went the throng as all London stopped …'

One of BBC TV's commentators this summer, joining Brian Johnston and Peter West, was Benaud: not yet quite retired as a player, but his future broadcasting path now starting to become clear. His last stint was at Lord's in early September, for the final of the Gillette Cup, English cricket's first one-day knock-out competition – the arrival, in effect, of the short form of the game, albeit at this stage a far from cursory sixty-five overs per side. In front of a large and noisy crowd (which included a disappointed one of us), Sussex beat Worcestershire by 14 runs, with the winning captain, Dexter, displeasing many neutral observers in the Stygianly gloomy closing stages as he took advantage of a loophole in the regulations to place his nine fielders around the boundary. Not displeasing, though, to the pragmatic Benaud, who recalled Dexter's tactics as 'impeccable'.

Sadly, his tactics were judged altogether more peccable in 1964, as England once again failed to recover the Ashes: first at Lord's, where on the last day he took too long to turn to his slow bowlers (Fred Titmus and Norman Gifford) in conditions which favoured them; but above all at Headingley, where on the second afternoon, as Australia's batsmen were visibly struggling against Titmus and Gifford, he took the second new ball and Burge, in a magnificent, game-changing innings, proceeded to punish Trueman and Flavell mercilessly. The season was not long over when, in the October general election that brought Harold Wilson to power, Dexter unsuccessfully stood in Cardiff South East as Conservative candidate against the shadow chancellor, James Callaghan; that winter, Warwickshire's M. J. K. (Mike) Smith captained the MCC team in South Africa, doing by general consent a good job; and ahead of the 1965 season it was far from certain that the role would revert to Dexter.

'Has he managed to get the best out of his men?' wondered *Wisden*'s Norman Preston. 'He has now led England in losing rubbers against India, Australia and West Indies.' 'No one who knows him,' added Preston, 'could suggest that Dexter has shirked his duties. He gives a tremendous amount of thought to the game, including tactics, bowling changes and field placings. He prefers to act alone and is usually reluctant to take advice.' An earlier assessment, and particularly perceptive, had come from Alan Ross in his 1962–63 tour book:

> Social responsiveness, affability, evenness of mood are not noticeably part of Dexter's personality ... Where he failed in his relations with his team was that he left them overmuch to

their own devices, often without guidance or consideration, when both would have been appreciated ... Often he seemed *distrait* during long partnerships, as if some opaque screen had come down between his private fantasies and what was actually going on. Unlike Benaud, who gives the appearance of identifying himself with every single one of his players all of the time, Dexter seems to abstract himself, as if the flow of events was no real concern of his ...

A sense of entitlement allied to huge natural sporting talent – such a combination does not by definition preclude empathy and imaginative sympathy, but it probably does not help. Peter Cook, two years younger at Radley College in the 1950s, would not have been surprised by Dexter's defects as England captain. 'Prefects were dazzling and terrifying,' recalled a schoolfriend of Cook. 'They could punish and harass at whim. But Dexter was even more astral than the rest, as a cricketing, rackets-playing, rugby-playing hero. He was also extremely lordly, elegant, rich, well-dressed and assured, with something of a "sneer of cold command". Can you imagine anyone more likely to get young Peter's goat?' Cook himself did not forgive or forget, telling his host on *Parkinson* in 1977 how 'he beat me for drinking cider at Henley Regatta' – which 'I thought a little unfair', given 'I'd seen him coming out of a pub with a bottle of Scotch'. It was the moment, reflected the great, iconoclastic comedian, 'when I got my sense of injustice about the whole world'.

England's last two Ashes campaigns of the 1960s followed the usual twofold pattern: 'amateur' captains (Smith in 1965–66; Cowdrey, bar one match, in 1968), and failing to achieve their principal objective. As in the 1940s, though with extenuating circumstances then, the Ashes stayed firmly down under during the whole decade. 'For all his qualities, Smith was not really worth his place in the side as a batsman,' comments Simon Wilde in his fine survey (*England: The Biography*) of the national team's ups and downs over the years; while as for Cowdrey, he 'found responsibility a constant struggle, being too diffident and indecisive'. Even so, whatever the individual explanations, the larger mystery remains for the decade as a whole: why was this 'amateur' quartet of May, Cowdrey, Dexter and Smith unable to exhibit, when it came to captaining England against Australia, those uninhibited qualities of boldness, of taking games by the scruff of the neck, of daring to risk defeat in the pursuit of victory, that were the best part of the amateur tradition? Hutton's dour legacy is of course relevant, so too is the increasingly defensive county cricket they participated in week-in, week-out. Yet, ultimately was it because these four men, May and Cowdrey in particular, knew (at some level) that they were out of sync with the meritocratic-cum-anti-establishment zeitgeist of the 1960s – and that deep awareness undermined their inner confidence? Put another way, the world was changing, quite fast, and the new world was not one that their very conventional public-school and Varsity education had prepared them for. Well, it can only be speculation; but that *something* was not quite right is surely undeniable.

There was an alternative. 'His leadership was inspiring, both by example and in a tactical sense,' praised *Wisden* about Close's first season, 1963, in charge of Yorkshire. 'He knew just what the men under him were capable of, and while expecting them to give of their best he never asked from them more than they could manage.' The plaudits continued, as in 1966, when Yorkshire again won the Championship: 'The bowling was invariably supported, indeed augmented, by enterprising fielding in which Close played the leading part expected of a captain. At either short leg or silly point he stationed himself alarmingly near to the bat and was fortunate to avoid injury, but his courage enabled him to create many spectacular catches and his example in concentration and effort was a vital factor ...' Or as Mike Brearley recalled years later about Close's very distinctive style of leadership in the field, as aggressive as it was shrewd, 'he would caper about at the batsman's feet as happy as a hippo in wet mud'.

In August 1966, not having played for England since 1963, he had the opportunity of demonstrating his captaincy on the biggest stage. England were 3–0 down in the series against the West Indies, with Smith once and Cowdrey twice the losing captains; for the final Test, at The Oval, the selectors dropped Cowdrey and replaced him with Close; and, almost incredibly, England won by a comprehensive innings and 34 runs in three and a bit days. The culmination came on the Monday morning. The great Garry Sobers came in; Close directed John Snow to try a bouncer first up ('Let him have one'); Snow obliged; Sobers went for the hook; nicked the ball onto his box; and the ball ballooned up, presenting an easy catch to a solitary Close himself, in at a very short forward short leg. 'It might have looked a dolly,' rightly noted Peter West about the unflinching Yorkshireman, 'but only to someone who had the guts to keep his eye on the ball rather than turn away in self-protection – as most very reasonably would have done.' The

Oval triumph was not, from an English point of view, quite the sweetest sporting moment of that immortal summer, but it came a very decent second.

There was no winter tour, but Close naturally retained the captaincy in 1967 against India and Pakistan, winning five of the six Tests and drawing the other. But by the last Test, played at The Oval towards the end of August, his position was in serious jeopardy, following in mid-August at Edgbaston a blatant display of time-wasting tactics by Yorkshire in order to prevent a win by Warwickshire and thereby gain two extra points (in a tight Championship race that Yorkshire would eventually win). Condemnation was immediate and, outside the Ridings, almost universal, leading eventually to the MCC Committee deciding, quite possibly in part because of Swanton's urgings, to replace Close (obstinately refusing to apologise) with Cowdrey as captain for the forthcoming tour of the West Indies.

This decision overrode the wishes of the selectors – one of whom, albeit perhaps in a minority, was May. Not every *Telegraph* reader was happy. 'Close is of outstanding talent as a cricket captain,' wrote C. B. Collins of Staines, Surrey. 'It is utter stupidity not to have chosen him as captain for the West Indies tour.' Instead, he went on, 'what should be "out" – thrown out – is the effete, inefficient, old-school-tie-cum-vicar's-tea-party mentality which haunts the MCC and its committees and bedevils this wonderful game in England.' In any event, Close was now the lost leader and would never captain England again. Or as the young Christopher Martin-Jenkins, for all his natural instincts as a privately educated southerner, put it in the *Cricketer*'s spring annual for 1968, 'amateurism is too often used almost as a synonym for good sportsmanship, professionalism as a by-word for the lack of it'. And: 'As a result English cricket seems afraid to exploit the reality of professionalism to the best ends. Blinded by the bad implications of the professional, legislators have been petrified into the misconception that there are no good ones.'

This is the moment perhaps to indulge in a little counter-factual history, for in addition to Close there were other cricketers apart from May, Cowdrey, Dexter and Smith who might have captained England – quite possibly more successfully – in 1960s Ashes battles. After all, given that none of the decade's five series in which England failed to recover the Ashes were remotely one-sided affairs, the question of captaincy was presumably relevant. Putting to one side Tom Graveney (who in one Test in 1968, in Cowdrey's absence, did actually skipper the team), we have three in mind. The first is Essex's Trevor Bailey: though in theory an amateur, but in practice a pretty well-paid shamateur, all his cricketing instincts were those of the pragmatic, clear-minded, hard-nosed professional. 'Astute' was *Wisden*'s word for his captaincy of Essex in 1962; two years later, and five since his last Test appearance, he was still topping his county's batting and bowling averages; and if in 1961 he had been in charge that final afternoon at Old Trafford, it is fair to assume that the batters after tea would not have been left in doubt about what they were trying to achieve.

Our other two candidates *were* professionals, starting with Tony Lock. Quite apart from being an aggressive spinner, a stubborn batter and a redoubtable fielder, he was also (to quote *Wisden* again, this time after his death) 'a driving captain'. Sadly, he never got the chance to lead

Surrey, but later in the 1960s he took not only Leicestershire to their then-highest position in the Championship, but Western Australia to just their second Sheffield Shield title – a remarkable double achievement. Finally, for our third possible, the endorsement comes from Bill Lawry. 'The England selectors have had the perfect captain right under their noses for years,' he declared in his 1966 autobiography, *Run-Digger*. 'And they just couldn't see him for looking.' Lawry went on:

> His name – Kenneth Frank Barrington – and he is the man who should have been at the helm for England during those fumbling years when the captaincy switched back and forth among Peter May, Colin Cowdrey, Ted Dexter and Mike Smith with England getting exactly nowhere.
>
> I suppose Barrington's hungry appetite for runs that turned so many of his innings into marathons counted against his choice as national leader. The selectors must have felt Barrington would place his own interests first, England's second. What stupidity!

'He is a knowledgeable cricketer, a likeable personality and a cricketer who automatically wins the respect of his colleagues,' added Lawry. 'What better qualities for a Test skipper?' But, given the governing assumptions of the day, it was never a realistic prospect, indeed seldom mooted; and the Australian reflected that whereas his own country's captains 'unfailingly have the full loyalty from the ranks', he had 'felt this is not always the case with English sides where maybe the old amateur-professional distinctions still cling on'.

In the event, in time for a new decade, the England team did get at the helm another bloody-minded, take-no-prisoners Yorkshireman in the Hutton-cum-Close mould. Ray Illingworth perfectly fitted that bill; but in the summer of 1970, as the focus intensified on who should lead England in Australia that winter, Swanton predictably favoured Cowdrey. 'I expect that most readers with a sporting interest', ran his essentially non-cricketing, ambassadorial argument, 'will have an inkling of the qualities needed in a man leading his country abroad without my needing to elaborate them.' But Illingworth it was; and in a controversial, fiercely competitive series, a man who had never been near a private school, let alone an ancient university, duly brought home the bacon. Soon afterwards, he and English cricket's great self-appointed arbiter found themselves having a ding-dong on the radio:

Illingworth: You wrote a summing up on the tour, Jim, and you did write that there'd been a lowering of standards on and off the field, and I wasn't very impressed with that ...
Swanton: I said there was a lowering of standards. Yes, I did say that, Ray, with very great reluctance. It's no pleasure to anybody like myself who loves to see England win and nothing else, to see certain of the things that went on. I thought I'd never hope to see an England captain threatening or seeming to threaten by wagging his finger at an Australian umpire with twenty or thirty thousand Australians looking on. If the game is going to come to this sort of pass where the umpire is going to be openly

challenged on the field, I think that the end of cricket in the Test match sense is really pretty near ...

There was little love lost between the two men. And when, near the end of the exchange, Illingworth apparently claimed that, unlike his predecessors, he was willing to speak his mind, Swanton responded with the haughtiness that was his speciality: 'We've had a great many captains who've spoken their minds very well, Ray. Don't imagine that because you're a Yorkshireman and tough, you're the only person who can speak your mind.'

Four years later – after Illingworth had retained the Ashes in 1972 but then the following year, after a humiliating defeat by the West Indies, lost the captaincy to Kent's more amenable Mike Denness, a move leading to a sharp spat between Michael Parkinson (calling the decision 'barmy') and Swanton – England were in Australia again. There they were blown away by Dennis Lillee and Jeff Thomson, with Ian Chappell's side then retaining the Ashes in England a few months later, despite the best efforts of new, not very gentlemanly, captain Tony Greig.

Two moments or episodes stick in the memory from the summer of 1975 as epitomising why, taking Ashes encounters as a whole since the late nineteenth century, a certain something about the Australian approach to cricket has meant they have tended to fare the better. The first came in the final at Lord's of the first men's World Cup. With Lillee and 'Thommo' last men in and gallantly throwing the bat in an attempt to overhaul a just-out-of-reach West Indies total, the crowd at the boundary edge mistakenly thought that the end had come and started rushing towards the middle; at which point – with chaos ensuing, the fielders mobbed, the ball lost – those two batters, all their competitive juices flowing, kept on frantically running, *just in case* the umpires were to decide not to call dead ball. Some two months later, one of us was at the third Test at Headingley, where shortly before lunch on the Monday the visitors set out in pursuit of 445 runs to win. Almost certainly an English team, of almost any era, would have spent the rest of the day laying a sure and steady foundation, with a view to upping the tempo on the final day; but that was not the Australian way, as they finished on 220 for three – virtually halfway there. Would they have won? Although sadly one will never know (the pitch vandalised overnight, the innocence of George Davis proclaimed), not all that many dispassionate observers would have bet against them.

By 1976 one of the very few still-playing survivors of Old Trafford 1961 was Close, who had made his Test debut twenty-seven years earlier and was now captain of Somerset, not Yorkshire. He was forty-five, it was nine years since he had played a Test, but to much surprise he got the call to face the West Indies. Three appearances ensued: at Trent Bridge he helped England secure an ill-deserved draw; at Lord's he faced down the fast men before on 60 holing out to a full toss from the solitary spinner – an innings that in some sense encapsulated his career; and at Old Trafford he batted with the utmost bravery against a fearsome short-pitched barrage from Michael Holding. Next season he bowed out of first-class cricket; but in 1978 he was playing as Todmorden's pro in the Lancashire League, including an away match at Bacup watched by the writer Geoffrey Moorhouse, whose vivid account of a mixed performance on the day culminates in appropriately tragi-comic vein:

> He is on 18 when Stansfield chips a ball from Fell through the slips. Some lingering sprite inside Brian Close makes him call for a single and he sets off on long legs towards the striker's end. Stansfield dashes past him before he is half-way there, already a slip has turned and has the ball, and those long legs are too stiff to carry Close to safety in time. He thunders past the broken wicket and carries on for several yards, head flung back in anguish at the loss of what was once so easily gained. Then he turns and comes in, grim-faced as he could be even in his salad days, but now with his chest heaving out of breath.

The same year saw the publication of Close's autobiography, *I Don't Bruise Easily*. Inevitably, some of the most heartfelt pages were devoted to the fateful Tuesday afternoon in 1961; and in essence his retrospective self-justification ran:

- That, sitting in the pavilion before either he or May had batted, he twice made the point to his captain that, with Benaud bowling into the dangerous rough, the England run chase was in danger of congealing if two left handers were together.
- That May's sole response was to murmur 'Mm – mmm'.
- That when, after May's dismissal, he did join Subba Row as one of two left handers at the wicket, he realised after a Mackay maiden that his partner was playing only for

himself and that he (Close) had no alternative but to attack Benaud.

- That with the ball turning and lifting out of the rough, it was too risky to play offside shots.
- And that, with the law limiting fieldsmen behind the wicket on the leg side to two, there was plenty of vacant space and it was perfectly rational to play the lap shot, especially once his straight-driven six to a ball landing on the true part of the wicket meant that Benaud was unlikely to drop many more there.

The dismissal itself? 'Another fraction of an inch higher and it would have been four; another fraction of an inch nearer the meat of the bat and it would have been four; another yard squarer of the fieldsman (Richie has since said that was actually where he wanted O'Neill) and it would have been four ...' The Close version ended on a perhaps understandably bitter note. 'Six wickets fell after mine. Had they nothing to do with our defeat?' And: 'Watching our later batsmen play some strange shots and get out I thought, "No one knows whether we are going for the runs or playing for a draw or what. No one has set any guidelines or laid down any policy." At least I knew what I was trying to do.'

The Packer revolution – irresistibly pointing the way to cricket's future, including night-time, white-ball cricket and the dominance of the short form – was by now under way. It probably could not have happened without Benaud's close and whole-hearted involvement, behind the scenes as well as behind the microphone. 'I've always been a cricketing public man and players' man, never an establishment man,' he insisted to an Australian newspaper a few months after agreeing in April 1977 to be Kerry Packer's consultant. 'I'm quite certain something is being pioneered,' he added, 'and it will be for the good of the game in the long run. It's the sort of thing that was always going to happen in Australia. Not least, the players will be able to earn a proper living for the amount of time they are putting into the game.'

Even for someone of Benaud's immense strength of character, the next year or so proved a rocky ride, including many cricketing friendships broken or severely damaged from Sir Donald Bradman downwards. 'I could not help wondering whether Benaud, for so long a supporter of established cricket, ever doubts the wisdom of joining Packer,' pondered Henry Blofeld in January 1978; while some months later a letter to *The Times* from Peter Cakebread of Birmingham packed a punch. 'Am I alone,' he asked, 'in finding the BBC's employment of Mr Benaud as a TV commentator for this season's Test matches offensive?' And: 'It is not unfair to call Mr Benaud a front man for Packer. I do not believe that Packer's cricket activities are compatible with the future well-being of Test cricket.'

Benaud himself remained, then and later, wholly unrepentant, declaring in a 1998 autobiography that World Series Cricket's legacy had been not only vastly improved conditions for the players, but also 'an astonishing increase in interest in the game, despite intense competition from other sports'. Fundamentally, of course, his master's motivation back in 1977 had been all about television and money. What then was WSC's legacy to the game? Gideon Haigh would reflect in 2016 – almost forty years on – how it had 'hastened the end of a world in which cricket was covered by national broadcasters as a kind of public trust', to be replaced by a world in which 'the game is funded by the sale of rights to televise it'. Good thing or bad thing? Swanton, not long before his death in 2000, had no doubt about the twenty-first-century perils – ultimately to cricket's traditional character and whole feel – which lay ahead. 'I think,' he told his future biographer David Rayvern Allen in a final interview, 'it's going to be a great struggle to keep cricket anything like the game that we've known and loved because now television has got it by the throat, and we need the money.'

*

Swanton was far from the only traditionalist finding it increasingly difficult in the 1980s and 1990s to come to terms with the modern game and modern cricketers. Another was Peter May, in many ways a man increasingly out of his time after his playing days were over. In 1982 – the year after England's memorable Ashes triumph, masterminded by Mike Brearley as a captain with Benaud-like qualities in man management as well as tactical ingenuity – he found himself, for all his undeniable cricketing greatness a quarter of a century earlier, painfully miscast as chairman of the selectors: a reluctant communicator; lacking in imagination; and responding to criticism (of which there was much) seldom if ever with any self-criticism, but instead blaming difficult circumstances. He could hardly have got off to a worse start – sacking Keith Fletcher as captain with the curtest, clipped-City-tones of phone calls – while over the ensuing years two successful Ashes series were counterbalanced by an abysmal record against the West Indies, partly down to May's inflexible adherence to (in

Scyld Berry's words) 'picking "balanced attacks" and sides to play against the most unbalanced team of all time'.

It is reasonable to ask why he had been given the job in the first place. The obvious answer is that it was all part of the old boy network, the cricket establishment looking after its own, perhaps even a deliberate and nostalgic reversion to the old amateur ethos after thirteen years of Alec Bedser as chairman. Although English cricket was now being run by the Test and County Cricket Board (TCCB), and no longer the MCC, there is probably a significant element of visceral truth in such an explanation. Yet it was a defensible appointment, given that in the late 1970s he had done a stint as chairman of the TCCB's cricket committee, lasting until autumn 1980, before becoming (for the customary one-year term) president of MCC. 'No Better Man to Follow Bedser than May' was *The Times*'s headline when in March 1981 the TCCB announced that he would be taking over the following year, with Richard Streeton calling it 'the best possible choice' and noting that May's 'stature as a player and administrator could be criticized by no one'. So, too, the *Daily Telegraph*'s Michael Melford, describing May as 'well acquainted with modern cricket and cricketers', and adding that he 'is respected by all and is known as a tough – though courteous – clear-thinking chairman'. The records of the TCCB (forerunner of the modern-day ECB) remain difficult to access; but it would be no surprise to discover that May's appointment went through on the nod.

Notwithstanding his occasional perversely stubborn selections (notably his almost suicidal insistence on playing two spinners against the West Indies in the crucial opening Test at Edgbaston in 1984, or taking only two openers to the West Indies two years later), and generally towards the end too much darting about, the real problem was less to do with cricket as such than human relations – as suggested by the early Fletcher episode, or indeed when in 1979 at the TCCB he had blocked Alan Knott from touring Australia because of Knott wanting his family to join him for several weeks. Probably no English cricketer of the 1980s had more to do with May as chairman than David Gower; and Gower's 1992 autobiography memorably characterised him as a man 'of the neutral suits, minimal communication and whose fluctuations of unease were reflected by the speed with which he revolved loose change in his pocket'. May, according to Gower, was seldom in the dressing-room ('he'd pop in early for a few quiet words, but that was about it'), and 'the only time he got close to animation was over the press. He used to refer to them as "those dreadful press chaps," probably because he was very sensitive to some of the criticism that he came in for from the media.' The relationship between chairman and captain ultimately foundered at Lord's in 1986, as the Indian visitors gave England their sixth successive Test loss (following a disastrous tour of the Caribbean) and May's long-standing dissatisfaction with Gower's relaxed style of leadership culminated on the fourth day when the curly-headed one was seen popping into the sponsors' lunchtime tent for a drink. Within minutes of the match ending, there was a new captain (Mike Gatting) in place. 'He didn't gel with our generation,' reflected Gower on May almost three decades later, 'and it created a gap in communication and attitude that could not be bridged.'

A gap in communication ... Inevitably, the old, piquant contrast with Benaud arises again – and certainly communication was never Benaud's problem, nor did he often have issues with the modern cricketer in the context of the game's rapidly changing ecology and mores. Still, the role of commentator is by definition always an easier, less exposed one than that of participant; and whatever his deficiencies in the role, May – nicely described by John Woodcock at one point in his chairmanship as 'a very private person doing a very public job' – undoubtedly felt a strong sense of duty as he endured the slings and the arrows.

Everything came to a head in the cumulative debacles of 1988, that season of four England captains against the West Indies, including for one match May's godson, Chris Cowdrey. 'A self-perpetuating oligarch' was Frank Keating's description midway through the series, before going on:

> In Alan Watkins's glorious description Mr May is a man who 'views life from behind his collar stud'. May is a City businessman and cannot afford much time to watch first-class cricket anyway, so I fancy he has probably less idea of who to put in the team than the average cricket lover who turns up with devoted regularity with his son and thermos round the midweek county grounds.
>
> Mr May says he 'takes soundings' from senior figures in the game, like managers, coaches, umpires and county captains. I have questioned many of these chaps during Mr May's disastrous stewardship, and have yet to meet one manager, coach, umpire or captain who has received so much as a single phone call from the wintery-faced mandarin, Mr May.

The mandarin, perhaps not unwillingly, stepped down in November, with England under his chairmanship having lost eleven out of eighteen series, including at home against New Zealand, Pakistan and India as well as the mighty West Indies. 'Mr Flop' was the *Sun*'s nuanced headline; Martin-Jenkins in the *Cricketer* identified extenuating factors (including injuries and the failure of the TCCB to prioritise the national team), but accepted that under May there had been poor decisions and little consistency as well as 'often a lack of strategic planning'; while Matthew Engel in *Wisden Cricket Monthly* frankly called him 'a very bad chairman, not merely unsuccessful but bad'. Damning criticisms followed, culminating in Engel comparing May as a general to the Great War's Field-Marshal Sir John French – 'dreaming of cavalry charges in an age of trench warfare'.[*]

The choice of May's successor owed almost everything to Raman Subba Row, chairman of the TCCB – a choice that, when it was announced in March 1989 three months ahead of an Ashes series, could hardly have stayed more firmly within the magic circle. Not everyone was thrilled. 'We respect Dexter as a first-class sportsman of the past,' declared Cliff Gillott, chairman of Nottinghamshire, 'but it doesn't necessarily follow that he will be the right man for the job.' While, according to another voice from the counties: 'What you are going to get from E. R. Dexter (Radley and Cambridge) is a P. B. H. May (Charterhouse

---

[*] It was during his chairmanship that May produced, in 1985, his characteristically reserved and unrevealing autobiography, *A Game Enjoyed*. On events at Old Trafford twenty-four years earlier, he reflected that 'Ted Dexter's brilliant innings of 76 ... with Raman Subba Row's support, gave us ideas above our station' – an oddly insouciant, almost self-excusing way to describe the consequence of Dexter's great knock.

and Cambridge) with better PR.' The press, making much of Dexter's 'Lord Ted' image and general hauteur, also quoted a current England player, apparently speaking for several others: 'I once walked towards Ted Dexter, with nobody else around, and said hello to him. He walked straight past me.'

Even so, among those making more welcoming noises – largely based on their entirely valid assessment that Dexter had an altogether keener, more original intelligence than May's, typified by the way he had recently pioneered the Deloittes rating system to evaluate current Test players – were not just the establishment-minded cricket writers. 'His appointment has been criticised,' noted the *Guardian*'s Mike Selvey, 'for perpetuating what some see as an insidious cabal of southerners who administer a game.' But, he went on, 'there is little to be said in support of these claims, least of all the one that he is from the May mould and a yes-man to boot. Dexter has flown often enough in the face of convention for that not to be a problem. He is most definitely his own man ...' Dexter himself spoke at the end of March to the International Luncheon Club at the Café Royal, where he set out the essence of his philosophy: 'What we want to see is heroic performances by individuals, chivalrous conduct – I believe that's important – and good, keen cricket. Yes, my goodness, we want to win but winning, I don't think, is everything.'

There was all too little winning that summer, as Allan Border's Australians, starting as underdogs, won the series by a crushing 4–0 margin, with England outplayed even in the two draws. Dexter before the start had promised continuity; but in the event he selected thirty-one players, including thirteen seamers. Mixed results followed over the next few years, including an unsuccessful Ashes campaign down under and a calamitous tour of India and Sri Lanka (with Dexter severely criticised for not taking David Gower), before in 1993 Border's men returned and again won comfortably. The nadir was at Lord's, for most of the match an embarrassingly one-sided affair. 'The England selectors and players must be pleased that we are not a revolutionary society, otherwise the sound of tumbril would have been heard in St John's Wood,' wrote Michael Parkinson in his *Daily Telegraph* column, revealing how he had found himself playing a word game in which he listed the contrasting qualities of the two sides:

Australia	England
Fire	Water
Mountain	Molehill
Rottweiler	Poodle
Brer Rabbit	Flopsy Bunny
Merv Hughes	Lord Ted
Torrent	Dribble
Team	Rabble
Dame Edna	Lord Ted

'Time Has Finally Run Out for Lord Ted' was the unsparing headline to Parkinson's piece, but after the match Dexter was still unrepentant, even flippant. 'We may be under the wrong star sign,' he told a bemused press conference. 'Venus may be in juxtaposition with the wrong planet.' Keating was among those watching and listening:

After another horrendous defeat for England yesterday, the umpteenth on the trot, Lord Ted sank into a long and tedious stream of consciousness wrapped up in woolly and patrician hauteur.

The drift was hard to get, but the gist seemed to be don't worry, chaps, everything will turn out okay, it is just a passing local difficulty and the opposition inconveniently keep knocking up five or six hundred and then bowling us out twice. Botheration and all, well the blighters can't keep it up, can they? – and then, hey presto, we will win the next four matches and regain the Ashes ...

Less than two months later – on the last day of the penultimate Test, as England succumbed to yet another heavy defeat – his resignation was announced, prompting loud applause from the Edgbaston crowd listening to their radios. Just as with May five years earlier, Martin-Jenkins made the case for the defence, but could not deny that overall it had been a poor record under Dexter's chairmanship, with six losing series and a drawn one out of the ten played; while, again just as five years earlier, Engel made a memorable comparison, observing that Dexter's manner 'increasingly came to resemble Basil Fawlty on a bad day', presumably with the cricket-loving major playing the part of the Greek chorus.

In almost every way, Mike Marqusee's 1994 book, *Anyone But England*, could hardly have felt more timely – indeed, the Indian historian (of cricket and much else) Ramachandra Guha called it 'stunningly topical'. Written by an American Marxist who had come to live in England in the 1970s and fallen in love with the game, his history-cum-polemic covered much of the same ground as Derek Birley's pioneering 1979 survey of English cricket, *The Willow Wand*, but with a significantly sharper, more political edge. English cricket in the mid-1990s, argued Marqusee, was, quite apart from the faltering fortunes of the national team, in a fundamentally bad place. Still dominated by a privately educated establishment elite; still imbued with the racist assumptions of empire; and seemingly unwilling or unable to resist the forces of greedy commercialism from wrecking the very essence – ultimately aesthetic – of the game's appeal. 'While devoting its energies to keeping women out of the Long Room at Lord's,' wryly observed Francis Wheen in his introduction to the 1998 edition, 'the MCC has done nothing to prevent rich corporations from disfiguring the arcadian scene – the boundaries, the players' shirts, the very pitches themselves – with logos and huxtering slogans. Even the umpires now wear the colours of a privatised electricity company ...'

Reaction to Marqusee was suitably divided. 'An excellent critical analysis,' reckoned the recently retired great Pakistan and Worcestershire/Sussex all-rounder Imran Khan; the product, according to Swanton, of 'a warped intelligence'; 'slightly barking' was Tim Rice's variant verdict; and David Frith's underwhelmed response that 'it all helps pass the time'. As so often, it was CM-J who spoke for the mainstream devotee. 'A very intelligent book, very cleverly written, with a lot that provokes thought,' he reflected on *Test Match Special*. 'But I am uneasy about the way that he has a go at just about everything cricketers hold sacred.'

Nineteen ninety-four was also the year of Peter May's death. Early that year he had told his son-in-law and executor, Simon Baker, that his losses as a Lloyd's Name meant that he was looking into a financial black hole. 'He borrowed to pay losses, but he had no means to continue,' recalled Baker. 'He was honest, straight, and he always met his obligations. He always believed in playing fairly. By the end, he became severely disillusioned.' May died just after Christmas, of a brain tumour, and as it happened just as England were being thrashed at Melbourne. John Major ('he played cricket and life in a way few people could match') and Richie Benaud ('he was the finest batsman I ever played against') led the tributes. 'He was also an outstanding captain,' added Benaud. 'But he was self-effacing, and was never one to push himself forward – not quite in keeping with the modern trend.' Yet in truth, about May as a captain, it was probably Arlott who had got it right in a 1986 profile: 'He was considered polite, but absolutely ruthless. It might also be said that he was unimaginative and inflexible.'

By chance, the last tourists to England in May's lifetime were the South Africans – visiting for the first time since 1965. Did he ever perhaps regret, in his dying months, that he had been on the wrong side of history over an issue which for many years during the apartheid era had divided the English cricket world? Or at the very least, did he regret that the issue had brought to a painful end his long and close friendship with David Sheppard, one of the most prominent opponents of sporting links with South Africa? In 1970, after MCC had with the utmost reluctance cancelled the South African tour following large-scale protests led by Peter Hain and eventual government intervention, Sheppard invited nineteen prominent 'cricketers and cricket lovers' to a supper intended to mend bridges. 'I don't think we have anything to talk about,' wrote May in a terse note declining to attend.

Yet perhaps one should not be too harsh. We are all products of our environment, and he was certainly a product of his: a privileged world of its own, with often little understanding of, and even less imaginative sympathy with, any worlds beyond. Nor, in terms of development of character and a rounded life, is it necessarily an advantage to be born, as May was, with a striking natural talent. Such people commonly find it hard to understand what makes the less gifted tick. But they do, in the exercise of their talent, bestow considerable pleasure; and during the 1950s, before things got complicated and old certainties eroded, the greatest English batter of the post-war era undoubtedly did that, creating imperishable memories for many thousands of cricket lovers.

Understandably, his obituarists did not dwell overmuch on the unfortunate events of 1 August 1961. But in 2002 that drama had one more outing with the publication of Alan Hill's biography of Close, including several retrospective takes – emotion recollected in less than complete tranquillity – on what had unfolded all those years before. Mainly they came from participants, but Hill also quoted Arthur Milton, insisting that Benaud going round the wicket had been 'a defensive measure', and Tom Graveney: 'It was the right-handers' fault for losing the match. They should have kicked Richie away to embarrass him. He would then have had to revert to bowling over the wicket.'

Hill's principal participant witnesses were Subba Row and Allen from the English side, Davidson from the Australian. 'Brian had to bat when Richie was bowling round the wicket into the divots,' recalled Subba Row. 'If I'd started in the same circumstances, I would have been in considerable trouble.' Even so: 'I'm not sure that Brian was correct in trying to sweep Richie. He played across the line when he had already hit one six straight. With his strength and ability that was the way to play.' Allen was also critical, though confining himself to the five timeless words, 'Play longer and play straighter'. By contrast, Davidson's views made much more enjoyable reading for Hill's still keenly interested subject. First, he laid into May for having that morning prematurely removed Allen from the attack: 'Peter should have stayed with David. I would then have had to attack like mad as I had previously done. There was no guarantee with the footmarks as a hazard that I would have been able to get away with it two overs in a row.' And then he turned to Close's controversial innings. 'If Closey had got away with a couple of clubs, Richie might well have had to change his plan,' he argued. 'It only needed a couple of overs from Brian achieving the success that I'd had [i.e. in his one-over assault on Allen earlier in the day], and the game would have gone the opposite way.' In short, seeking as he did to regain the initiative, Close had been 'playing the Australian way'.

The same year as Hill's book appeared, Nasser Hussain took his England team to Australia. Over the seven previous Ashes series, going back to 1989, Australia had won an overwhelming twenty-four Test matches compared to England's miserable six, with only one of those six wins, in 1997, being when the Ashes were still at stake. Even so, hopes were reasonably high – up to that moment when, on the morning of the first Test at Brisbane, Hussain won the toss and chose to field, a move which simultaneously stunned and divided his dressing-room. Australia finished the most humbling of days on 364 for two.

'An England captain finally calling correctly in Australia for the first time since 26 January 1995 and then doing precisely what the opposition would have liked was incredible,' Selvey despaired from the Gabba. 'This is an area of severe drought. The pitch is rock hard and cracking, the sky is blue and the humidity low. England simply had to bat first.' Why had he done it? Selvey's view was that it had been a 'defensive' move – wanting at the start of the series to postpone the evil hour when the English batters had to face the potent Australian attack – and most pundits took a similar line. Less than a month later, and still three and a half weeks before Christmas, Australia had gone 3–0 up in the series and, once again, retained the urn, seemingly almost without breaking sweat.

'Will England *ever* win the Ashes again?' wondered the *Observer*'s Jon Henderson even before that third Test; and in his pessimistic analysis he identified a crucial reason not only for the continuing failures of the national side, but also for why the game was starting to slip away from the centre of the larger sporting conversation:

Private schools, at which a tiny percentage of our children are educated, are the only place where good facilities for young cricketers are guaranteed any more. One of these schools, Radley College in Oxfordshire, has produced three players who are on the books of Middlesex, who have just gained promotion to the first division of the county championship. Good for Radley, but shouldn't Middlesex be brimming with talented players from London state schools? ...

Cricket is still a wonderful recreational sport to be played in high summer, but it is no longer a young Englishman's fantasy that one day he will play in a Test match at Lord's.

It's hardly hip to have an Andy Caddick poster adorning your bedroom wall ...

Engel for his part counselled a sense of perspective and deprecated the increasing way in which 'the fate of English cricket has become hopelessly bound up with the fate of the England team'. After all, the fact was that Australia 'palpably now have one of the greatest groups of cricketers ever assembled' (including, of course, in Shane Warne an even greater 'leggie' than Benaud); and accordingly, 'allowing the marvellous institution of English cricket to wither because the national team happens to be inferior to one other country's team is absurd. It is like losing a lifetime's savings by putting the lot into Enron shares. Sports, like investors, need a balanced portfolio to survive.'

Then came 2005: at the very least, among the handful of most enthralling Ashes series, as at last the urn changed hands again. Heartbeat of the English team was Andrew Flintoff, displaying – like Ian Botham back in 1981, that other instantly semi-mythical year – the quintessential 'Australian' qualities of aggression and fearlessness. So, too, England's South African import, Kevin Pietersen, who after lunch on the final day at The Oval took on Brett Lee in much the same game-changing way that Burge had taken on Trueman at Headingley in 1964. As it happened, that climactic, nerve-wrecking Monday was Benaud's last day behind a microphone on an English cricket ground – prompting the packed crowd to rise as one when the PA system reminded them of the fact. It was the end, for British viewers anyway, of four decades of a wholly distinctive commentary style: dry, laconic, penetrating, unsentimental, sometimes not even using a word when one would do. The finish of his last stint coincided with Pietersen's dismissal. 'Whereupon,' reported *The Times*'s Ivo Tennant, 'one of the greatest and most knowledgeable of all sports commentators moved to the back of the Channel 4 box and sat impassively next to a case of Veuve Clicquot champagne presented to him by the ECB. There was nothing misty-eyed about his countenance or tremulous about that celebrated lower lip.'

The final day's play was also the end of terrestrial TV coverage of English Test cricket for many years – perhaps for ever – following the spectacularly short-sighted decision of the ECB (chairman of marketing: the entrepreneur Giles Clarke) to take Sky's millions. Just when cricket, in the course of five riveting, larger-than-life matches, had captured the nation's heart, the timing could not have been worse; and the sorry process of the game's marginalisation, already under way for the previous decade or so, would now only speed up.

11

Old Cricketers Leave the Crease

For Ashes aficionados, there was, taken as a whole, something unsatisfying about the nine series between 2006 and 2022: too many one-sided series; and even within the more competitive series, too many one-sided matches. Home advantage came to matter more than ever, with Andrew Strauss's England, in 2010–11, the only side to win an away series. Overall, there were four series wins apiece; but strikingly, whereas England won thirteen Tests in the course of the nine series, Australia won twenty-four – not far short of double, and a discrepancy largely caused by England's almost uniformly dismal performances (apart from 2010–11) down under.

An ominous sign that Ashes contests were no longer gripping the English public as a whole came in late 2015 when, only months after Joe Root's outstanding batting had played a large part in enabling England to regain the urn, nominations were announced for BBC Sports Personality of the Year: twelve men and women from nine different sports – but none of them cricket. It felt a fitting tenth-anniversary reminder of the dire consequences of the loss of terrestrial TV coverage. But at least, in these years up to 2022, there was one day when the nation *was* gripped and, for an afternoon, all the clocks stopped. It came at Headingley in August 2019, as Ben Stokes played one of the very greatest of Ashes innings, and Jack Leach held firm at the other end, with England squeaking home by one wicket.

It was an illusion, of course; but just for a moment, coming hard on the heels of the remarkable World Cup final at Lord's, cricket seemed once again the national game. Stokes had also been to the fore in that day's intense drama; and in summer 2022, after dispiriting English tours of Australia and the West Indies under Root's captaincy, he took over the reins of the Test team, with Brendon McCullum as coach. Stokes had been brought up in New Zealand until the age of twelve; McCullum was the former New Zealand captain who through his free-spirited approach had revolutionised his country's international fortunes; and right from the start, it was as if they had been reading Jack Fingleton's stirring words in *Wisden* after the historic Brisbane tie about how 'there is as much virtue in losing as in winning if the game has been played honourably, with courage, with character and with challenge'. Together they now brought to England's cricket a breath of fresh air – confident, aggressive, allowing players in a mutually supportive team atmosphere to express themselves without fear of failure, a willingness indeed to accept Benaud-style that defeat could sometimes be the price of attempting victory – which was not just exciting to watch, but also highly successful. By June 2023 and the eve of a new Ashes series, they had won eleven out of thirteen Tests, with one of the two losses being by a single run at Wellington. The series itself was the most keenly anticipated since 2005, though with patriotic fervour tempered by a consensus among the pundits that so-called 'Bazball' would be facing, by some way, its severest challenge, especially given that Australia were (after defeating India at The Oval) the newly installed world champions of Test cricket.

Neither set of cricketers disappointed, as five compelling contests unfolded. At Edgbaston, on a wretchedly lifeless wicket in a match in which England were for the most part ahead, the Australian tail held its nerve on the final afternoon, as the tourists got home by two wickets; at Lord's – where the controversial stumping of Jonny Bairstow by wicketkeeper Alex Carey generated arguably more heat than light about 'the spirit of cricket' – Australia deservedly won, by 43 runs, despite the last-day heroics of Stokes; at Headingley, it was the turn of the English lower order to hold its nerve, as the home team won, again deservedly, by three wickets; at Old Trafford, where the England batters (led by Zak Crawley) thrillingly and memorably put a quality attack to the sword, it needed rain to rescue Australia, thereby enabling them to retain the Ashes; and at The Oval, another gripping encounter saw England come out on top by 49 runs, to give an overall series score of 2–2. Named as England's player of the series was the understated, often undervalued, Chris Woakes: a yeoman cricketer, one of the game's Caleb Garths, and a choice which surely would have pleased Arlott.

Throughout it all, a running theme was the range of views – from highly enthusiastic to distinctly sceptical – about the ultimate merits of the fast-scoring and inherently more risky English approach, an approach often in stark, role-reversing contrast to the essentially conservative tactics of Australia under Pat Cummins's captaincy. Inevitably it was an approach which produced moments of considerable frustration for home supporters, certainly those of a traditional cast of mind. Perhaps none more so than on the penultimate morning at Edgbaston, in retrospect the pivotal Test, the one where England 'should' at the least have come out with a draw if they were going to reclaim the Ashes. Root – wonderful batter, admirable cricketer and man – was well set in the forties, looking entirely untroubled; at which point he ran down the wicket to Nathan Lyon, made an ugly heave to leg, missed the ball and was stumped, for the first time in his Test career. The obvious comparison was with Australia's Usman Khawaja, who in both innings batted long and played with the utmost focus and self-discipline: in other words, cricket's eternal verities writ large, and in this case making the decisive difference.

Yet overall we are with Mike Atherton, when on the eve of the final Test he looked back on a series so sharply 'splitting opinion between those who see sport as a glory game, with entertainment its primary purpose, and those who take a more practical, utilitarian view'. 'It doesn't', he argued in *The Times*, 'have to be one or the other and it seems to me to be entirely laudable that England are trying to weave a precious, if difficult, route that touches both.' And as he ended his piece: 'Attempting to win in style – what could be a more admirable objective than that?'

The series had been compressed into barely six weeks between mid-June and late July – a reflection of how utterly different the shape of the English cricket season had become by comparison with the traditional rhythms of summer familiar to generations of cricket followers. The county championship was now largely squeezed into the early and late parts of the season (or, in Engel's chilly words, 'banished to the coat-and-Thermos-flask days of April and September'); the Vitality Blast, the One-Day Cup, and, of course, The Hundred, most sharply divisive of all competitions, all vied for space; the five Ashes Tests were but part of the extensive international programme; and, in general, it could almost seem a lottery what sort of match was going to start when. The season had once had a reassuring certainty about it, almost a stateliness, as the days of the calendar inexorably passed: in 2023, as its contribution to the modern world's unbearable lightness of being, not so much. In fact, little if anything felt certain any more in cricket at large.

'A bewildering act of self-harm,' which risked causing the game's structures to 'implode', was how Lawrence Booth, in his editor's notes to the 2023 *Wisden*, described the proliferation of T20 franchise competitions. 'Test cricket has become jetsam, tossed overboard to make room for simpler cargo,' he wrote. 'The national boards have handed the keys to the self-interested few, and lost control of players they nurtured. The Indian franchises have been allowed to take over the house, one T20 knees-up at a time.' Could anything be done? 'A plea for balance and moderation – including an unrapacious IPL, a better spread of commitments, and the sense that cricket's big'uns will look after the little'uns – no doubt sounds idealistic,' accepted Booth. 'Yet', he concluded, 'it may be the only way to avoid implosion.'

More parochially, what did not help the outlook was how by this time the ECB's great cry, 'Cricket is a sport for all' (as proclaimed in its mission statement, *Inspiring Generations*), was all too liable to raise a hollow laugh. The number of people in the UK playing cricket at least once a month fell sharply from 365,000 in 2016 to 229,000 in 2021, a fall not attributable solely to the pandemic; around 30 per cent of recreational cricket players by this time were of South Asian origin, as compared to 4 per cent of those playing first-class cricket; and the dominance of the privately educated had quite possibly never been so great. 'I think that in the Middlesex sides of which I was a member, only Mike Brearley had a public school background,' recalled Mike Selvey shortly before the 2023 season. 'The sale of school playing fields in the 1980s began the slide away from this equal opportunity. Today, almost half of professional cricketers have come through private education despite only 7 per cent of the school population attending such establishments.' In short, and he is surely broadly right even allowing for sports scholarships at private schools, 'the game has reverted to one of privilege'.*

Such was also broadly the argument of Duncan Stone, whose path-breaking 2022 book, *Different Class: The Untold Story of English Cricket*, examined in detail the history of recreational cricket, a largely class-based analysis founded on extensive primary research. 'Cricket's future as a sport with broad popular appeal,' he predicted on his final page, 'will remain in doubt unless the game better understands its own past and, crucially, begins to reflect the nation that

---

*Ironically, it was during the May/Dexter era of chairing the selectors that England cricket teams were probably more socially and ethnically diverse, not to mention diverse by national background, than they had been before or would be later. As for the larger story, not just relating to cricket, of how the privately educated have in recent decades recovered from an apparent decline in their influence, and instead achieved a seemingly ever-greater degree of dominance in many walks of national life, see: Francis Green and David Kynaston, *Engines of Privilege: Britain's Private School Problem* (2019).

is England today.' Put another way, cricket's only realistic long-term way to go was genuinely towards inclusivity, with any alternative a slow but sure route to semi-oblivion. This must be the case; and it was disappointing that few of the reviews did anything like justice to the book's mix of scholarly originality and urgent concerns. Yet perhaps it was not so surprising – for this was also the time when the MCC, after making a welcome commitment to end the annual, hugely symbolic Eton v Harrow fixture at Lord's, then in early 2023 backed down in the face of strong internal opposition. It was a retreat which made a sad mockery of all the sterling outreach work that the MCC Foundation had done since the 1990s; and it sent a dreadful signal about what the club really stood for, making it impossible to claim with any conviction that the MCC was not, deep down, still motivated by considerations of class. For one of us, a member since 1970 and in his naivety starting to travel hopefully about where the club was heading, it felt a peculiarly dismal, shameful moment.

Full chapter and verse for much of this came with the publication in June 2023 of the 317-page report of the Independent Commission for Equity in Cricket – a report commissioned, to its credit, by the ECB. It was a major, highly detailed piece of work, involving evidence from well over 4,000 players, coaches, administrators and fans. Its key findings included that racism remained 'a serious issue', continuing 'to shape the experience of, and opportunities for, many in the game'; that 'the ethnicity of male and female players at professional level does not reflect the ethnicity of the adult recreational playing base, nor the wider population of England and Wales'; that 'women are not even nearly on an equal footing with men within the sport today'; that there still seemed to exist 'a widespread culture of sexism and misogyny'; and that 'a prevalence of elitism and class-based discrimination' was driven not only by 'the lack of access to cricket in state schools', but also by 'the way in which the talent pathway is structurally bound up with private schools'.

Given that for many years the question of social class – as opposed to ethnicity or gender – had often been strangely absent from wider discussions about diversity and inclusivity in British society at large, this report was notable for giving class its due weight, including a refreshing willingness to call out the historic, still flourishing, still lavishly funded prime engines of privilege. 'Although we started our work with a general understanding of the dominance of private schools in the talent pathway, we were nevertheless shocked by the starkness of the class divide,' reflected the commission – two days before England took the field at Lord's against Australia with nine of the (all-white) team having benefited from private education. 'The lack of cricket provision in state schools, the way the pathway is structurally bound up with private schools, and the apparent reluctance for cricket to move away from this as a model: these issues present significant barriers ...' So they did to a significant degree back in the 1960s; so they do even more in the 2020s; and sadly, it is hard to feel any great optimism that it will be all that different in the 2080s.

*

Inevitably, most of the participants in our match were beyond caring one way or the other. By the time of the 2023 iteration of the Ashes, sixty-two years on, only one of the England team was still alive, compared – perhaps tellingly – with four of Australia's. In reverse batting order, 'Garth' McKenzie had post-1961 become for a time the youngest bowler to reach 100 Test wickets, before later in his career doing sterling service for Leicestershire; Neil Harvey, no unqualified admirer of the modern cricketer ('they play on flat wickets all the time and they grizzle if the ball does a little bit off the pitch'), was not only one of the survivors of Old Trafford, but, following the death of Arthur Morris in 2015, the last of the 1948 'invincibles' left standing; Bobby Simpson had been Australia's coach in the years 1986–96, when they had been transformed from no-hopers into world conquerors; and Bill Lawry, that dour and immovable limpet at the crease, had spent forty-five excitable, patriotic, endearing years in the TV commentary box.

Of the seven departed souls, Wally Grout (1968) and Ken Mackay (1982) had long gone, with 'Slasher' in his *Times* obituary rubbing shoulders alongside Marie Rambert and King Khalid of Saudi Arabia, a disparate trio possibly beyond even the capacity of a latter-day John Buchan to find connections between; Peter Burge had died in 2001, only seven years after being the match referee at Lord's and having a famous run-in with England captain Mike Atherton in what became known as The Dirt-In-The-Pocket Affair; Norman O'Neill died in 2008, four decades after the end of a career which had ultimately flattered to deceive but still left golden memories; Richie Benaud, at the age of eighty-four, died in April 2015; six and a half years later, in November 2021, he was followed by his single most important player, Alan Davidson, reckoned by one obituarist (Peter Mason) as, with the possible exception of Wasim Akram, 'the greatest left-arm pace bowler in the game's history'; and Brian Booth, in Swanton's words that 'blamelessly self-effacing' person and cricketer, died in April 2023, having spent many years as a schoolmaster and Anglican lay preacher, while creating the odd wave as he laid into Steve Waugh's Australian team for its systematic sledging tactics.

As with Bradman fourteen years earlier, and Shane Warne seven years later, Benaud's passing seemed like a huge moment. 'Everyone loved Richie, he was above the prime minister in Australia,' said Warne at the time, and he was right: it was a major national event, even though Benaud's family, in accord with Richie's wishes, followed the Don's example and declined a state funeral. Bradman, Benaud, Warne: three Australian deaths in barely twenty years that transcended cricket and moved millions. Can one – with perhaps W. G. Grace's death in 1915 as the sole exception, albeit overshadowed by the war – think of any comparable English examples in the entire history of the game? It is a striking comparison between the two countries and what cricket means to them.

England's living survivor in 2023 was Raman Subba Row, subject of Douglas Miller's careful 2017 biography – its subtitle, *Cricket Visionary*, a nod to Subba Row's key role (at Surrey, at the MCC, at the TCCB) in furthering and consolidating the marriage between cricket and the forces of commercialism, whether for good (as in his biographer's view) or for ill. As for the other ten old cricketers, it was now forty-two years since the first had left the crease: Ken Barrington, suddenly in Barbados in March 1981, while serving as an inspirational assistant manager on the England tour captained by Botham. 'Unflinching bat, kindest of men' was the title of Arlott's tribute, ending with a lovely, very human touch: 'Many a night he has gone home late and oily-fingered from a cricket match because he stayed on to repair another player's broken-down motor car and then brushed aside all thanks with "Forget it, mate."'

Then came May in 1994, followed by the three quick men. First, in 2000, was Lancashire's modest, unassuming, deadly accurate 'Gentleman George', aka 'the Whippet' or 'the Greyhound'. 'Brian Statham was our idol for all the right reasons that great sportsmen should become heroes,' recalled Colin Shindler, who had grown up watching him at Old Trafford. 'He combined outstanding achievement with an uncomplaining willingness to bowl all day uphill into the wind so that Tyson and Trueman could steal the headlines. Whether it was on the flat pitches of the West Indies and Australia or on a green top at Chesterfield, Brian Statham bowled his heart out for his country and his county and we loved him for it.' Then, four years later, Jack Flavell, who had only played twice for England after 1961 but had been pivotal to Worcestershire in 1964 winning the county championship for the first time and then retaining it the following year. Finally, in 2006, Fred Trueman. Those long years on *Test Match Special*, becoming almost a parody of himself as the growling, old-timer Yorkshireman unable to see any good in the modern game, had sorely tried the patience of listeners and done him few favours; but his death reminded all older cricket followers what a wonderful, larger-than-life player he had been – someone fully deserving of the fine, admirably three-dimensional biography that Chris Waters would produce in 2011, complete with Ian McMillan's affectionate poem ('Remember the hair/Flopping over the face/Before the long run-up …').

An eight-year gap ensued before another flurry: in May 2014, the side's off-spinner, David Allen, whose most famous moment in Test cricket had come at Lord's in 1963 as he managed to fend off the last two balls from Wes Hall and secure an honourable draw;* later in 2014, Subba Row's opening partner, Geoff Pullar, who among other business activities during a cheerful post-cricket life of fluctuating financial fortunes had run fish and chip shops near Wigan and at Chorlton-cum-Hardy; and in September 2015, five months after Benaud's death and at the same age, Brian Close. 'Farewell to Close, the Bravest of All' was *The Times*'s headline, with Ray Illingworth recalling his fearlessness at short leg: 'This was in the days before players were like Michelin men with all their protection. It takes them ten minutes to get ready nowadays. Closey just wore a box, if anything at all.' Or as Eric Morecambe had once put it, the return of summer was signalled each year by 'the sound of leather on Brian Close'. But perhaps the tribute he would most have appreciated came from Ian Botham, fondly remembering him from apprentice Somerset days in the mid-1970s as 'the best captain a young player could ever have wished for'.

Three years later, in July 2018, after watching a day's play at Lord's, it was the turn of the elegant gloveman John Murray, who according to many judges should have made far more than his twenty-one Test appearances. That was certainly the

---

*If that loomed large in his memories after his playing career had ended, so too did the final day at Old Trafford 1961, including the fulcrum moment of May's failed 'sweep' to Benaud. 'Like all the university boys he didn't lap,' Allen told Stephen Chalke in 2009. 'Nobody had ever bowled like that at him. He didn't even get down on one knee.'

view of Christopher Sandford, who not long after Murray's death brought out a sympathetic biography, *Keeper of Style*, informed by lengthy conversations with him. These touched at one point on the 1961 Old Trafford Test and included an intriguing revelation. Australia may have won and thereby retained the Ashes; but, wrote Sandford on the basis of what his subject had told him, 'there was at least some consolation for the home team during their six-night residency at the nearby Mere Country Club, particularly for those players who took a more relaxed view of their wedding vows than Murray himself did.' No names, no pack drill; but again the contrast was with the opposition, staying in the city centre and concentrating on the business in hand.

The last of the English departed was Ted Dexter, in August 2021, a year after the publication of his enjoyably rounded autobiography, *85 Not Out*, with all royalties donated to the MCC Foundation. This octogenarian, whose life had begun in Italy and had encountered its fair share of brickbats as well as bouquets, was now playing for stumps in the rather incongruous surroundings of less than glamorous Wolverhampton. In his touching last page, he reflected on how similar tastes – in films ('not too violent, and certainly not spooky'), in music ('the old ballads with the clever, subtle lyrics'), in food ('from Indian curries to French and Italian cuisine and of course, good old Rosbife') – contributed to continuing harmony with Susan, his wife for sixty-one years. Finally, added Dexter with words that, to put it mildly, very few former England captains would conceivably have written, 'once our sex lives inevitably though sadly came to an end, we agreed, instead, always to have a proper *hug* before going to bed. I recommend it.'

*

Both of us have sometimes enjoyed and relished the literature of cricket as much as cricket itself. So we end with two poets: one taking the bigger view; the other, rather less so. First, Alan Ross's short poem 'Watching Benaud Bowl', probably written not long after Old Trafford and first anthologised in 1964. Ross himself may have keenly felt England's loss that Tuesday afternoon; but his poem, a tribute to cricket's most difficult and tantalising art, transcends such prosaic concerns:

> Leg-spinners pose problems much like love,
> Requiring commitment, the taking of a chance.
> Half-way deludes; the bold advance.
>
> Right back, there's time to watch
> Developments, though maybe too late.
> It's not spectacular, but can conciliate.
>
> Instinctively romantics move towards,
> Preventing complexities by their embrace,
> Batsman and lover embarked as overlords.

Our other poet, on 3 August 1961, is not so metaphysical. 'Certainly an exasperating affair,' Philip Larkin laments in a letter to Monica Jones about the recent Test – in essence, he goes on, 'the same old story: they can do it, we can't.' Not always perhaps, not always; but sadly, during our lifetimes, all too often.

Three Puzzles

WHAT HAPPENED AT SATURDAY TEATIME?

'At tea, when the score of 361 for seven justified it, I did tell
Ken Barrington to open up,' Peter May next day informed
the *Daily Express*'s Frank Rostron about the change of
batting tactics which had led to England's last three wickets
falling after tea so precipitately – and almost suicidally – to
the less than threatening leg-breaks of Bobby Simpson. But
was it purely May's decision? Not according to Ted Dexter,
who in his autobiography five years later recalled in highly
critical fashion how Walter Robins – dynamic amateur all-
rounder for Middlesex between the wars, a former and
future Test selector, and a man of strong opinions – had,
uninvited, come into the England dressing-room at the
tea interval and 'insisted that we should get on with it'.
A quarter of a century later, Barrington's biographer, Mark
Peel, identified Gubby Allen as the person who had
'entered the dressing-room and ordered an acceleration in
the run-rate'. But Dexter, in his 2020 second autobiography,
remained adamant it was Robins, apparently the worse for

wear after finding a drinking companion for the afternoon session: 'He stormed into the dressing room to shout at Barrington, telling him to "Get a bloody move on!"' One can only guess; but it is entirely plausible that May's main wish, in giving his instructions to Barrington (and implicitly the others), was to placate Robins – perhaps even to get him out of the room. Either way, as Dexter reflected ruefully almost sixty years after the event, 'wickets fell quickly, offering Australia a squeak of a chance [i.e. of victory] they should never have had'.

WHOSE FOOTMARKS?

It soon became the conventional wisdom, especially following Jack Fingleton's account in the 1962 *Wisden*, that it was Freddie Trueman who had been largely responsible for the footmarks at the Warwick Road end that Richie Benaud had so skilfully and resourcefully exploited on the final afternoon. But is that right? After all, we know that Trueman bowled at least some of his overs (including the match's opening over) from the other end; while in 1981 his fellow Yorkshireman C. D. Clark, in his book *The Test Match Career of Freddie Trueman*, not only made the point that Trueman had bowled from both ends, but argued that Brian Statham, Jack Flavell and Dexter all deserved a share of the blame. Furthermore: 'At least one leading ex-England cricketer, who cannot be named, has every reason for believing that it was, in fact, Dexter who was the main culprit.' And Clark went on: 'It is true to a degree that a bowler of Dexter's height, and with his action, would bring his front foot down from a greater height than any of the other bowlers.' As it happens, for all the whiff of special pleading, the recent posting on YouTube of selected highlights from the match has added a sliver of circumstantial detail in favour of this revisionist thesis. It comes at 30.13, as Dexter, having completed on the Monday an over at the Warwick Road end, appears to take a meaningful look at the footmarks. But Trueman it was who took the rap – as so often, it is tempting to add, with matters of north and south.

CLOSE FLYING SOLO?

Our view of Brian Close's much-maligned innings on that fateful Tuesday is reasonably straightforward. After the fall in rapid succession of Dexter and May, he was perfectly entitled to try to knock Benaud off his length and score some quick runs, maybe even induce Benaud to take himself off; but when it became clear that his policy of hitting with the spin from out of the rough was not working – as clearly it wasn't – then he should have switched to a Plan B, which he either did not have or was unwilling to do. At the moment of his dismissal, Swanton's tone of resigned-cum-exasperated inevitability was a justified one. But was Close batting under orders? His captain was asked at the end of the match if he had given him any special instructions. 'No,' May replied to Rostron, 'I merely told him [as they crossed after May's second-ball duck?] to play his natural game.' Do we know anything else? One of our Old Trafford eyewitnesses has related to us how, a few weeks later at a benefit match in Worcestershire, he met Flavell, who on being asked said that May had told Close that he was indeed to try to hit Benaud off his length. Yet according to another of our eyewitnesses, meeting Close not long before his death and asking him about his Old Trafford innings, 'nobody told me what to do' (Close's own words). Which version of events to believe?

A Note on Sources

Our two key sources have been the contemporary press and YouTube, with the latter fortunately posting some fifty-five minutes of Old Trafford highlights not long before we started work on this book. Particularly helpful accounts of the match are the relevant chapter in Richie Benaud's *A Tale of Two Tests* (1962) and Abishek Mukherjee's 2017 online essay, 'Ashes 1961: Richie Benaud routs England at Old Trafford; Australia retain the urn'; while Stephen Chalke's conversation with a rueful David Allen almost half a century later (*Wisden Cricketer*, September 2009) features some illuminating as well as evocative memories about the last day. Likewise evocative, and recalling with wry affection his childhood experience of watching that final day on TV, is John Taylor's essay which appeared in the *Journal of the Cricket Society* (autumn 2023) as our book was being copyedited. Gideon Haigh's *The Summer Game* (1997) includes a typically accomplished chapter on the 1961 tour, full of interesting detail from an Australian perspective. This was still the era of the tour book, and in addition to Brian Booth's tour diary – Brian Booth and Ronald Cardwell,

On Tour with Brian Booth: England 1961 (2009) – we were grateful to have at our disposal these six accounts:

John Arlott, *The Australian Challenge: John Arlott's Cricket Journal – 4* (1961)
Bill Bowes, *Aussies and Ashes* (1961)
Charles Fortune, *The Australians in England, 1961* (1961)
Jim Laker, *The Australian Tour of 1961* (1961)
Ray Lindwall, *The Challenging Tests* (1961)
R. A. Roberts, *The Fight for the Ashes, 1961* (1961)

There aren't biographies and/or autobiographies for all the Old Trafford participants; but happily enough there are for most, with these the ones with significant material for us (and apologies for any inadvertent omissions):

Ken Barrington, *Running into Hundreds* (1963)
Mark Peel, *England Expects: A Biography of Ken Barrington* (1992)
A. G. Moyes, *Benaud* (1962)
Mark Browning, *Richie Benaud: Cricketer, Captain, Guru* (1996)
Richie Benaud, *Anything But … An Autobiography* (1998)
Richie Benaud, *Over But Not Out* (2010)
Brian Matthews, *Benaud: An Appreciation* (2016)
Brian Booth, *Booth to Bat: An Autobiography* (1983)
Brian Close, *I Don't Bruise Easily* (1978)
Alan Hill, *Brian Close: Cricket's Lionheart* (2002)
Alan Davidson, *Fifteen Paces* (1963)
Ted Dexter, *Ted Dexter Declares* (1966)
Derek Lodge, *The Test Match Career of Ted Dexter* (1989)

Alan Lee, *Lord Ted: The Dexter Enigma* (1995)

Ted Dexter, *85 Not Out* (2020)

Wally Grout, *My Country's 'Keeper* (1965)

Ashley Mallett, *Neil Harvey: The Last Invincible* (2021)

Bill Lawry, *Run-Digger* (1966)

Bill Lawry, *Chasing a Century* (2018)

Peter May, *A Game Enjoyed: An Autobiography* (1985)

Alan Hill, *Peter May: A Biography* (1996)

Ed Jaggard, *Garth: The Story of Graham McKenzie* (1993)

Christopher Sandford, *Keeper of Style: John Murray: The King of Lord's* (2019)

Norman O'Neill, *Ins and Outs* (1964)

Bobby Simpson, *Captain's Story* (1966)

Douglas Miller, *Raman Subba Row: Cricket Visionary* (2017)

John Arlott, *Fred: Portrait of a Fast Bowler* (1971)

Chris Waters, *Fred Trueman: The Authorised Biography* (2011)

Many other books were helpful, including:

John Arlott, *Australian Test Journal: A Diary of the Test Matches Australia v. England, 1954–55* (1955)

Richie Benaud, *Richie Benaud's Way of Cricket* (1961)

Derek Birley, *The Willow Wand: Some Cricket Myths Explored* (1979)

Andrew Bradstock, *David Sheppard: Batting for the Poor* (2019)

Michael Burns, *Seven Summers: Surrey Making History in the 1950s* (2022)

Neville Cardus, *Cardus on the Ashes* (1989)

Mike Carey, *Les Jackson: A Derbyshire Legend* (1997)

Stephen Chalke, *Micky Stewart and the Changing Face of Cricket* (2012)

Stephen Chalke, *Summer's Crown: The Story of Cricket's County Championship* (2015)

Colin Cowdrey, *M.C.C.: The Autobiography of a Cricketer* (1976)

Jack Fingleton, *Four Chukkas to Australia: The 1958–59 M.C.C. Tour of Australia* (1959)

Guy Fraser-Simpson, *Cricket at the Crossroads: Class, Colour and Controversy, from 1967 to 1977* (2012)

Gideon Haigh, *On the Ashes* (2023)

Tony Lewis, *Double Century: The Story of MCC and Cricket* (1987)

Mike Marqusee, *Anyone But England: An Outsider Looks at English Cricket* (1994)

Michael Marshall, *Gentlemen & Players: Conversations with Cricketers* (1987)

Geoffrey Moorhouse, *The Best-Loved Game: One Summer of English Cricket* (1979)

Amol Rajan, *Twirlymen: The Unlikely History of Cricket's Greatest Spin Bowlers* (2011)

Simon Raven, *Shadows on the Grass* (1982)

Alan Ross, *Australia 55: A Journal of the M.C.C. Tour* (1955)

Alan Ross, *Cape Summer and the Australians in England* (1957)

Alan Ross, *Through the Caribbean: England in the West Indies, 1960* (1960)

Alan Ross (ed.), *The Cricketer's Companion* (1960)

Alan Ross, *Australia 63* (1963)

Duncan Stone, *Different Class: The Untold Story of English Cricket* (2022)

E. W. Swanton, *Gubby Allen: Man of Cricket* (1985)

Frank 'Typhoon' Tyson, *In the Eye of the Typhoon: Recollections of the M.C.C. tour of Australia 1954/55* (2004)

John Waite, *Perchance to Bowl: Test Cricket Today* (1961)

Simon Wilde, *England: The Biography: The Story of English Cricket, 1877–2018* (2018)

Charles Williams, *Gentlemen & Players: The Death of Amateurism in Cricket* (2012)

John L. Williams, *CLR James: A Life Beyond the Boundaries* (2022)

Finally, some specific references:

Cardus on Benaud in the nets: *Manchester Guardian*, 21 June 1956. Insole on May's captaincy: 1995 *Wisden*. Larkin on Beckett/Benaud: David Kynaston, *A Shake of the Dice: Modernity Britain, 1959–62* (2014). Eliot's lecture: *Yorkshire Post*, 3 July 1961; for the official (probably revised) version, see T. S. Eliot, *To Criticize the Critic: and other writings* (1965). Grout's question for Cowdrey: Haigh, *Ashes*. Trueman's action: Arlott, *Fred*. Allen, Gloucestershire and his 1959 season: Stephen Chalke, *The Way It Was: Glimpses of English Cricket's Past* (2008). Hutton's question for Keating: *Guardian*, 30 June 1997. Benaud and get-well card: *Daily Telegraph*, 5 August 1961 (letter from N. A. Thompson). Selbourne diary quote: David Selbourne, *A Doctor's Life: The Diaries of Hugh Selbourne M.D., 1960–63* (1989). Trueman declining to bowl: Sandford, *Keeper*. Benaud's blue suede shoes: *Times*, 1 August 1961 (John Woodcock). Benaud/Lindwall conversation: *Daily Herald*, 2 August 1961. Yardley on

Close: recollection of Kit Wright. Illingworth on southern bias: Huw Turbervill, 'Ashes Chronicles – Part 5', *Cricketer* online, November 2021. Wheen on James: foreword to 1998 edition of Marqusee. Rhodes on James: *Catalyst*, summer 2022. Keating on Dexter's blade: *Guardian*, 20 May 2005. Dexter at Radley: Harry Thompson, *Peter Cook: A Biography* (1997). Benaud on Packer: *Guardian*, 6 August 1977. Haigh on WSC's legacy: 2016 *Wisden*. May sacking Fletcher: *The Times*, 9 March 1995 (Alan Lee). Berry on May's inflexibility: *Observer*, 27 November 1988. May blocking Knott: Wilde, *England: The Biography*. Gower on May: David Gower, *Gower: The Autobiography* (1992), *An Endangered Species* (2013). Woodcock on May: *The Times*, 4 August 1988. Keating on May: *Guardian*, 6 July 1988. Khan, Rice and Martin-Jenkins on Marqusee: quoted in 2005 paperback edition. Frith on Marqusee: *Wisden Cricket Monthly*, August 1994. May's losses: *Mail on Sunday*, 13 August 1995. Engel on the county championship: *New Statesman*, 12 May 2023. Selvey on cricket and class: *Cricketer*, March 2023. Shindler on Statham: *Guardian*, 17 June 2000. Ross on leg-spinners and love: Jack Pollard (ed.), *Six and Out: The Legend of Australian Cricket* (1964). Larkin on Old Trafford Test: Kynaston, *Shake of the Dice*.

Acknowledgements

We are grateful to the following for allowing us to reproduce copyright material: Tim Arlott (John Arlott, *The Australian Challenge*); Christopher Sandford (*Keeper of Style*); Jane Ewart (Gavin Ewart, 'The Cricketers' Arms'); Jane Rye (Alan Ross, 'Watching Benaud Bowl'); and Ian McMillan ('Remembering Fred').

Three of the living participants kindly spoke to us about the match: Bill Lawry; Graham McKenzie; and Raman Subba Row (the meeting generously arranged by Norman Parks). We are also grateful for the recollections of four eye-witnesses: Charles Barr; Victor Black; Barry Rickson; and Geoffrey Shindler. Introductions to the last three were kindly provided by Malcolm Lorimer. Kit Wright recalled listening to the radio commentary on the final afternoon; John Kemp-Welch remembered watching those dramatic events unfold on the only television at Cazenove & Co at 12 Tokenhouse Yard in the City of London; and a particularly distinctive memory of the same Tuesday afternoon belongs to Tim Elliott. 'Our family holiday was in South Cornwall, and Carne Beach the exact location,' he wrote to one of us. 'Mum and Dad quite liked cricket and were fascinated by the happenings in the

Old Trafford Test. Another family about 100 yards along the beach had a transistor radio tuned into the cricket from Manchester, and my elder son role (I was nearly eight) was to wander along every 15 minutes or so and ask the score which was then dutifully relayed back to my parents.' 'That was when', he added, 'I got hooked onto cricket for life.'

We owe a considerable debt to those who kindly read all or part of the draft and offered constructive suggestions: Charles Barr; Mike Brearley; Mike Burns; Ramachandra Guha; Gideon Haigh; Simon Rae; Jamie Ricketts; and John Taylor. Responsibility for the final text remains, of course, ours.

In addition, we are grateful to Stephen Chalke for sending us a transcript of his 2009 conversation with David Allen; to Sancintya Mohini Simpson and Bridget Simpson for locating contemporary Australian newspaper accounts of the Old Trafford match; to Alan Rees at the congenial as well as excellent MCC Library at Lord's; to John McKenzie for supplying books from the world's best cricket bookshop; to Amanda Howard (Superscript Editorial Services) for transcribing tapes; to Richard Collins for copy-editing; to Vicki Robinson for compiling the index; to Catherine Best, for reading the proofs; to our agent Georgia Garrett and her assistant Honor Spreckley; and, at Bloomsbury, to our editor Ian Marshall, as well as his colleagues Francisco Vilhena, Shanika Hyslop and Brittani Davies.

Our friendship began at school in 1968. There, we were fortunate to encounter Michael Curtis, a gifted English and History teacher whose enthusiasm was matched by his demanding of the highest standards. Over half a century on, we remain indebted.

New Malden and Wellington, January 2024

Image Credits

Benaud and May shake hands: Keystone/Getty Images; Benaud and other Australian cricketers with Birmingham schoolboys: Trinity Mirror/Mirrorpix/Alamy; MCC fixture list: Armoret Tanner Collection/Alamy; May hitting out: Dennis Oulds/Central Press/Getty Images; Subba Row dropping Lawry: Trinity Mirror/Mirrorpix/Alamy; Benaud Bowling round the wicket: V. Wright/Central Press/Getty Images; Benaud getting Dexter caught behind: Dennis Oulds/Central Press/Getty Images; Simpson catching Allen: Dennis Oulds/Central Press/Hulton Archive/Getty Images; Davidson bowling Statham to win the match: Trinity Mirror/Mirrorpix/Alamy; Benaud's moment: Central Press/Getty Images; Peter May in 1981: Patrick Eagar/Popperfoto/Getty Images; Benaud wig tribute: Mark Evans/Getty Images.

Index

A Note on the Type

The text of this book is set in Linotype Stempel Garamond, a version of Garamond adapted and first used by the Stempel foundry in 1924. It is one of several versions of Garamond based on the designs of Claude Garamond. It is thought that Garamond based his font on Bembo, cut in 1495 by Francesco Griffo in collaboration with the Italian printer Aldus Manutius. Garamond types were first used in books printed in Paris around 1532. Many of the present-day versions of this type are based on the *Typi Academiae* of Jean Jannon cut in Sedan in 1615.

Claude Garamond was born in Paris in 1480. He learned how to cut type from his father and by the age of fifteen he was able to fashion steel punches the size of a pica with great precision. At the age of sixty he was commissioned by King Francis I to design a Greek alphabet, and for this he was given the honourable title of royal type founder. He died in 1561.